The Evolution of Rights in Liberal Theory

The Evolution of Rights in Liberal Theory

IAN SHAPIRO

Yale University

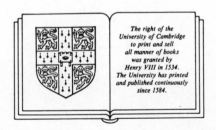

The right of the
University of Cambridge
to print and sell
all manner of books
was granted by
Henry VIII in 1534.
The University has printed
and published continuously
since 1584.

Cambridge University Press

Cambridge

London   New York   New Rochelle

Melbourne   Sydney

Published by the Press Syndicate of the University of Cambridge
The Pitt Building, Trumpington Street, Cambridge CB2 1RP
32 East 57th Street, New York, NY 10022, USA
10 Stamford Road, Oakleigh, Melbourne 3166, Australia

First published 1986

Printed in the United States of America

Library of Congress Cataloging-in-Publication Data
Shapiro, Ian.
The evolution of rights in liberal theory.
Bibliography: p.
1. Civil rights – History. 2. Liberalism – History.
I. Title.
JC571.S45   1986   323.4'09   86–2657

British Library Cataloguing in Publication Data
Shapiro, Ian
The evolution of rights in liberal theory
1. Rights (Philosophy)
I. Title
323.4'01   B105.R5

ISBN 0 521 32043 7 hard covers
ISBN 0 521 33853 0 paperback

To the memories of
H.A.S. and S.M.

Contents

Acknowledgments

To discuss seriously ideas that one knows to be half-baked, and to criticize them constructively in the early stages of their formulation, is never easy, and without Douglas Rae's enthusiastic execution of these tasks this book would not have been written. Debts to others have also accumulated at various stages. In this regard I should like especially to thank Michael Walzer for diligently reading the long and often painfully roving drafts of an author who, as he once observed, has a tendency to chew more than he has bitten off. I hope I have done enough swallowing for him, and certainly I have benefited greatly from his advice. I also owe substantial debts to Quentin Skinner and Richard Ashcraft, both of whom went well beyond the call of duty in reading the entire manuscript and commenting extensively and constructively on it. Both will find arguments in the final version with which to disagree, but both have helped me develop my thesis while saving me from myself in more ways than I care to think about; for this I remain indebted.

Others who have read and commented helpfully on large parts of various drafts, or offered important advice in other ways, include Carol Fessler-Mendoza, William Galston, Jennifer Hochschild, Jeffrey Isaac, David Johnston, John Kane, Adolph Reed, Jr., Rogers M. Smith, and Steven B. Smith. Research assistance was provided by Frederick Bartol and Chihoe Hahn. I would like to thank, without in any way implicating, all of the above.

Financial assistance was provided by fellowships from Yale University between 1978 and 1982 and a Newcombe Fellowship from the Woodrow Wilson National Fellowship Foundation in Princeton for 1982–83. I am grateful to both these institutions.

Finally I must thank Judy for helping in innumerable ways with the manuscript itself and for tolerating long periods of absence when writing was in progress – and worse periods of presence when it was not.

Part I
Introduction

1

Anatomy of an ideology

This is a book about the evolution of an ideology. Its goal is to show, in a more detailed and systematic way than has hitherto been attempted, why particular ways of talking about economic, social, and political rights became central to the Western liberal tradition around the time of the English Civil War, how these ways of talking have since evolved in that tradition, and in what respects they condition, shape, and constrain arguments about politics and public morality in contemporary Anglo-American political discourse.

The Western liberal tradition that will concern us is the one espoused by the principal architects of its political theory. This is not to say that the study of influential traditions of political theory is the only, even the best, way of trying to penetrate the many complexities that constitute a political ideology, but it is my claim that a detailed analysis of the writings held in great esteem in the established institutions of a culture can reveal much of importance about its underlying values and predispositions that might otherwise go unnoticed. My outlook is thus explicitly anthropological. My goal is to grasp, explain, and think critically about the values and beliefs that constitute our contemporary political culture. This I hold to be integral to discerning how, and in which directions, those values and beliefs might evolve in the future, and how, if at all, they might be influenced to evolve.

I. THE HISTORICAL STUDY OF CONTEMPORARY IDEAS

The basic goal is critically to evaluate contemporary arguments about right and justice, but my approach is necessarily historical for four related reasons. It is, first, a striking feature of the recent contractarian revolution in American political theory that its most influential proponents make explicit appeal to the intellectual authority of a contractarian tradition believed to have emerged in England in the seventeenth century and to have established itself in France and Germany in the eighteenth. John Rawls regards Locke's *Second Treatise,* Rousseau's *Social Contract,* and Kant's ethical works beginning with the *Foundations of the Metaphysics of Morals* as "definitive of the contract tradition." His aim is to "present a conception of justice which generalizes and carries to a higher level of abstraction" their arguments (1971:11; cf. also 32 ff, 112, 132). Although more equivocal about Hobbes, he is nonetheless impressed by his greatness and employs some of the main arguments of *Leviathan* in the course of developing his own views (ibid.: 11n, 240, 269). Robert Nozick, too, develops his account in *Anarchy State and Utopia* by building on what he takes to be Locke's state of nature (1974:10–25). In addition to such appeals, these writers (like many more minor figures they have influenced) rely heavily, as we will see, on conceptual tools, modes of reasoning, and assumptions about human nature and rationality that they take to be characteristic of this older contractarian tradition, particularly in its early English variants.

One should not, however, overlook the fact that the modern contract theorists have been deeply influenced by other powerful intellectual currents as well, most notably utilitarianism and legal positivism (against which they reacted but which left indelible marks on their arguments), post-Kantian deontological moral philosophy, and developments in modern economic and psychological theory. I will try to show how these various movements have been adapted to fit within the evolving contractarian tradition, which latter in important and usefully identifiable ways continues to define the basic outlook of the modern writers: they articulate and reproduce it.

Second, the liberal rights tradition, viewed more broadly, has itself evolved over time and these modern writers are to some extent products of that evolution. They are products in that they invoke the tradition's authority, but also because they are influenced by it in ways of which they are frequently unaware. In contrast to those commentators who identify "mod-

4

ernity" with a single unit-idea, be it the decline of objective moral standards, the supremacy of "possessive individualism," or "the emotivist self,"[1] I argue that the liberal view of rights is an ensemble of related doctrines, beliefs, and assumptions about the nature of persons, value, legitimacy, and ends. The relations among these are complex and have changed over time, more as an internally complex organism with many (and often conflicting) needs adapting to a changing environment, than as a radical disjunction with the past or a single characteristic simplifying assumption that constitutes the motif of modernity. The tradition as I describe it has been through four distinct incarnations or "moments," which I designate as transitional, classical, neo-classical, and Keynesian. These are not presented as historically or conceptually exhaustive categories and their heuristic utility is intended primarily to be thematic and comparative. I do hold, however, that some sense of the changing socioeconomic conditions that gave rise to them is essential to grasping why the modern arguments are presented in the forms that they are, why they confront the particular difficulties that they do, and why, these difficulties notwithstanding, they retain such powerful intellectual and ideological appeal.

A third reason for an historical approach derives from this fact of evolution. From an intellectual point of view (though not, as we will see, necessarily from an an ideological one) the modern arguments can usefully be thought of as lethal mutations of the earlier ones. The seventeenth-century arguments confronted important intellectual difficulties within their own terms of reference, but they exhibited an underlying intellectual coherence which the modern arguments lack, mainly because they relied on a view of scientific knowledge that was not to survive the eighteenth century. The modern writers try to combine a substantive appeal to the arguments of the early English contract theorists with a methodological appeal to Kant's ethics; in this conjunction reside some of their most intractable difficulties. My argument on this point is comparable in form, though not in content, to the claim in the opening

1 See Strauss (1953), Macpherson (1962), and MacIntyre (1981).

5

pages of *After Virtue*. Like MacIntyre I argue that contemporary writers have fragmented an older tradition by appropriating parts of it while leaving behind crucial premises that gave those parts their underlying coherence. Like him I argue that an understanding of the processes by which this occurred is essential to a full critical evaluation of the modern arguments. I do not, as MacIntyre (1981:35) does, locate the reasons for these changes in the mere follies of philosophers, or in what Richard Rorty (1979:136ff) has, with unintended irony, referred to as our "optional" commitment to the enlightenment epistemology of Descartes and his successors – which can be jettisoned once we come to understand its muddled genesis.[2] The history of dominant ideas is far more intertwined with the evolution of social structures and practices than this therapeutic metaphor suggests. Philosophical predispositions are deeply embedded in peoples' consciousnesses, at levels of which they are typically unaware. These beliefs hold together less abstract views which serve important material ends. In contrast to these voluntarist accounts of the historical evolution of ideas, I argue that a much greater role has been played by extraintellectual factors and I am skeptical of the extent to which we might return to the arguably more coherent contentions of earlier writers. Many of our most fundamental philosophical beliefs are integral to social practices in which we engage unreflectively every day. Those beliefs are required, in nontrivial ways, by those social practices, thus generating important limitations on how we might reasonably expect beliefs to change. Understanding the intricate relationships between theory and practice and how these relationships have evolved historically will reveal the dimensions of the task facing those who advocate altering the beliefs that constitute the dominant intellectual culture. We need to take much better account of our actual circumstances, how they have come to be what they are, and how they influence our own values and actions, if we are seriously to argue for the pursuit of significantly different values in the contemporary political world.

2 For discussion of Rorty's historical thesis and its implications for the history of ideologies, see Shapiro (1982:550–3ff).

A final, and related, reason for an historical approach is that it helps to get at the tenacity of this ideology over time; to grasp the historical power of its core ideas, which have persisted through the various mutations and been reproduced as dominant institutions and practices have replicated themselves. To speak of the tenacity and continuing dominance of a liberal ideology of individual rights in this way is to some extent to take issue with recent work by historians of political thought. In particular, no one who comes to this field of inquiry can fail to admire and come to terms with J.G.A. Pocock's brilliantly argued thesis in *The Machiavellian Moment* and elsewhere, seriously questioning the claim that liberal ideas have been as influential historically as is often supposed. I do not doubt that a powerful strand of republican ideology, emphasizing civic virtue and idealizing the values of civic humanism and republican citizenship (in contrast to the characteristically liberal focus on jurisprudence and the centrality of individual rights), can be traced from the Florentine Renaissance through the writings of some seventeenth-century followers of Harrington. Nor do I doubt that these ideas, which might usefully be characterized as an Atlantic republican tradition, played a significant role in shaping American revolutionary ideology, or that they have since continued to play important (if changing) roles in the evolution of American political ideas. I do question, however, the extent to which these two ideologies have evolved exclusively of one another historically, either in their geneses or in all the historical periods in which Pocock holds them to have been distinct, but it would take a different book to show this definitively.[3] In concentrating here on the evolution of liberal ideas and in trying to document and explain their continuing historical influence, I am not supposing that these are the only ideas of significance in shaping the values dominant in Anglo-American culture, or that they have evolved uninfluenced by the evolution of republican political thought. My interest is in understanding why liberal ideas have retained their powerful appeal over

3 For a recent summary of Pocock's views on this incommensurability before the Scottish jurisprudence of the eighteenth century and after 1789, see Pocock (1981:353–68).

time, these and other competing influences notwithstanding. We might say that I am concerned to explain the ideological appeal of the view that Pocock is concerned to debunk.

II. THE STUDY OF IDEOLOGY AND THE ANTHROPOLOGY OF POLITICAL THEORY

If my concern is with a major intellectual tradition and the canonical figures who comprise it, my venture differs at root from conventional studies of The Greats, whose principal focus tends to be on interpreting what are taken to be their Fundamental Insights into the human condition. The questions I am asking concern why they are thought to have these Fundamental Insights; my interest in them is from the point of view of an evolutionary anthropology of establishment values. Such an enterprise requires interpretation of canonical texts, but it is interpretation undertaken from a different point of view, with different goals in mind, than most modes of textual exegesis.

My enterprise differs, also, from the attempts by Quentin Skinner and his followers to reread the history of ideas as what they take to be the history of ideologies. My disagreements with these writers, and my realist alternatives to their hermeneutic procedures, have been set out and defended elsewhere, and need not detain us now.[4] Skinner and his followers focus exclusively on an internal reading of texts, geared toward the detailed recovery of authorial intention. My view is that, insofar as we are concerned with the history of *ideologies*, such analysis, while necessary, will never be sufficient. It must be supplemented by an external analysis that goes beyond the realm of authorial intent and locates the texts, as well as the traditions they constitute, in the broader processes of socioeconomic change that give rise to them *qua* ideological entities, and which they are instrumental in reproducing.[5] This is not to relegate the text to the realm of the

4 See Shapiro (1982:335–78).
5 There are some affinities between my use of the terms "internal" and "external" and H.L.A. Hart's use of them in his discussion of the relation between moral and legal rules in *The Concept of Law* (1961:168–80). For more extensive discussion of my uses of them see Shapiro (1982:554–63).

epiphenomenal (the relationship between ideologies and the causal reproduction of the social world is vastly more intricate than this notion suggests), nor is it to hold the quite fashionable view that authorial intent is intrinsically irrecoverable, and, anyhow, irrelevant, to textual exegesis – which latter depends exclusively on the meaning imputed by the reader. The intentions of the authors of canonical texts are indeed manipulated by subsequent generations (it is doubtful that the process of canonization could otherwise occur). Attention to the ways in which this process occurs can be highly instructive in tracing the evolution of an ideology and in thinking critically about it. Although texts become relatively autonomous of their authors once written or, as Pocock (1984:31) has noted, there is a certain "refraction and recalcitrance" to uttered speech or written language, which means it can be manipulated by others, such processes of manipulation are never without limits. These limits derive partly from the meanings of the words themselves, not because they do not change over time, but because they exist in weblike, mutually interdependent, relationships with other parts of our conceptual vocabularies. As Hanna Pitkin (1972:175–6ff) has pointed out in relation to the concept of justice, the very fact that we use this term and its cognates in a whole mesh of interrelated and overlapping ways places limits on its manipulability in a given usage. We do (or fail to do) justice to meals as well as criminals, to an author's intentions as well as to a corrupt politician, to our convictions as well as to our students, and this whole network of overlapping meanings cannot simply be detached from a single substantive use for a particular ulterior purpose. The web of connected meanings ensures a certain amount of continuity over time and space, although the degree of this will vary and is unlikely to invite much that is useful in the way of theoretical generalization.

The debate on whether or not we impute meanings to texts tends to be conducted at so high a level of abstraction that it entirely misses these issues, which are frequently crucial to grasping in concrete historical terms how ideologies evolve. It may be that the arguments of canonized writers are systematically misapplied in ways that they would never have endorsed or perhaps in some cases even have understood, but this is typically the result of bending, stretching, and pulling at parts of arguments, of subtly manipulating the contexts in which they are held to apply, of being half-true to an author's intentions, not of distorting them wholesale. Just as powerful ideologies invariably have some significant connection with reality, make straightforward sense of some realm of experience, and depend on these facts for their justificatory appeal when missapplied in other contexts for other purposes,[6] so it would be a mistake to think that there are not elements of Locke's argument, as the argument he made, which, while doubtless manipulable into the service of various competing political goals, nonetheless retain a powerful straightforward appeal in their own right and contribute to his continuing influence in the liberal tradition as a result. For this reason close attention to the internal aspects of the argument and their connection with evolving external aspects of it can be essential to getting at its ideological force over time. Nozick's "misreadings" of Locke, Rawls's of Kant, we will see, reveal a great deal about the modern evolution of liberal ideology.[7]

In short, though I follow Skinner in conceiving of ideologies in functional terms and in analyzing them by reference to the practices they are instrumental in legitimating or attacking, we differ both in our accounts of what such analysis requires and in that we are not, ultimately, interested in the same social practices. Skinner focuses on an internal hermeneutic analysis to get at the ideological force of the argument for its author. I supplement this with an external analysis in which I try to get at the more complex relationship between the meaning of the text for the author and its role in the evolving tradition, and to locate these in the broader processes of socioeconomic reproduction and change of which they are

6 I am here following Walzer's discussion of the concept of ideology (Walzer, 1983:12ff).
7 This does not go to the question of whether I, as reader, can be certain I understand the text in the sense of being sure I know what Locke's intentions in writing it really were, or that I can be certain of having grasped Nozick's reading of Locke's intentions. Obviously to say that Nozick misreads Locke is to presume a correct reading of Locke (and of Nozick). For reasons given elsewhere (Shapiro, 1982: 575–8), I see no a priori reason to suppose that such correct readings are intrinsically unavailable.

a part. Finally, where Skinner's focus is exclusively historical, my emphasis is on comprehending contemporary ideas historically: my interest in the evolution of the liberal rights tradition is geared toward a better critical understanding of its dominant contemporary manifestations.

III. THE LIBERAL IDEOLOGY OF INDIVIDUAL RIGHTS

If the liberal rights tradition is to be thought of as an internally complex set of doctrines, beliefs, and assumptions that have evolved over time while retaining a relatively enduring underlying structure, more needs to be said about how these processes of change and persistence occur, and about the underlying structure itself. We need a better sense of our animal's basic anatomy and of how this directs and limits its activities in an environment that is itself evolving over time.

i. Ideologies as conservative adaptive mechanisms

A useful start to thinking about this problem can be made by considering W. V. Quine's seminal discussion of knowledge and belief in "Two Dogmas of Empiricism." The two "dogmas" that Quine was concerned to overturn were Kant's analytic/synthetic distinction and the related correspondence theory of truth, which in his view rested on a misleading reduction of the relationship between language and experience. In contrast to the empiricist view of beliefs deriving from sense-data, which in turn correspond to particulars in the world, he averred:

The totality of our so-called knowledge or beliefs, from the most casual matters of geography and history to the profoundest laws of atomic physics or even of pure mathematics and logic, is a man-made fabric which impinges on experience only along the edges . . . [it] is like a field of force whose boundary conditions are experience. A conflict with experience at the periphery occasions readjustments in the interior of the field. Truth values have to be redistributed over some of our statements. Reevaluation of some statements entails reevaluation of others, because of their logical interconnections – the logical laws being in turn simply certain further statements of the system, certain further elements of the field. Having reevaluated one statement we must reevaluate some others, which may be statements

11

logically connected with the first or may be the statements of logical connections themselves. But the total field is so underdetermined by its boundary conditions, experience, that there is much latitude of choice as to what statements to reevaluate in the light of any single contrary experience. No particular experiences are linked with any particular statements in the interior of the field, except indirectly through considerations of equilibrium affecting the field as a whole. (Quine, 1953:42–3)

For Quine there is no simple correspondence between language and experience (although there is a more complex adaptive relationship), and there is no analytic/synthetic distinction. Beliefs that are commonly thought to be analytic are those toward the center of the "field" on which a great many others depend, and our "natural tendency to disturb the total system as little as possible" leads us always to focus revisions on specific statements (often but not necessarily empirical) as close to the edge of the system as possible (ibid.:44).

Leaving aside the issue of whether this constitutes an adequate ontological account of the nature of knowledge,[8] as a descriptive account of how beliefs generally, and political ideologies in particular, operate and evolve, Quine's account seems to me deeply plausible and, for reasons that will emerge shortly, very useful. For one thing, Quine's analogy captures the intrinsically messy nature of peoples' beliefs, and of the relations among those beliefs. In contrast to one predominant Whiggish tendency, to expect beliefs to exist in neat, tidy structures of ascending levels of generality, this view captures their fluid nature and the much looser notion of consistency with which people actually operate. Second, Quine's account captures the complexly interlocked nature of more and less general beliefs which requires us always to go to the more general to understand the less general, without making large and implausible claims about the transcendental validity of some list of "key" terms or categories. Third, the field analogy makes it clear that from this point of view there is no sharp distinction between theoretical principles and empirical beliefs, which intuitively conforms to the way ideologies preserve

8 Aspects of this issue are taken up in the final chapter.

12

themselves. Consider how monetarists can find a construction of "the facts" to support the view that Reagan's policies have worked while Keynesians can find a different one to show they have failed; how Marxists can produce constructions of "the facts" to show that there is a long-term declining tendency in the rate of profit, though neo-classical economists can hold that "the facts" disconfirm this. Quine's analogy captures the verity that empirical beliefs need not necessarily be less "basic" than theoretical beliefs; some empirical beliefs will be closer to the center of a "field" and less amenable to revision than some theoretical beliefs, and the desire to hold onto particular empirical beliefs may generate complex theoretical modifications. Fourth, Quine's account is sensitive to the truth that many parts of a system of beliefs can be implicit or unconscious, at least until they meet with recalcitrant experiences, or need to be adapted to accommodate other adaptive changes. Even in these cases agents may be more or less conscious of the ways in which they modify their beliefs. People can quite consistently hold mutually inconsistent beliefs, so long as these inconsistencies are not seen to be mutually threatening. Finally, an advantage of this view of ideologies over, for instance, a Wittgensteinian one, is that though it requires no correspondence theory of truth, it does rest on a view of language as situated in and adapting to a world that is at least partly external to itself, and it therefore directs our attention to those features of the world to which particular elements of language adapt, in addition to the internal imperatives generated by the requirements of language itself.[9] This account of the structure of belief systems is thus broadly consistent with the realist account of ideologies which I have defended elsewhere.[10]

ii. Anatomy of an ideology

If Quine's analogy supplies a general account of how ideologies operate, how does this help us to probe the underlying structure of the modern liberal tradition? At the heart of this tradition is a particular view of rights that powerfully con-

9 For a good critical account of the Wittgensteinian view see Bloor (1983).
10 Shapiro (1982:563f).

strains arguments about politics and public morality in the contemporary Anglo-American world. Its influence is sometimes latent, sometimes manifest, and the forms it has taken have varied historically, but its continuing power cannot be overestimated. Indeed, as I will suggest, its influence is so great that we should reject as misleading the widespread belief that liberalism faces a fundamental choice between contractarianism and utilitarianism: this view of rights is integral to them both.

The underlying structure of rights. People who talk or make assumptions about rights are talking or making assumptions about one of a family of moral and political concepts that are essentially formal and relational. These concepts express complex substantive relationships among different terms or variables. A claim about rights generally involves a fourfold assertion about the *subject* of entitlement, the *substance* of entitlement, the *basis* for entitlement, and the *purpose* of entitlement.[11] It generally makes sense, therefore, to ask: *who* is entitled, to *what*, on what *basis*, for what *purpose?* All users of the term do not typically address themselves to all aspects of its fourfold relational nature, nor are they necessarily aware that all these aspects exist. We will see that some of the greatest difficulties modern writers confront derive ultimately from a systematic blindness to some of them. The relational schema should be conceived of as part of the underlying grammar of the term "right," and just as in other areas speakers can be more and less aware of the grammatical rules which structure their discourse, so here these rules of intelligibility will often function invisibly. They are part of the core meaning of the term; they constitute that component of its meaning which is essentially reapplicable over its various intelligible uses.

A full philosophical defense of this claim would take us far afield and is not necessary for my purposes here.[12] Some gen-

---

11 This relational account is similar to, and based on, MacCallum's (1972:174–93) discussion of the concept of freedom as a triadic relation among accounts of persons, restraining conditions, and actions.
12 For a summary discussion of "core" theories of meaning see Shapiro (1982:540–46). For a fuller account see Graham (1977:94–102).

eral remarks will, however, be helpful in fleshing out this analytical schema and in explaining its usefulness and limitations.

Consider for a moment what things would be like if the
term "right" were used without conforming to these relational
requirements. Imagine someone who said that there were
rights that attached to no one, they were just *there*, as if they
fell off trees in the fall and grew again in the spring. Or
imagine how you would react to someone who said: "Oh yes,
people have rights, but they are not rights to anything at all:
they are just rights." We should make no sense of this kind of
usage and would doubt that the speaker understood what it
meant. So also with a claim that people have rights, but not by
virtue of any natural, rational, moral, or positive authority—
they just have them in the same way as they have teeth. The
meaning of the idea of right is inseparably bound up with that
of legitimacy. If someone said he had a right and responded
to our question "By virtue of what authority?" with "None"
(not "None of your business," "My own," "Because I am a
human being," or "Because I say so," but simply "None") we
would doubt that he understood what the word meant. We
would encounter comparable difficulties with a claim that
rights existed and attached to people but served no purpose
(not that they had become redundant like an appendix, or
were seldom or never invoked, or that we did not know what
their purpose was, but simply that they served no purpose
whatsoever). The claim, then, is that it is a condition for the
intelligibility of talk about rights that it be expressible in terms
of the quadratic schema, that intelligible claims about rights
must be able to supply answers to the fourfold question: who
is entitled, to what, on what basis, and for what purpose?

It might reasonably be asked what the "historical status" of
this schema is. My use of the Austinian tactic here of what
"we" would find intelligible glosses over the historical or cultural ranges within which these claims are held to be true. Let
us leave aside the question of whether there could be a culture
in which no rights existed at all. Could there be a culture in
which people used the term in such a way that it had some
affinities with our understanding of it but did not conform to
this schema, at least in some respects, or perhaps in a way that

bears no resemblance to our usage at all? The response that in that case we should not be able to understand it is never very satisfactory, partly because the issue in arguments about the indeterminacy of translation is often not this type of case, but the one where we think we have a correct translation but someone questions our grounds for thinking this. There are tremendously complex philosophical problems raised here, but it is legitimate to sidestep them for two reasons.

First, no special epistemological status is claimed for this schema. It is offered as an analysis of the core meaning of the term "right," which should be taken only to mean that if the term is used in such a way as to violate the injunctions entailed by this analysis, it is difficult to see how it could be intelligible. To this extent we could say that these conditions for the use of the term are quite close to the centers of our metaphorical Quinean fields. In addition, we are talking here about conditions for the intelligibility of utterances about rights, not conditions that make them plausible or convincing.[13] This is not to say that first and second order questions are unrelated. Part of my historical thesis will be that the negative libertarian view of rights that has had so much influence in the liberal tradition rests on a misconception of the second order nature of the term "right." The claim is simply that assertions about rights will be translatable into the schema if they are coherent, because the schema embodies what is essentially reapplicable in what the term means. It is part of the internal grammar of the term which functions independently of whether people who use the term coherently realize this, and this is partly why it can be a useful heuristic device in bringing hidden assumptions to the fore and in comparing different arguments. For instance, we will see that one influential substantive account of rights holds that it is possible to specify the right independently of the good, indeed that the idea of right, if taken seriously, requires that we do this. My schema, if accurate, reveals such claims to be fallacious, because reference to the

---

13 My claim thus differs, for instance, from the much stronger (and in my view implausible) claim of Rawls (1971:48ff) that our "considered judgments" on substantive questions of right and justice can be expected to command unanimity. Rawls's claim is discussed in Chapter 5.

substance of rights and their purposes clearly requires a conception of the good. And indeed when we examine the substantive arguments of defenders of this "independence" thesis, we find that they obviously do embody conceptions of the good in what they say, or imply, concerning the second and fourth terms in the relation. It is in this sense that intelligibility requires conformity to the schema whether protagonists typically realize it or not.

Second, this study is quite historically and culturally specific. It is concerned with developments in the Anglo-American liberal tradition since the English Civil War. From points of view such as that of the narrative historian this range might be thought to be very broad, but it means that many of the formally possible problems relating to indeterminacy of translation do not arise. Whether the term "soul" means something different than it does to us in a culture where people believe that they carry their souls in boxes, whether two people could systematically believe they both have the same understanding of the same term when they do not, whether I could invent a private language, these questions are not presented in this context. There can be, however, substantial difficulties in recovering enough of the contexts in which people wrote to see why they made the assumptions they did, or in being sure that we have grasped the argument in its own terms of reference. But these are questions of a much lower order, and do not entail anything about the intrinsic inaccessibility of old books.

Underlying structure and substantive argument. Assuming, then, that the schema is taken on trust, what does it tell us about the concept of a right? On its own, very little: conformity to the schema is a necessary condition for an assertion being about rights, but it is by no means sufficient.[14] The formal, empty

14 Parent (1974:154) makes this point in relation to MacCallum's triadic account of freedom. This is something of a misplaced criticism, however, since the object of MacCallum's analysis was to demonstrate that arguments that often purport to be about alternative definitions of freedom are often in fact arguments about the different (substantive) characterizations of the variables in his triad. His point was not that conformity to his triad is a sufficient condition for talking about freedom but rather that it is necessary. MacCallum would be the first to acknowledge that talking about freedom involves talking about many other things as well. It is precisely to those things that he wished to direct our attention.

17

character of the schema points to the fact that assertions about rights rest on and entail a great many substantive propositions about other things, some abstract, some normative, and some empirical. This is a point of far-reaching implications, for it militates against the tendency of the whole deontological ethical tradition to treat substantive moral and political questions as questions of "ideal theory" which are then applied to the "second best" situations of the actual world. We will see that moral arguments about rights are deeply embedded in assumptions and beliefs about how the world actually operates causally, and claims which purport to be purely hypothetical and theoretical invariably require such assumptions. This should not surprise us once we think about the problem in terms of the schema. If a claim about rights, for instance, is partly a claim about what there are rights to, about the substance of rights, or the things that have value, this will obviously rest on assumptions about how those things are in fact created and distributed. Thus an apparently purely normative question concerning whether we ought to have a right to what we make is intrinsically empirically loaded with assumptions about how things are made, what constitutes "making," and why different persons have different capacities to make different things. For a moral claim to our right to what we make to have substantive content, it engages these questions willy nilly. It is a virtue of the schema that it brings such engagements to the surface and makes them explicit.

If the schema places some basic limitations on intelligible uses of the term "right," this is not all that constitutes the skeleton to its main uses in the liberal tradition since the English Civil War. The Anglo-American liberal tradition has evolved, since the seventeenth century, in such a way as to view certain substantive characterizations of the terms in the relation, certain ways of talking about rights, as central and basic to moral and political philosophy. These ways of talking have evolved with, and been functional to, changing circumstances, although I will argue that it is misleading to think, as Macpherson and others appear to, that they merely reflect those changing circumstances, or that these ways of conceiving of rights have not themselves undergone significant changes.

In Part II, I trace the emergence and consolidation of individual rights theories in their early modern forms. Employing my quadratic schema to delineate the domain of investigation, I examine the accounts of rights in the writings of Hobbes and Locke, who are held to typify the emergence and classical consolidation of the liberal ideology of individual rights. In Part III, I undertake a parallel analysis of the modern rights theories of Nozick and Rawls who are argued to typify the neo-classical and Keynesian moments in this ideology.

Each chapter is divided into an "internal" discussion of the argument and an "external" analysis which focuses more explicitly on its ideological consequences. In the first of these I try to recover the meaning of the argument within its own terms of reference. Such critical judgments as are offered do not seek to question those terms of reference. In the second half of each chapter I move beyond those terms of reference, examine their consequences for the evolving liberal tradition, and offer more general critical judgments. Part IV begins with a comparative discussion of the earlier and later theories. It is argued that, although all these arguments have had (different) powerful ideological components, the seventeenth-century arguments were generally more coherent and made better intellectual sense, within their own terms of reference, than the modern arguments. For various historical and conceptual reasons, however, I contend that it is unrealistic to suppose that the seventeenth-century arguments can fruitfully be applied to our contemporary reality and its characteristic political dilemmas. I conclude with a more general discussion of the limits to a coherent general theory of rights or justice in our contemporary world, and with a critique of the deontological turn in modern liberal theory.

Part II
The early arguments

2

The transitional moment

I. INTRODUCTION

My aim at the outset is to exhibit the subject of our investigation
in its earliest recognizably modern form, through an analysis of
the account of rights at the heart of Hobbes's political theory.
My interpretation of Hobbes's argument shares some affinities
with C. B. Macpherson's, but it differs in three main respects.
First I will argue that, although the major socioeconomic forces
that influenced Hobbes's argument were intimately bound up
with the emergence of capitalism in England, Macpherson's
"possessive market" model misses the transitional character of
English society during this period, and that partly for this
reason it provides an inadequate and misleading basis for understanding the historical role of Hobbes's argument in the
evolution of liberal ideology. Second, if Hobbes's argument
contained many elements of what was to become the classical
variant of the liberal ideology of individual rights, several ideas
central to that later ideology were absent, the most important
being the concept of equilibrium. This made a vast difference
to the ideology's practical imperatives, particularly with respect
to the social, economic, and political functions of the state in an
emerging market economy—for it entailed very different assumptions about how markets functioned in practice. Macpherson's excessively general "possessive market" model leads him
to miss these and other important implications of Hobbes's arguments. Finally, although Hobbes played a central role in articulating much of the vocabulary and underlying grammar of
the modern liberal rights tradition, and in transforming the
language of natural rights he inherited into a recognizably
modern form, his argument was embedded in a view of the
nature of moral knowledge which (while essential to his own

argument's underlying coherence) is anathema to the modern liberal consciousness. In this regard Hobbes's argument is undeniably premodern, but it remains useful for understanding some of the greatest difficulties the modern arguments confront.

II. HOBBES'S THEORY OF RIGHTS

Hobbes is renowned for the view that man in a state of nature has a right to life, that this right is perpetually threatened by the chaos that prevails in the state of nature, and that he consequently agrees, in a simultaneous act with all others, to submit to an absolute sovereign. The precise nature and basis of the rights and obligations thus generated have been the subject of intensive dispute,[1] but it is clear that although some residual right to life remains (the moral status of which is somewhat ambiguous), to all intents and purposes man's positive political rights are those granted by the sovereign at his pleasure. An individualsit theory of contract thus generates a command theory of law. Hobbes's account of rights, however, contains a good deal more of interest which can be gleaned by looking at it more closely.

i. The subject of rights

Hobbes was a member of a ruling class and, whatever the complex redistributions of power and wealth occurring within that class during this period,[2] he exhibited the ruling-class fear of the masses, quite widespread in Tudor and early Stuart England, so convincingly documented by Christopher Hill. Hill points out that a recurrent theme in early Stuart literature was a strong upper-class mixture of fear of and contempt for the "many headed monster" (Sidney's phrase in *Arcadia*), the marauding rabble of dispossessed poor. It can be discerned in the writings of Spenser, Barnable Googe, Sir Thomas Browne, Thomas Fuller, and many others. The same sentiment is re-

---

1 Warrender (1957:278–98ff, 1965:89–100), Plamenatz (1965:73–87), Pennock (1965:101–16), Wernham (1965:117–39), Tuck (1979:119–39).
2 Stone (1965:1–134). For a useful summary of Stone's views as they relate to Hobbes see Wood (1980:437–52).

flected in many political tracts of the propertied class. Richard Morison, for whom "all men almost [are] at war with them that be rich," Francis Thynne, Sir Thomas Ashton, the Duke of Albermarle, Sir John Oglander, and Sir Thomas Wentworth all expressed views similar to that of Deloney, who asserted in 1597 that "[t]he poor hate the rich because they will not set them on work; and the rich hate the poor because they seem burdensome."[3] Such rulling-class sentiments intensified during the extensive lower-class unrest in the decades immediately preceding the Civil War.[4] The fear was a natural response to visible social consequences of economic and demographic changes in progress: urbanization (particularly in the south) and the growth of a wage laboring class (by the time of the Civil War comprising close to one half the population of England) at a time of prolonged economic crisis marked by extensive unemployment and underemployment.

Although demographic statistics for the period are uncertain, it appears that the trend of increasing population growth characteristic of the sixteenth century continued throughout the seventeenth (Hill, 1961:23). Nominal wages rose in the century before 1640, but this rise was more than offset by the continuous rise in prices, which began in the 1520s (Outhwaite, 1969:7–15) and took on sudden spurts in the 1540s, 1590s, and 1630s, producing a decline in the real purchasing power of wages (Bowden, 1967:594–616). In 1641 the opinion was expressed that "the fourth part of the inhabitants of most of the parishes of England are miserable poor people, and (harvest time excepted) without any subsistence," and in the 1680s King estimated that laborers, cottagers, and paupers constituted as much as 47 percent of the population (ibid.:598). Real wages fell by about two thirds over the sixteenth century, and although they began to rise slowly at the end of the century, a worker born in 1580 would never earn half of his grandfather's wage (Hill, 1961:24; Everitt, 1967:435). This marginalization produced a large and growing population living at or near the poverty line and concentrated in the towns, especially London, whose population may have increased eight-fold between 1500

3 Quoted in Hill (1968:302. Cf. also 300–1).
4 For further discussion and evidence, see Hill (1961:23–8, 1968:306–14, 1972:39–56).

and 1650. These "masterless men" were not tied to the feudal system and were thus threatening to it. In 1569 a government inquiry concluded that there were 1300 of them, mainly in the north; by the turn of the seventeenth century it was estimated that there were 30,000 in London alone (Hill, 1972:39–41).

Hobbes's attitude to the new urban masses was ambiguous. At one level he obviously felt the ruling-class fear; he thought uncontrolled mobs had provided one of the forces necessary to make the rebellion against the king successful. Since they were not in fear of the law they would fight for money and the merchants who had more of it than the crown were hence able to buy their allegiance. In *Behemoth* Hobbes wrote:

Truly, I think, if the King had had money, he might have had soldiers enough in England. For there were very few of the common people that cared much for either of the causes, but would have taken any side for pay or plunder. But the King's treasury was very low, and his enemies, that pretended the people's ease from taxes, and other specious things, had the command of the purses of the City of London, and of most cities and corporate towns in England, and of many particular persons besides. (Hobbes, 1966, VI:166)

In Hobbes's view, the masses were a powerful and potentially dangerous force, willing "to serve under them that had the greatest plenty of money," and it is in this context that his discussion of the state of nature should be comprehended.[5] *Pace* Macpherson (1962:20), for Hobbes the state of nature was no theoretical construct; he thought it actually prevailed in much of the world and had prevailed in England with the breakdown of legal order during the Civil War:

It may peradventure be thought, there was never such a time, nor condition of warre as this; and I believe it was never generally so, over all the world: but there are many places, where they live so now. For the savage people in many places of *America*, except the government of small Families, the concord whereof dependeth on naturall lust, have no government at all; and live at this day in that brutish manner, as I said before. Howsoever, it may be perceived what manner of life there would be, where there were no common

5 For a useful discussion of Hobbes's views of the role of the masses in the Civil War, see Ashcraft (1978:27–62).

Power to feare; by the manner of life, which men that have formerly lived under a peacefull government, use to degenerate into, in a civill Warre. (Hobbes, 1968:187)

Yet, despite his fear that society must inevitably degenerate into civil war once the masses cease to be controlled by an absolute power, Hobbes recognized with a kind of Tocquevillean foresight that these masses were to be the stuff of the politics of the future. Dangerous and threatening as they were, a political system, to survive, must appeal to their interests – not as a member of this or that class and not for some higher good: these "overmighty subjects" had to be appealed to in terms of their individual interests.

Leviathan was not directly aimed at the masses. For Hobbes the war of all against all and the relentless drive for power infected the entire social landscape, and was present not least within the ruling classes themselves. He was a first-hand witness to the decline of the aristocracy that Lawrence Stone has so masterfully chronicled, to the corruption and squabbling for advancement that accompanied and exacerbated the inflation of honors, and to the growing sale of titles and offices to meet the urgent financial needs of the crown.[6] It seems certain that Hobbes regretted the breakdown of aristocratic values that these events appeared to accelerate, and that he disliked the growing influence of merchants and money in politics (Thomas 1965:189–215).[7] He saw these as events to be reckoned with – again perhaps the comparison with Tocqueville's attitude toward equality is instructive – in the attempt to generate the social consensus necessary for political stability. For Hobbes thought it essential for people, in their own interests, to assent to the arrangements he advocated if political stability was to be assured. This is reflected in his opening remarks in *Leviathan* where he says:

[Y]et, when I shall have set down my own reading orderly, and perspicuously, the pains left another, will be onely to consider, if he also

6 See Stone (1965:37–61, 71–88, 191–232), Wood (1980:441–7).
7 In section II(ii) of this chapter it is argued that Thomas's account, while a useful corrective to Macpherson's, nonetheless understates the significance of Hobbes's views for the liberal ideology of individual rights.

27

find not the same in himself. *For this kind of Doctrine, admitteth no other Demonstration.* (Hobbes, 1968:83, emphasis added)

The ways in which his principles are to be communicated to the common people are bound up with a complex theory of political education which need not concern us in detail now.[8] Suffice it to note here that Hobbes did not believe that the masses must be terrorized into submission, as Thomas (1965:203ff) and others have suggested. He had a powerfully egalitarian conception of rationality, and believed that the major barriers to the universal acceptance of the laws of nature as he articulated them derived neither from any constitutional inadequacy of the common people, nor from any difficulties with the ideas themselves. (These latter, we will see, he held to be unambiguously and conclusively demonstrable.) The political confusion of the common people derived instead, for Hobbes, from ideological distortions generated by religious, economic, and intellectual groups for partisan political reasons.[9] He thus responded to critics who maintained that "though the Principles be right, yet Common people are not of capacity enough to be made to understand them" in the following terms:

I should be glad, that the Rich, and Potent Subjects of a Kingdome, or those that are accounted the most Learned, were no lesse incapable than they [the common people]. But all men know, that the obstructions to this kind of doctrine, proceed not so much from the difficulty of the matter, as from the interest of them that are to learn. Potent men, digest hardly any thing that setteth up a Power to bridle their affections; and Learned men, any thing that discovereth their errours, and thereby lesseneth their Authority: whereas the Common-peoples minds, unlesse they be tainted with dependance on the Potent, or scribbled over with the opinions of their Doctors, are like clean paper, fit to receive whatsoever by Publique Authority shall be imprinted. (Hobbes, 1968:378–9)

The implications of this for modern doctrines of individual consent will concern us in detail later. Notice here that in

8 Aspects of this issue are taken up in section II(iii) of this chapter. For a comprehensive discussion of Hobbes's theory of political education see Johnston (1981: 189–91).
9 For a useful discussion of Hobbes's views on ideological distortion of political beliefs see Ashcraft (1978:27–62).

ascribing rights indiscriminately to all in the state of nature, and holding that all must be convinced individually that the Leviathan functions in their interests, Hobbes is doing more than just rejecting the feudal order. He is acknowledging that the breakdown of that order has radically changed the whole basis of politics.

It would thus be misleading to suggest that Hobbes was entirely against all the developments that had produced mass politics as he understood them. The many attacks on knowledge from authority throughout his writings and his belief that scientific principles are rationally demonstrable to and understandable by all bespeak considerable enthusiasm for the possibilities generated by this "new subjectivity." It was the fact that peoples' rational capacities had been sullied and exploited in the service of various religious, economic, and political causes that was the problem, which he saw it as his task to address.[10]

ii. The substance of rights

For Hobbes there are no restrictions in the state of nature on what people have rights *to* (in the absence of some system of authority all have a right to everything against all), but following the contract people are entitled only to what the law permits. Even property rights are regarded as postcontractual, distributed by the state, an anticommon-law view that clearly identified Hobbes with the royalist position that all property is subject to the crown (Thomas, 1965:223ff). There is a powerful authoritarian component to this view, as is often pointed out, but to pay too much attention to it obscures other elements of his account that are important here. It is true that Hobbes allows the state unlimited power, but it is also clear that the "absolute and arbitrary" power of the sovereign should be exercised through published rules, that its functions are seen as fundamentally regulative of private interaction, and that a very wide area is envisaged where private rights of exclusive dominion (over objects and actions) prevail. It is important not to conflate a regulative state with a minimal one.

10 For further analysis of Hobbes's views on these issues see Johnston (1981).

For Hobbes, writing in a situation of political and social chaos, where national markets in important commodities such as land, labor, and food were still in the process of establishing themselves, regulation could and often did mean very considerable intervention.

Hobbes's view of the relation between state and society can perhaps best be gleaned by considering his account of the economic functions of the state. In chapter 24 of *Leviathan*, entitled "Of the Nutrition and Procreation of the Common-Wealth," he outlines the following six such functions: first, the sovereign arbitrarily distributes land among the subjects and thereby creates property rights. This constitutes *"Mine,* and *Thine,* and *His* that is to say in one word Propriety" (Hobbes, 1968:296). The existence of a civil law, Hobbes argues, is a necessary condition for the creation and maintenance of property rights, and should it be *"abandoned, or but negligently guarded . . . there is nothing that any man can be sure to receive from his Ancestor, or leave to his children"* (ibid). This account may sound remarkably unbourgeois but two points should be noted. First, Hobbes is at this stage dealing with the original endowment of property rights. In his account of commutative justice subsequent changes among individuals are effected through voluntary contract. It is only initial distribution that Hobbes deals with in this way, and it is worth pointing out that it was to become characteristic of liberal accounts of property that they would fail to offer a satisfactory treatment of the initial endowments of property rights – focusing exclusively on the mechanisms of subsequent distributional change, and assuming that questions of initial endowment were of now more than historical concern.[11] It is thus to Hobbes's account of commutative justice that modern liberal theories of property ownership and exchange most closely conform. Commutative justice "is the Justice of a Contractor." It concerns "Performance of a Covenant, in Buying and Selling; Hiring and Letting to Hire; Lending and Borrowing; Exchanging, Bartering, and other acts of Contract." In all such transactions the value of things contracted for "is measured by the Appetite of the

---

11 This issue is taken up in Chapter 4.

Contractors: and therefore the just value, is that which they be contented to give." It is on this basis that Hobbes rejects the traditional distinction between commutative and distributive justice, arguing that the notions of merit to which the latter was tied are not relevant to the justice of market transactions (Hobbes, 1968:208).

Hobbes's refusal to grant property rights against the state, and his medieval views on the rights of the starving poor to relief through theft if this was the only alternative to starvation, separate his view from a developed bourgeois account of property as Thomas (1965:223, 225–7) has argued. This should not, however, lead us to overlook the significance of Hobbes's account for the evolution of liberal views. Hobbes grounds all property rights in positive law and thereby links the state to the preservation of private property. The subject has no property right against the sovereign (and can therefore legitimately be taxed) but his property right against other subjects is inviolable: "The Propriety which a subject hath in his lands, consisteth in a right to exclude all other subjects . . . and not to exclude their Soveraign" (1968:297). It is simply not true, then, that Hobbes "provided no effective guarantees for private property" as Thomas claims. For Thomas, "in the one issue where property rights . . . were seriously disputed, Hobbes abandoned the interests of possessing classes altogether" (Thomas, 1965:224, 223). Even if this were accurate historically (which is hard to imagine when we think of the social and political implications of enclosure or the more general perceived threats to property before and during the Civil War),[12] it misses the fact that Thomas elsewhere acknowledges: for Hobbes "the commonwealth exists to provide a framework of security in which wealth may be pursued, but [that it is] not to interfere with its distribution," and that "he favoured what we should regard to-day as an extreme state of internal *laisser-faire*" so that in general his economic position was, "in the context of his age, extremely advanced and it constitutes the most obviously *bourgeois* aspect of his thought" (ibid.:228–9).

12 See section II(i) of this chapter.

Second, Hobbes was writing in a volatile political and legal context. The state had for over a century been taking a powerfully active role in the destruction of feudal property relationships and the creation of modern transmissibility in land. Both through its own confiscation and sale of church lands after the Reformation and through its central role in dismantling feudal land law, the state in late Tudor and early Stuart England *was* distributing "initial" property rights in their modern form of exclusive transmissible dominion. This is, in significant part, how "bourgeois" property relations were created in England.[13] In simultaneously adhering to a view of ownership in terms of exclusive dominion, and charging the state with responsibility of distributing property in accordance with it, Hobbes was, however unconsciously, sanctioning changes in English land law that had been in motion for some time and which were to become central to the modern system of private law on which developed capitalism would rest.

The second function of the state concerns taxation. The sovereign may tax the subject when the public need arises:

In the Distribution of land, the Common-wealth it selfe, may be conceived to have a portion, and possesse, and improve the same by their Representative; and that such portion may be made sufficient, to sustein the whole expence to the common Peace, and defence necessarily required. (Hobbes, 1968:298)

The amount of taxation that will be required is to be determined by circumstances, but what is interesting from our point of view is that Hobbes was clear that it must be limited to whatever is necessary for the maintenance of internal peace and national security. He thus opposed the creation of a stock of public property on the grounds that it would invariably generate waste and corruption:

[T]he nature of men being as it is, the setting forth of Publique Land, or of any certaine Revenue for the Common-wealth, is in vaine; and tendeth to the dissolution of Government, and to the condition of meere Nature, and War, as soon as ever the Soveraign Power falleth into the hands of a Monarch, or of an Assembly, that

13 For discussion of evidence see sections II(iii) and III of this chapter.

are either too negligent of mony, or too hazardous in engaging the publique stock, into a long, or costly war. (Ibid.)

Thus Hobbes advocated limited taxation to finance a regulative state whose economic functions were seen as confined to those necessary for the maintenance of civil peace and national security. This interpretation is reinforced by his account of public goods: although the twelfth law of nature dictates, on the basis of equity, that those things held in common should be equally available to all, things should only be held in common to begin with if they "*cannot be divided*" (1968:212). Since all were held to have an equal interest in the limited public functions ascribed to the state, Hobbes was later able to argue that people should all be taxed equally: "Seeing then the benefit that every one receiveth thereby . . . is equally dear to poor, and rich; the debt which a poor man oweth them that defend his life, is the same which a rich man oweth for the defence of his" (ibid.:386).

Third, the state regulates foreign trade to ensure that no individual can furnish a foreign power with "means to hurt the Common-wealth" (ibid.:299) or import things inimical to its safety. Fourth, the sovereign regulates the mode but, significantly from our standpoint, not the substance of contract.

[I]t belongeth to the Common-wealth (that is to say, the Soveraign,) to appoint in what manner, all kinds of contract between Subjects (as buying, selling, exchanging, borrowing, lending, letting, and taking to hire,) are to be made; and by what words and signes they shall be understood for valid. (Ibid.:299)

Fifth, the sovereign establishes and regulates the value of money, which is the "Bloud of a Common-wealth" (ibid.:300); and sixth, it ensures the "procreation" of the commonwealth by licensing the founding of colonies abroad. A seventh function is dealt with in the course of Hobbes's discussion of the province of the sovereign: the state should provide maintenance for the unemployable, for "as it is Uncharitablenesse in any man, to neglect the impotent; so it is in the Soveraign of a Common-wealth, to expose them to the hazard of such uncertain Charity" (ibid.:387). But the able-bodied idle should be forced to work. To ensure that employment be available, laws should be passed to encourage "all member of Manifacture that requires labour." The state should not intervene directly in the production process to create employment, but it should create conditions conducive to the expansion of private generated employment. If this does not solve the problem, the unemployed should be "transplanted into Countries not sufficiently inhabited" (ibid.).

These constitute a complete list of the economic functions of Hobbes's state. Within the limits imposed by them individuals are free to enjoy liberty by "praetermission":

The Liberty of a Subject, lyeth therefore only in those things, which in regulating their actions, the Soveraign hath praetermitted: *such as is the Liberty to buy, and sell, and otherwise contract with one another, to choose their own aboad, their own diet, their own trade of life, and institute their children as they themselves think fit, & the like.* (Hobbes, 1968:264, emphasis added)

The state, then, remains silent as to the substance of individual trades and contracts (which it nonetheless regulates and enforces), as well as most other activities that contemporary liberals typically regard as comprising the private sphere.

We seem to be confronted by the paradox that Hobbes the political absolutist advocates a highly restricted state in matters economic, as Letwin (1972:163–4) has noted. Despite the state's absolute power, its actions are conceived of as indirect and regulative, as revealed in the discussions of unemployment and taxation; it is supportive of the institution of the market, revealed in the account of contract and individual freedom; and it is limited, revealed in the discussion of the limits to public property as well as by the fact that Hobbes does not ascribe any further economic roles to the state.

How are we to reconcile this economic minimalism with Hobbes's political absolutism? This has not been squarely confronted in the Hobbes literature. Commentators have tended to ignore his chapter on the economic functions of the state and Letwin's explanation, that Hobbes was a complicated thinker (1972:162–4), is less than fully satisfactory. To address this issue three factors should be borne in mind. First, it seems clear that Hobbes perceived no necessary connections between economics and politics. Ashcraft (1978:27–62) points out that, in his history of the Civil War, Hobbes acknowledged the social usefulness of merchants and the social cohesion that could result from an order based on "market-friendship," but that he inveighed against the prevalent view that only republicanism was compatible with the development of commercial wealth. He thought it misleadingly false, for instance, to suggest a connection between Dutch republicanism and prosperity. In Hobbes's view as expressed in *Behemoth*, the true interests of merchants were quite compatible with those of the monarchy; it was their ignorance of this and their being "passionately carried away" that led them to oppose the king. Since for Hobbes all ideas originate from "the motions of the mind," the place to deal with deceptive ideologies was in the universities (ibid.:49–50). He believed there was no necessary relationship between a country's economic prosperity, or lack of it, and its type of government.[14]

Second, Hobbes could hardly on the one hand subscribe to the increasingly widespread view that production for exchange is the source of society's wealth, and on the other condemn the activities of the merchants who appeared to be the driving force behind this production. The view that the capacity to produce for exchange is the source of wealth had become common currency among English economic and political writers by the mid-seventeenth century. During the middle third of the century dozens of writers, simultaneously concerned with the problem of the poor and the sources of national wealth, began to reject the mercantilist identification of wealth with precious metals, as well as medieval conceptions of wealth as "the bounty of a dread God or in the gifts of a reluctant Nature" (Johnson, 1937:239). Instead they began to define national prosperity as inhering in the capacity to produce for exchange. Appleby has shown that the belief that the capacity to labor is a source of wealth was affirmed in much of the pamphlet literature on

---

14 On this subject see also Thomas (1965:214–15).

trade and the poor throughout the century, a view which reflected the "dawning realization that art could produce more than nature" (Appleby, 1978:135–57).

Perhaps the most systematic formulation of this view came from Hobbes's contemporary William Petty (whom Marx regarded as the founder of political economy).[15] Petty formulated a labor theory of value in which he distinguished the "natural," "real," or "true price current" (which depends on "the few or more hands requisite to necessities of nature") from the "political" price (which depends "upon the paucity of Supernumerary Interlopers into any trade over and above all that are necessary"). He thereby set out the terms of the central problem that would preoccupy the classical economists of the eighteenth and nineteenth centuries, how labor and demand interact in the determination of value or price. Petty himself tried to compute relative prices in terms of comparative labor times: If a man can bring an ounce of silver to London from Peru in the same time as he can produce a bushel of corn, "then one is the natural price of the other." If, in virtue of technological innovation, he can bring two ounces in the same time as he formerly did one, "then Corn will be as cheap at ten shillings the bushel, as it was before at five shillings, *caeteris paribus*" (Petty, 1899 [1662], I:89–91, 50–1). Petty recognized that such computations implied some basic unit of value in terms of which commodities are commensurable with one another. This brought him, in *The Political Anatomy of Ireland*, to what he regarded as "the most important Consideration in Political Oeconomies" which is "how to make a *Par* and *Equation* between Lands and Labour, so as to express the Value of any thing by either alone" (ibid. [1691], I:181). To tackle this Petty developed the notion of simple labor, to which all labor can be reduced.[16]

Hobbes and Petty had worked together in the 1640s, and although Petty's discipleship of Hobbes was primarily for his

---

15 See the discussion in *Theories of Surplus Value* (1963, I:178–82, 354–63).
16 Appleby uncovering in the seventeenth-century English literature on trade and the poor, long before the demise of physiocratic ideas in France, so much of the language of what was to become classical political economy, is an important corrective to the assertions of Tribe (1978) and others that the language of classical economics did not emerge before the eighteenth century.

politics, it is possible that Hobbes influenced Petty in his formulation of the labor theory of value.[17] That Hobbes embraced a version of this view is indicated by his comments on
the poor already mentioned, by his celebrated assertion in
chapter 10 of *Leviathan* that the *"Value,* or WORTH of a man,
is as of all other things, his Price; that is to say, so much as
would be given for the use of his Power. . . ." (1968:151–2), by
a discussion of labor as a commodity and source of wealth in
Behemoth where Hobbes claims that merchants produce wealth
". . . by making poor people sell their labor to them [mer-
chants] at their own prices" (1966, VI:321), and by his discussion of labor-value and trade in chapter 24 of *Leviathan*. In
this instance Hobbes is arguing that few countries are large
enough to be self-sufficient and few do not produce surpluses
in some commodities. Thus:

the superfluous commodities to be had within, become no more superfluous, but supply these wants at home, by importation of that
which may be had abroad, either by Exchange, or by just Warre, or by
Labour: for a mans Labour also, is a commodity exchangeable for
benefit, as well as any other thing: And there have been Commonwealths that having no more Territory, than hath served them for
habitation, have nonethelesse, not onely maintained, but also en-
creased their Power, partly by the labour of trading from one place to
another, and partly by selling the Manifactures, whereof the Materials
were brought in from other places. (Hobbes, 1968:295)

Clearly this passage reveals no mercantilist predisposition for
particular types of imports over exports, or balance of trade –
anything, including labor, which can be exchanged for benefit
brings advantage. It is true that Hobbes treats just war as an
alternative mechanism of accumulation to production for exchange. War was a principal mode of accumulation under late
feudalism and the fact that Hobbes acknowledges both these
mechanisms signals the transitional juncture in English economic history at which he stood. This should not, however, be
overstated. Hobbes was for the most part in the mainstream of

17 This is suggested by Charles Hull, editor of Petty's economic writings; see Petty
(1899 [1691]:lxi, lxiii, lxxiii). See also Reik (1977:79, 210). On the influence of
early versions of the labor theory of value in seventeenth-century writing on
wages, employment, depopulation, and the poor see Coleman (1956:280–95).

the advanced economic thinking of his day in regarding the capacity to labor as the source of wealth, and production for trade as indispensable to the health of a commonwealth. It is therefore not surprising that he did not criticize the economic activities of merchants. He was compelled to endorse their economic behavior and claim that it was compatible with the political arrangements he advocated.[18]

A third point concerns the absence of the concept of equilibrium from economic and political writing during this period. It was not until the turn of the eighteenth century that writers began seriously to contend that the economic system could regulate itself without any interference from the state; it was much later still that the notion of equilibrium would be directly applied to politics generally. This meant, in Hobbes's England, that one could quite consistently advocate market-based social and economic organization without holding anything like the view that the system could be self-regulating. Indeed for Hobbes absolutist political institutions would be essential to sustain this organization. The driving force behind his politics was that without decisive control by the sovereign, society would collapse into disorder. In the early eighteenth century Mandeville would become notorious for his metaphorical understanding of the social mechanism in terms of the harmonious activities of bees. Hobbes, by contrast, employs this analogy in reverse: where bees (and ants) were correctly labeled political by Aristotle because they "live sociably one with another," this is because among them the "Common good differeth not from the Private" so that although "by nature enclined to their private [goods], they procure thereby the common benefit." But man differs in that he is continually in competition for honor and dignity, his "Joy consisteth in comparing himselfe with other men," he "can relish nothing but what is eminent," and his rational capacities enable him to question the "administration of their

18 As Ashcraft puts it, Hobbes could "leave the bourgeois economic arrangements of society – in so far as they existed – as they were, provided the political *ideas* of merchants and educated gentlemen were reformed in accordance with Hobbesian principles" (Ashcraft, 1978:49).

common businesse" (1968:225–6). In these circumstances the common good must be preserved by the state. It will otherwise be undermined by the private activities of individual men.

Hobbes's account of the state as essentially regulative of economic activity, the substance of which latter is inherently private, rests on a broader negative libertarian view of society summed up in his epithet that "The Greatest Liberty of Subjects, dependeth on the silence of the Law" (1968:271). Hobbes conceives of social relationships as essentially private, their form, but never their content, regulated by the state. This view was significant not only for economic life, it was central to the demands for religious toleration that dominated so much of English politics at this time, and is required by the Protestant view of man's religious life as essentially private. Although Hobbes took great pains to argue that his laws of nature were compatible with the laws of God, he made a sharp distinction between civil and ecclesiastical law and acknowledged the privacy of man's relationship with God. Indeed, he used this to deny the legitimacy of Catholicism against the English crown on the grounds that a "private opinion" (of the Pope) could never be set up against the "Publique Person" of the civil authority. He even defended freedom of the individual rational conscience (which Locke was accused of plagiarizing in *The Reasonableness of Christianity*). Although this did not generate any political guarantees of toleration for nonconformists, it did recognize the sanctity of religious beliefs. Hobbes held that "true" religious beliefs by definition could not conflict with civil power, since they require acknowledgment of the legitimate authority and domain of that power; in this way he largely avoids the *political* question of religious toleration. He does acknowledge, however, that it would be madness for someone knowingly to condemn himself to eternal damnation at the command of the sovereign, and in the case where the sovereign is an infidel, defiance will in some circumstances be understandable, but "if they do [defy], they ought to expect their reward in Heaven" (ibid., 625ff). Hobbes believed that if religion does not overstep its legitimate (private) boundaries and interfere with civil matters, conflict between church and state will not arise.[19]

So although Hobbes's sovereign is allowed unlimited power, we have seen that the sphere in which private rights are to function is expected to be quite extensive in economic, social and religious life. People will make voluntary agreements with one another that will be enforced by the state; they will be free within the limits of the law, to make, do, exchange, and believe as they please.

iii. The basis for rights

Hobbes is perhaps best known for introducing into English political theory a view of law as resting on a generalized agreement among equal individuals, which both constitutes civil society and confers legitimacy on the actions of the state. All positive rights are embedded in a command theory of law whose legitimacy derives from this contract. The aim of the contract is the preservation of man's natural right to life that would otherwise be perpetually threatened. This view is rightly regarded as innovative not only because of its fundamental egalitarianism, the centrality it attached to the notion of individual consent, its secularism and its rationalism, but also because it marks a decisive break with feudal conceptions of law. With the Royalists, Hobbes rejected outright the common-law case that the law derived its legitimacy from an Ancient Constitution which was older than, and placed limits on, the authority of the crown. But unlike conventional defenders of absolutism such as Filmer, who linked their patriarchal defenses of prerogative to theories of divine right, Hobbes defined legitimate authority as the power to command obedience, the de facto presence of which was regarded as decisive evidence for the existence of the contract. Hobbes's view of

---

19 I do not claim to do justice to the highly contentious and voluminous literature currently emerging on Hobbes's religious views, and on the relevance of his religious arguments to his political theory. I would only claim, *pace* Warrender, that had Hobbes not offered a secular formulation of his argument, the logic of which was in principle separable from his religious arguments, he would never have been canonized in the liberal tradition. For this reason I sidestep the debates on his religious views. For a reinterpretation of their significance in light of Hobbes's changing views on the political importance of rhetoric, see Johnston (1986).

the contract was thus innovative in its accounts of the parties to the contract, the nature of their agreement with the sovereign, and the consequences of that agreement.

For Hobbes, man's rights in the state of nature seem at first sight to have a purely descriptive status. He defines natural right as:

THE RIGHT OF NATURE, which Writers commonly call *Jus Naturale* [which] is the Liberty each man hath, to use his own power, as he will himselfe, for the preservation of his own Nature; that is to say, of his own Life. (Hobbes, 1968:189)

This is sharply contrasted with, and separated from, natural law:

For though they that speak of this subject, use to confound *Jus*, and *Lex, Right* and *Law;* yet they ought to be distinguished; because RIGHT, consisteth in liberty to do, or to forbeare; Whereas LAW, determineth, and bindeth to one of them: so that Law, and Right, differ as much, as Obligation, and Liberty; which in one and the same matter are inconsistent. (Ibid.:189)

Natural rights thus indicate the human capacity for free action. This conceptual division marks an important shift in the Western tradition away from emphasis on natural law to the centrality of individual natural rights, as can perhaps be gleaned from the fact that in European languages other than English there is not the same linguistic distinction. The German word *Recht*, the Italian *diritto* and the French *droit* are all used to signify law in the abstract as well as right, so closely bound up are the etymologies of these ideas historically. They all exhibit the conflation Hobbes identifies in the Latin *ius* when he detaches the idea of right from that of law by insisting that natural rights are mere capacities, quite independent of any conception of law. Hobbes's natural rights do not even have the status of what Hohfeld referred to as "privileges" (and which his followers have come to refer to as "liberties"), rights that correlate only with the "no-right" of others to interfere with one's right – while imposing no additional affirmative obligations on those others.[20] For Hobbes man's natural

20 Hohfeld (1923:7, 38f). For a useful account of Hohfeld's views see Flathman (1976:38–47).

state is literally a state in which the right of all *against all* prevails and people's rights are limited by nothing more (or less) than their capacities for enforcement.

Morality inheres in the laws of nature which Hobbes regards as postulates for rational action and derivable from a correct understanding of the human condition. They are not, strictly speaking, laws at all, for a law, "to speak properly and accurately, is the speech of him who by right commands somewhat to others to be done or omitted" and natural laws, even though they are "delivered by God in the holy Scriptures," are not "in propriety of speech" laws at all; they are "nothing else but certain conclusions, understood by reason, of things to be done and omitted . . . as they proceed from nature" (Hobbes, 1966, II:49–50). The exact moral status of these natural laws is complex and elusive, but in one important respect Hobbes stands traditional natural law arguments on their heads: the various Ockhamist, Gersonist, and neo-Thomist traditions, while significantly different from one another, had all recognized the existence of *some* relationship between natural right and law, such that natural rights were either derived from natural law or at least limited by it. Even if the relationship was not one of symmetrical correlativity – as in the writings of the "subjective" theorists influenced by the revival of the Roman law conception of a right as a *facultas,* a liberty or power – natural law placed some limitations on man's natural rights, as will be seen in the next chapter.[21] To Hobbes, however, natural laws are derived from his account of man's natural capacities, which are taken to be, or at least in isomorphic correspondence with, man's natural rights.

Man's *civil* rights, those rights granted (or indirectly secured) by the actions of the sovereign, have an important moral force which inheres in the legitimacy of the contract. Once we try to pin down the nature of this moral force, however, we seem to find two distinct arguments. First is the claim that *in making* the agreement man authorizes the actions of the sovereign, that the act of agreeing is itself morally decisive. Second is the claim that the contract confers legitimacy be-

21 Chapter 3, Section II(iii). For useful discussions of the evolution of these various traditions see Skinner (1978, vol. I), Tuck (1979), and Finnis (1980:205–10).

cause it is *rational* for men to make it; it is a rational imperative dictated by the laws of nature which are in turn derived from a scientific analysis of the human condition.[22] On the face of it these appear to be very different arguments, perhaps even mutually contradictory. The 'first, supported by Hobbes's accounts of free action, promising and mutual renunciation of rights, corresponds most neatly with modern rights-based theories of contract. The second, which allows Hobbes to defend the imposition of commonwealths by force, the denial of any individual rights against the state, and the granting to the state of unlimited power, reads far more like a theory of interests. It is these features of his account that are generally singled out by liberals for criticism.

In fact, there was no contradiction here for the historical Hobbes because he had a different view of the ontological status of moral knowledge from that which the preceding dichotomy implies. Though Hobbes believed subjective assent played an important role in validating moral judgments, he was not a subjectivist in anything like our sense of the word. He thought that moral predicates could only meaningfully attach to individuals, that terms like "good" had no intrinsic meaning, that Aristotle was wrong in defining "good" simply as "that which all men desire . . . since different men desire and shun different things, there must need be many things that are *good* to some and *evil* to others . . . one cannot speak of something as being *simply good* since whatsoever is good, is good for someone or other" (1972:47). He thought moral knowledge to be radically mind-dependent in that it depended ultimately on introspection. None of this, however, was thought to entail that it could not be known with absolute certainty. On the contrary, one of his central aims in writing *Leviathan* was to supply such a conclusive demonstration. This apparent paradox can be explained only by reference to his theory of scientific knowledge.

It should be remembered that although *Leviathan* is a study of the "matter, form, and power of a commonwealth ecclesiasti-

---

22 Hence the so-called Taylor thesis which postulates a kind of schizophrenia between moral and psychological theory in Hobbes's argument. See Taylor (1965:35–55). For a useful critical discussion of this view see Minogue (1972:70–84).

cal and civil" Hobbes begins it with an account of the nature of sense-experience and scientific knowledge. He outlines a sense-data theory of perception, remarkable in its anticipation of Hume, according to which all knowledge is reducible to sense-impressions. Knowledge is divided into two classes, history, which is knowledge of fact, and science, which is knowledge of consequence. These classes are further subdivided into knowledge that in some way depends on man's will, such as civil history or civil philosophy, and that which does not, such as natural history or physics.[23] It is important to recognize that in classifying a mode of activity as scientific, there is no distincton between different types of consequences. Similarly, although all factual knowledge is reducible to sense-data, there is no ontological difference between objects of sense experience that exist inside the mind and those which exist outside it.[24] A desire is as much an object of sense-experience as a tree and a triangle. This is not to say that Hobbes makes no distinciton between a priori and a posteriori knowledge – we will see in a moment that he does – but simply that he regards all knowledge, even mind-dependent knowledge, as grounded in sense-experience. Scientific knowledge consists in the rational deduction of true consequences from true premises, which latter are either unambiguous "definitions" or accurate reflections of sense-experience.

Reason is defined in terms of, and held to be wholly reducible to, addition and subtraction. Its purpose is the discovery of "consequences," but these are conceived of far more broadly than entailment relationships. They include logical consequences, causal consequences, and moral consequences. Thus

23 Hobbes's classifications of the different sciences are not altogether consistent through the different writings. In *Leviathan* (1968:147–9) ethics is regarded as part of natural philosophy and politics part of civil philosophy, suggesting that only the latter depends on the human will, but in the (later) *de Homine* (1972:41) they are classified together as both being will-dependent and hence open to a priori demonstration.

24 There are, however, methodological differences in how these different phenomena can be known. Since the hallmark of genuine knowledge is subjective certainty, the kind of certainty we can have of a mathematical proof we understand, it follows that phenomena in the mind can only be known, ultimately, by introspection. In this regard there seems to be an essentialist component to Hobbes's view of science despite the epistemological nominalism (and ultimately, one must suspect, in tension with it) that has been well analyzed by Dorothea Krook (1956:3–22). This will be evident in my discussion of his view of truth in the next paragraph but one.

arithmeticians teach us to add and subtract in numbers, logicians to compute with the "consequences of words," political writers "add together *Pactions,* to find mens *duties;* and Lawyers, *Lawes,* and *facts,* to find what is *right* and *wrong* in the actions of private men." Reason, then, is applicable to "what matter soever there is place for *addition* and *subtraction*" (1968:110–111). All men reason alike in the sense that coherence requires conformity to the basic laws of addition and subtraction, but reason is not a natural capacity such as sense or memory. It is learned by "industry," through language, commonly misused, and its correct and unambiguous use is the source of all scientific knowledge (ibid.: 110–16).

Truth is a slippery concept in Hobbes's writing. It is held to be an attribute of language, not of the world, and is defined as "the right ordering of names in our affirmations" (1968:105). This is actually a definition of coherence or consistency and in many places Hobbes uses the term in precisely this sense. But it is clear from his discussion of the uses and abuses of speech, of absurdity, and from his sense-data theory of perception that he thinks true statements reflect or correspond to, or are reducible to, statements that reflect or correspond to, particulars in the world. Thus truth consists in the right ordering of names, but the names correspond to particulars in the world, "there being nothing in the world Universall but Names; for the things named, are every one of them Individuall and Singular" (1968:102). An important class of these are "Names positive" which are "put to mark somewhat which is in Nature" (ibid.:107). Although absurdity can result from unclear definitions and confusion of predicates with the subjects of which they are predicated, it can also result from misidentifying particulars in the world as universals or confusing our descriptions of bodies with the bodies themselves (ibid.:114). In his discussion of historical knowledge, Hobbes asserts that "[w]hatsoever . . . we conceive, has been perceived first by sense, either all at once, or by parts; a man can have no thought, representing any thing, not subject to sense" (ibid.:99). His various attacks on Cartesianism and scholasticism turn on his claims that such notions as "immaterial substance" and "incorporeal substance" are meaningless because they have no real referents. Despite his nominalism Hobbes clearly operates, at times, with a conception of truth as unambiguous correspondence.

When Hobbes comes to distinguish a priori from a posteriori knowledge his prototypical empiricism begins to wane. For Hobbes this distinction is not between knowledge which is true by definition and knowledge which depends on experience; the essential distinction is between truths which are functions of the human will and those which are not. A priori knowledge can be known with certainty because we *make* it. This is a so-called "workmanship" or "creationist" theory of knowledge which conferred on the moral sciences an epistemological status in pre-Humean empiricist thought vastly superior to any they have enjoyed in the Anglo-American tradition of philosophy ever since. For Hobbes the pure or "mathematical" sciences can be known a priori, but the "mixed mathematics" such as physics depend on "the causes of natural things [which are] not in our power" and the "greatest part of them . . . is invisible" (1972: 42). He put it more fully in the Epistle Dedicatory to his *Six Lessons to the Professors of Mathematics:*

Of arts, some are demonstrable, others indemonstrable; and demonstrable are those the construction of the subject whereof is in the power of the artist himself, who, in his demonstration, does no more but deduce the consequences of his own operation. The reason whereof is this, that the science of every subject is derived from a precognition of the causes, generation, and construction of the same; and consequently where the causes are known, there is place for demonstration, but not where the causes are to seek for. Geometry therefore is demonstrable, for the lines and figures from which we reason are drawn and described by ourselves; and civil philosophy is demonstrable, because we make the commonwealth ourselves. But because natural bodies we know not the construction, but seek it from the effects, there lies no demonstration of what the causes be we seek for, but only what they may be. (Hobbes, 1966, VII:183–4)

It is this geometrical, or pure "mathematical" model which is taken by Hobbes to be paradigmatic of the moral sciences,[25] so that:

25 For further discussion see Child (1953:271–83).

politics and ethics (that is, the sciences of *just* and *unjust*, of *equity* and *inequity*) can be demonstrated *a priori;* because we ourselves make the principles – that is, the causes of justice (namely laws and covenants) – whereby it is known what *justice* and *equity*, and their opposites *injustice* and *inequity*, are. For before covenants and laws were drawn up, neither justice nor injustice, neither public good nor public evil, was natural among men any more than it was among beasts. (1972:42)

This argument implies that the central task for a science of ethics must be an account of the human will, and in offering his account of this Hobbes bridges the gap between the argument from rights and that from interests for the legitimacy of the contract. His aim is to give an account of the will that enables him to deduce the indubitable rationality of the contract, to show that given the nature of the human will it must be in man's interest to contract – at the same time arguing that the state derives its legitimacy from man's decision to make it.

For Hobbes the will is an appetite, one of the "voluntary motions" that has "interior beginnings" in the mind; it is the result of man's deliberative capacity to do or forbear, the "last Appetite, or Aversion, immediately adhaering to the action, or to the omission thereof" (1968:127), but that it resides in the mind does not mean that its consequences cannot be scientifically studied. This view of moral knowledge being characterized by subjective certainty grounded in the purposive acts of individual wills has had a lasting impact on liberal moral and political thought. With geometry it lost its preeminent status as the archetypical science, not because of changes in conceptions of moral knowledge but because of changes in what came to be regarded as criteria for genuine science: specifically the replacement of apodictic certainty with intersubjective demonstrability, prediction, and experiment that came to characterize empiricist thought in the nineteenth century. *These* developments turned the subjective certainty that the early empiricists considered the hallmark of moral knowledge into "mere" subjectivism, opening the way for the emotivist revolution in ethics. Hobbes perceived no tension between his identification of moral knowledge with subjective certainty and his scientific pretensions; for him the mind-dependence or otherwise of

47

facts had no bearing on their epistemological status, and the will-dependence of moral actions made them understandable with the certainty of geometry.

If Hobbes was not himself a subjectivist in anything like the modern sense of the term, it is nonetheless true that in the political and moral isolation of the individual he made several decisive moves that would be crucial for the incorporation of a subjectivist ethos into liberal rights theories. His account of the contract was innovative politically because of its treatment of the relationship between man and the state. The state, as we saw, derives its legitimacy from a universal reciprocal agreement among all men to renounce the right of nature. Although the idea of legitimate government resulting from some sort of contract was by no means new in the seventeenth century, medieval conceptions of contract had assumed powerful corporatist views of society and were interlaced with ascending and descending feudal rights and obligations. Hobbes's account differed not only in its treatment of the makers of the contract as equal, but, as Gierke (1934, I:61ff) long ago pointed out, because his account rules out the possibility of any legitimate social or political institution – such as the church, local or regional associations, or the common law – other than the state and thus leaves the state and the individual as the only significant political actors in society.

One of the main reasons that Hobbes's account proved to be of such lasting influence lies in its compatibility with the monumental changes in English public and private law that occurred in the seventeenth century, providing the basis for the modern, secular, national states of the post-Enlightenment period. Central among these changes was the destruction of an independent basis for public law, and the growing tendency to perceive it as secondary to, and derivative of, the system of private law. This was implied, for instance, in the act abolishing the office of king in 1649. After declaring void "all fealty homage and allegiance which is or shall be pretended to be due unto any of the issue and posterity of the late king, or any claiming under him," the act decisively separates the public interest from any autonomous rights the ruler might be thought to have had, by declaring the ruler unnecessary to the public interest, where previously he had been regarded as the embodiment of it; and by convicting the king of treason, where treason previously had been defined in terms of thoughts or deeds against the crown.[26] Never again would an English monarch be granted rights that were not ultimately a function of the rights of the people. This denial of any other source of legitimate authority is also embodied in the act of the same year abolishing the House of Lords.[27] The Lords had derived their rights through the feudal hierarchy from the crown. Once the crown ceased to have any legitimate independent authority so too must the Lords. This dismantling of the medieval system of public law was not reversed at the Restoration. Although vestiges of medieval public law have remained, in characteristic English fashion, down through the present, when Royal institutions were reinstated they were firmly grounded in and limited by the private law rights of the common law. The abolition in 1641 and 1642 of the Star Chamber, High Commission, and other prerogative courts also sharply underscores these developments.[28] These courts, which had functioned independently of the common law and had expanded their jurisdictions throughout the later fifteenth and sixteenth centuries, had been principal mechanisms of Royal control over the legal system. Their abolition more than any other single development signaled the triumph of the doctrine of the rule of law. Thus, though Hobbes opposed the innovative anti-Royalist claims of the common lawyers, by grounding the authority of his absolutist state exclusively in the contract among individuals he was sanctioning a view of public law that had elective affinities with the larger historical changes in English law that were in motion. His claim that power is absolute and indivisible is not to be confused with the traditional defenses of absolutism, such as Filmer's, which invariably argued for a legitimating lineage of Royal power that

---

26 Act of March 17, 1649, reprinted in Gardiner (1889:294–6).
27 Act of March 19, 1649, reprinted in Gardiner (1889:296–7).
28 Thus the act abolishing the Star Chamber laid it down that "neither His Majesty nor his Privy Council have or ought to have any jurisdiction, power or authority . . . to examine or draw into question, determine or dispose of the lands, tenements, hereditaments, goods or chattels of any the subjects of this kingdom, but that the same ought to be tried and determined in the ordinary Courts of Justice and by the ordinary course of the law." Reprinted in Gardiner (1889:183).

49

functioned independently of, or was a source of, the rights of the subject.[29]

Hobbes isolated the individual morally by making him the only meaningful subject of moral predicates, and by considering his wants, needs, and aspirations in isolation from those of all others, except insofar as these latter can assist or retard the pursuit of his own goals. We have already seen that he rejected what today we should refer to as intuitionist and extrinsic conceptions of the good in favor of a relational view tied to the wants and needs of individuals. If, for Hobbes, moral predicates can attach only to individuals, they are individuals of a very special sort, for they are conceived of in this (moral) context in their prepolitical state. In his taxonomy of the sciences in *Leviathan* (1968:149), ethics and the sciences of justice and injustice are regarded as subdivisions of natural philosophy, derivable from the nature of the human passions and speech. Ethics is thus quite separate from civil philosophy which results from "the accidents of *Politique* bodies" which generate the institution of commonwealth and the political rights and duties of sovereign and subject. For Hobbes, moral questions are in no sense a function of political relationships; on the contrary, morality is prior to and gives rise to political relationships via the contract. This view was reinforced by the radical antiholism implied by Hobbes's resolutive-compositive method: the way to understand a complex social mechanism such as a commonwealth is to take it to pieces and examine the component parts—in this case the agents who have contracted to create it—ruling out the possibility that the whole might in any epistemologically loaded sense be more than the sum of its parts, or that the nature of those parts can be grasped only in relation to the mechanism as a whole. When Hobbes makes the further move of considering man *qua* moral agent only after he has completed this disassembly, he is able to supply a philosophical basis for treating all moral questions in terms of

29 This independent lineage rested on patriarchial conceptions of authority—taken over from Bodin in Filmer's case—in terms of which governmental authority was held to be identical to both familial and monarchical authority. The ultimate basis of all three kinds of authority was held to be divine. See Tully (1980:55f). This issue is taken up further in Chapter 3 section II(ii).

private individuals, and for deriving all moral and political relationships from relationships among individuals.

Hobbes's conception of morality is derived directly from his account of natural man's passions. It is this that enables him to make the prepolitical individual's wants, needs, and aspirations the foundation of his system of ethics, and hence his naturalist account of political legitimacy. The only sense in which Hobbes considers social relationships in his ethics is where individual desires are overdetermining and thus generative of conflict. He never considers moral questions as arising from man's political interrelationships. They result directly from man's natural capacities and passions, which are taken as axiological.[30] His refusal to regard man's passions as in any sense even conditioned by civil relationships led to the objection of Rousseau and countless others that he attributes obviously civil characteristics of the society of his day to "natural" man. There is truth to such claims but more to the point is this whole view of morality as predicated of isolated individual wills in the first place. This generates the notion that it is possible to have a science of morality that is entirely ahistorical and ignores all social facts, and which makes morality essentially a private affair, since man *qua* moral agent is logically prior to and a condition for the creation of a public sphere. This provides a new legitimating basis for the system of public law.

The historical tenacity of Hobbes's account must be understood in terms of its elective affinity with historical changes that were in process. While the system of public law was coming to be exclusively based on and legitimated by the common law, this latter was itself in a period of innovative change. The notion that the common law had existed since time immemorial, that it was rooted in an Ancient Constitution lost in the mists of time, was being displaced due to the discovery by Spelman and others that English law was largely feudal in character and German in origin, and had been imported at

30 Although Hobbes pays serious attention to the distinction between "vital" motions that include basic animal needs and "voluntary" motions (1968:118–30) this is not to be confused with a nature/nurture distinction of any kind. For Hobbes, as we have seen, all issues about morality fall into the latter (voluntary) category. This has no bearing on their presocial or, better, asocial character.

the time of the Norman Conquest (Pocock, 1957:70–123).[31] The doctrine of the rule of law could thus not be based on an historical claim; it must rest on a direct moral claim about the nature of the relationship between ruler and people. It is in this period that the common law begins, in the two critical areas of land law and contract, to take on the appearance of modern private law.

Although in many respects feudalism never became fully established in England,[32] the system of land law was the exception. Following the Conquest, all land became part of the system of tenures that derived ultimately from the crown.[33] If English land law was more perfectly feudalized than any in Europe, it was also the first to go into decline. England's relatively powerful medieval monarchy was able to destroy local suzerainties which the French, for example, were unable to do successfully. Henry VIII's seizure of church land (about one-sixth of all the land in England was seized during the 1530s) and subsequent sale of much of the land to pay for his wars in Scotland and France, did much to create the beginnings of modern transmissibility in land (Tigar and Levy, 1977:203–6). Although it is mistaken to imply, as Tigar and Levy do in many places, that there was a single homogeneous bourgeoisie which until the Civil War allied itself to the crown against the church and feudal landowners, and then against the crown in alliance with the common lawyers,[34] and although it is true

31 More recent scholarship has shown that this development was not as revolutionary as Pocock, in *The Ancient Constitution and the Feudal Law*, thought. Some of Hobbes's contemporaries believed that an historical view of the common law was compatible with a Hobbesian view of sovereignty. See Tuck (1979:83, 132ff). I sidestep these debates noting only that Hobbes's detaching the theory of sovereignty from all considerations of history and tradition was to be decisive for its incorporation into the ideological grammar of the modern liberal tradition. This is taken up in section III of this chapter.

32 See Maitland (1920:161–3).

33 For discussion of the impact of the Conquest on English land law see Nasmith (1875:561–88).

34 Thus the constant references to "the legal ideology of the bourgeoisie," to "the alliance of the bourgeoisie and the common lawyers," and to the partial responsibility of "the bourgeoisie" for the creation of the absolutist powers of the Henrican monarchy. They refer to the "alliance of the bourgeoisie and the common lawyers" during the Civil War, and to Coke as a "major architect of the alliance's ideology" (Tigar and Levy, 1977:216–18, 226–7). This is gross oversimplification, since it presumes a homogeneous bourgeois class that simply did not exist. See Brenner (1973:53–107).

that the redistribution of land took several centuries,[35] there is no doubt that Henry's actions spelled the beginning of the end of feudal land law. By the end of his reign not only had he established the fact of a considerable market in land, but he had also enacted statutes enabling the buying and selling of land and its effective transmissibility through wills (Tigar and Levy, 1977:196–210).

The legal consolidation of these developments began in the mid-seventeenth century. A statute of 1660 abolished a great many feudal tenures[36] and although tenures continued, nominally, to be granted by the crown, this meant the de facto end of the large majority of feudal rights and obligations. It was at this time that the common law shed much of its medieval machinery, either by statute or simply by being allowed to obsolesce, and was replaced by modern conveyancing in land (Holdsworth, 1937, VI:624–9). Property assumed its modern form of exclusive dominion and became a predicate of its owner, conferring rights and powers of exchange on him, no longer entailing social or political obligations. The individual property owner became the central figure in the land law.

These developments were critically helped by the incorporation of the commercial side of the law merchant into the common law. First in relation to internal trade and, by the end of the century, in relation to all trade, the special law and courts of the law merchant were replaced by common law courts, and the principles of the mercantile side of the law merchant were absorbed into the common law. Although the complete incorporation of the law merchant was not achieved until the time of Lord Mansfield, by the late seventeenth century it had ceased to be a separate body of laws administered by separate courts (Holdsworth, 1956, I:568–73). This is the principal mechanism by which modern principles of contract entered the common law and transformed its entire basis, replacing the feudal system of rights and obligations with the individual contractor as the linchpin of the system of private law. And this is why, although Bacon and Hobbes lost the battle with the common lawyers, they ultimately won the war. It was the Hobbesian

35 See Hexter (1979:71–116).
36 The statute is reprinted in Nasmith (1875:588).

conception of contract as individual voluntary agreement that was to triumph, even if gradually, and from within. The survival of the common law was only achieved via its immense modification, the decisive beginning of which was Coke's declaration, in 1601, that the law merchant was part of the common law (Tigar and Levy, 1977:217–27). Many vestiges of the medieval system of conveyancing survived well into the eighteenth century, but the movement of the contracting agent to the center of the common law implied by this incorporation ensured that in triumphing the common law would spawn a new system of private law.

iv. The purposes of rights

For Hobbes, the purpose of natural rights, or the right of nature, is self-preservation. He breaks, as we saw,[37] with much of the natural law tradition in not deriving his right to self-preservation from natural law, but by turning it instead into an axiom, taking to a logical extreme a position that had first been developed in its seventeenth-century form by Hugo Grotius.[38] All civil rights and obligations, although the immediate result of the command theory of law, derive ultimately – via the contract – from this right to self-preservation. As we saw,[39] however, Hobbes envisaged an organization of society which sustains many other broadly defined civil rights, a wide area of negative freedom, created and regulated by the state, in which people have rights of exclusive dominion over their actions and property against one another. Hobbes regards the institutional relationships guaranteeing these civil rights as essential to man's survival, but he also sees them as central to the realization by man of his natural capacities. It will thus be necessary to look more closely at his account of those capacities to get at the purpose of these institutional relationships, and of the rights and obligations he believed that they entailed.

Hobbes believed that man's capacity to desire is such that

37 See section II(iii) of this chapter.
38 See Finnis (1980:207ff).
39 See section II(ii) of this chapter.

there are no limits to the number of things that will be desired or to the quantities in which they will be desired. The renowned axiom that man has a "perpetuall and restlesse desire of Power after power, that ceaseth onely in Death" (1968:161) is paradigmatic of a view of man as driven by an imperative to accumulate power, wealth and prestige. This is partly the result of man's insecurity in the state of nature, but it is important to realize that Hobbes regards it as a permanent part of the human condition, and as such it infects his account of the purpose for which civil rights, indeed all the institutions of civil society, exist. Hobbes's view of man's capacity to desire as intrinsically insatiable rests on a pluralist conception of human goods which in turn generates an essentially utilitarian rationale for the civil rights and institutions he envisages. There are four different but mutually reinforcing roots to this pluralism.

To begin with the definition of goods, Hobbes makes two moves which combine to locate the value of an object in the state of mind that it evokes rather than any property intrinsic to the object itself. The first is his argument, already discussed,[40] that goods must always be understood relationally in terms of individuals; that the only sense in which assertions about goods are meaningful is when they take the logical form "good for x" where x is an individual. The second move is to reduce all conceptions of good and evil to the desires of individuals. "*Good* and *Evill*," he says with an almost Stevensonian ring, "are names that signifie our Appetites, and Aversions" (1968:216). In this way it is the individual appetite which is the ultimate measure of value.

The second source of pluralism concerns the variability of goods. Goods can differ not only for different individuals, but for the same individual over time. The appetites and aversions that determine good and evil

in different tempers, customes, and doctrines of men, are different: And divers men, differ not onely in their Judgment, on the sense of what is pleasant, and unpleasant to the tast, smell, hearing, touch, and sight; but also of what is comformable, or disagreeable to Reason, in the actions of common life. Nay, the same man, in divers

40 See section II(iii) of this chapter.

times, differs from himselfe; and one time praiseth, that is, calleth Good, what another time he dispraiseth, and calleth Evil. (Ibid.: 216)

It is partly this plurality of individual conceptions of the good which, in Hobbes's view, generates inevitable conflict and ultimately war in the state of nature, and which dictates the necessity for a state to prevent that conflict by implementing rational imperatives that function in the interests of all. Although all men are in principle capable of rational behavior, their private appetites and mutual distrust mean that, although they know that peace, and hence the laws of nature which are conducive to peace, is desirable, they cannot (individually) implement the laws. The laws of nature thus in part derive their force from an appeal to the plurality of private conceptions of the good, which Hobbes regards as endemic to the human condition.

A third, related, source of pluralism is that Hobbes sees the value of goods as dependent in practice on something very like effective demand. Hence the controversial assertion in chapter 10 of *Leviathan* that value "is not absolute; but a thing dependent on the need and judgment of another." The following passage gives an even clearer illustration of this view of effective demand as the determinant of a good's value:

An able conductor of Souldiers, is of great Price in time of War present, or imminent; but in Peace not so. A learned and uncorrupt Judge, is much Worth in time of Peace; but not so much in War. And as in other things so in men, not the seller, but the buyer determines the Price. For let a man (as most men do,) rate themselves as the highest Value they can; yet their true Value is no more than it is esteemed by others. (1968:152)

The "true value" of a good is thus its market value. This operationalist view is connected to Hobbes's identification of goods with individual states of mind, because in the absence of any alternative basis for the value of an object, the object becomes synonymous with what is taken to be its value; once this move is made, the only way in which we can know the value to society of an object is to observe what social agents, by their actions, implicitly agree to be its value. In other words Hobbes commits himself to something very like a doctrine of revealed preference. It is thus an important consequence of his view of effective demand as the determinant of "true value" that it imports the idea of individual agreement, or consent as revealed through the market, into the heart of his theory of value.

The final source of pluralism in Hobbes's conception of the good derives from his subsumption of wants and needs under the general category of desires. Here the claim is not that Hobbes makes no distinction between wants and needs (we will see in a moment that he does) but rather that his identification of both needs-based and wants-based desires with individual states of mind makes them behaviorally equivalent psychological imperatives. For Hobbes, desires are a species of the "Voluntary Motions" (1968:118). In addition to the purely "vital motions," the things necessary for the physical continuation of life, man's imagination generates desires and capacities of a quite different order. Hobbes sees all desires as needs in the sense that they result in irresistible psychological drives, and the intrinsic insatiability of the human capacity to desire means that there is no simple threshold between essential and inessential desires. All desires are wants, on the other hand, in that their satisfaction or nonsatisfaction involves deliberative acts of the will.

Although there is thus no basic distinction between needs and wants, there are two importantly different classes of things desired: those things which are universal goods in the sense that all men must rationally desire them, and particular goods which lack this quality. The primary universal goods are self-preservation, peace, and security, but it is Hobbes's argument that all the laws of nature embody goods of this type; given his account of human nature they must be desirable to all. It would be a mistake, however, to attribute to Hobbes some kind of threshold notion, a view of primary or basic goods; the laws of nature are conceived of rather as structural conditions which enable individuals to pursue their private goals without generating chaos, war, and death. The laws of nature are general injunctions – to seek peace wherever possible, to preserve oneself, to observe basic norms of reciprocity, to keep promises – without which social life would, in Hobbes's view, be impossible.

57

A law of nature is a "Precept, or generall Rule, found out by Reason, by which a man is forbidden to do, that, which is destructive of his life, or taketh away the means of preserving the same . . ." (1968:189). Although these laws are discoverable by reason and in principle knowable to all, the fact that in practice reason is subordinated to the passions means that people will not abide by these rules without being forced to. But the rules themselves, defined as rational imperatives for the most effective realization of individual desires, have more in common with modern doctrines of rule-utilitarianism than traditional conceptions of natural law. Hobbes's account of the good is not fully utilitarian because his individuals are power-maximizers not pleasure-maximizers, and because he was more concerned with the avoidance of civil war than with the promotion of happiness. The blueprints for social engineering that consumed the attention of the classical utilitarians could only emerge in a vastly more stable, expansionary, and optimistic age. Yet the fact that he takes individuals as maximizing their subjectively identified goods as the basis for his account of the social good, together with his transformation of natural law from a set of divine injunctions which give rise to natural rights into a set of rules for the most effective realization of individual goals, means that the seeds of a utilitarian conception of the good are deeply embedded in his own. The quasi-rule-utilitarian status of Hobbes's natural laws is of cardinal importance because these are the injunctions he expects the sovereign to enforce in civil society. They shape the basic institutional structure of the Leviathan and reinforce the role of the state as regulator of the interactions of private individuals in pursuit of their separate goals.

A final point that should be noticed concerning Hobbes's account of human desires is that, though the capacity to desire is intrinsically insatiable, there is no sense in which this generates a dialectical or developmental view of human nature. It is natural man who is conceived of as having these capacities and drives and they are regulated, but in no way altered, by the institutions of civil society (as they are altered, for example, in different ways, according to Rousseau, Hegel, and Marx). There is no developmental theory of needs or capacities, which would require that they be seen, at least in part, as functions of social institutions and relationships. Human desires, drives, and capacities are seen as presocial, or, better, nonsocial, and, when man *is* in society, essentially private except insofar as their effective realization requires regulation. Each individual strives continuously after his goals, but this has no intrinsic effect on either his own needs or capacities or those of anyone else. It is worth stressing again that in offering this interpretation I am not attributing to Hobbes the doctrines of individualism or subjectivism in their modern forms. His view of the ontological status of moral knowledge, discussed in section II(iii) of this chapter, as well as his belief that he could deduce a predictive account of man's voluntary behavior from a materialist theory of the passions, decisively separates him from these traditions. My claim is that he made moves that constituted important necessary conditions for the emergence of individualism and subjectivism in their modern forms.

III. IDEOLOGICAL CONSEQUENCES OF HOBBES'S ARGUMENT

What were the consequences for the liberal ideology of individual rights of Hobbes's account? What is so special about his argument that gives Hobbes his immense status in the liberal tradition and shapes so powerfully both the vocabulary and the grammar of that tradition? In the foregoing analysis of Hobbes's discussion of rights I have begun to sketch answers to these questions. Here my aim is to spell out in greater detail the implications of that analysis via a discussion of five consequences for the liberal tradition of the Hobbesian account.

A central and basic consequence of the Hobbesian view is that the private individual becomes the subject of all legitimate rights. At the most general level, Hobbes regards all moral assertions as meaningfully predicable only of individuals, and his science of morality is deduced from his theory of man in his natural state. The moral imperatives embedded in the laws of nature are rational imperatives for the survival of naturally private individuals. These imperatives do not become unnecessary, as they do for Rousseau, after the institution of civil society. The rational imperatives of the laws of nature are embedded in and enforced by the laws of the Leviathan and the actions of the sovereign; they regulate the interaction between private individuals *in* society, and indeed they make such interaction possible. In this way Hobbes is able to identify natural man with private man, and so present a view of society as based on and reducible to relationships between private individuals as part of the natural order of things. Hobbes is able to reduce society to a collection of private relationships and render the notion of a public sphere unintelligible except as a complex description of these private relationships. Whereas defenders of absolutism had hitherto derived the rights of the ruler either directly from his supposed relationship with God or from a complex structure of patriarchal authority inherited from Adam; whereas medieval theories of natural law had attributed rights and jurisdictions to the church quite independently of the secular rights in society; whereas the feudal land law had reinforced a complex asymmetrical structure of ascending and descending rights and obligations; and whereas medieval public law had acknowledged independent local and regional jurisdictions, Hobbes denied the existence of any legitimate rights other than those of the individual and the sovereign, and those of the latter he derived directly from those of the former. All social interaction was made by definition private. The existence of a public sphere was merely to facilitate private interaction. This is a move of immense ideological significance because it provides for the germination of the liberal notion that the state, as representative of the public sphere, is fundamentally undesirable, an illegitimate intruder except where its actions facilitate private interaction. What was to be decisive in the creation of a liberal conception of law was not that the private sphere should be considerable in size (in many ways this sphere was greater in the preabsolutist feudal period than at any time since) but rather that the public sphere was seen as derived from, reducible to, and legitimated by the private sphere. This was central to Hobbes's account of legitimacy.

A second consequence of Hobbes's account concerns his separation of rights from obligations. Instead of conceiving of rights and obligations in terms of reciprocal correlative relationships, both being grounded in natural law, or some other theory of the good, rights are conceived of as indicative of the basic human capacity for autonomous action. In the state of nature man's rights are conceived of as whatever he can in fact do, and in civil society this is limited only by the law; it is not changed in any essentials, except that the law imposes limitations on others to respect a person's right through the machinery of voluntary agreement. Property rights are regarded as individual rights to exclusive dominion and are taken as the basic model of rights generally; they are seen as spheres of private action. Rights become religious, economic, legal, social, and moral spheres surrounding individuals that can only be entered by other individuals via mutual consent. The only sense in which this view of rights entails a theory of obligation is that all are obliged not to violate the private spheres of others. The definition of these spheres is quite general. For this reason Hobbes's *civil* rights might be thought of as Hohfeldian "liberties" as they relate to all other individuals (but not as they relate to the state), since they impose "no-rights" on others which are enforced by the state. There are endemic problems for general accounts of this kind in that they are overdetermined. The condition of one individual's satisfaction of his right becomes the violation of another's; the spheres, as it were, overlap. Whatever the drawbacks attending this view of rights (and we will see in subsequent chapters that they are considerable), it has been immensely influential in shaping the liberal tradition, in which it has become axiomatic to regard private property rights and moral rights thus conceived as analytically identical indicators of human freedom.

A third consequence of the Hobbesian account is that the substance of rights is defined in terms of negative freedom. Apart from those natural rights that are never given up, man's civil rights are defined as those areas where he is not prohibited by law from acting as he chooses – what Hobbes refers to as liberty the sovereign has "praetermitted": the liberty to buy and sell, make contracts, choose where to live, what to eat, what work to do, and how to raise children. "The Greatest Liberty of Subjects, dependeth on the silence of the Law"

(1968:271). Hobbes's plural theory of the good reinforces this negative libertarianism. Since individual conceptions of the good differ, except in cases where it leads him into conflict with the law, the individual should define and pursue his own individual goals. Hobbes did not go as far as Mandeville, for whom the pursuit of private good was synonymous with promotion of the public good, but he thought it inevitable that people would in fact pursue what they took to be their private goods and that a political system, if it is to survive, must acknowledge – even build on – this fact. One of Hobbes's principal explanations in *Behemoth* of the outcome of the Civil War was that the king and his followers lacked the resources to appeal to the self-interest of the masses.

Although Hobbes gives no clear definition of the size of and limits to the private sphere (he thinks this will vary with circumstances in the same way as will the level of taxation), we have seen that he expects it to comprise the vast majority of day-to-day social and economic interaction. It is unquestionably intended to include activities relating to the production, exchange, and consumption of wealth, all of which are conceived of as intrinsically private activities, grounded in the individual capacities to work and desire. Little as Hobbes liked the merchants whom he blamed, in large part, for causing the Civil War, and strong as was his personal distaste for excessive preoccupation with material gain, Hobbes recognized the importance of merchants from the point of view of generating wealth. His criticisms of the merchants were political and ideological, not economic. He thought the merchants had been misled concerning ways to attain their self-interested goals, but he accepted the inevitability, even desirability, of those goals (Ashcraft, 1978:46–51). Hobbes's assumption that there is a radical distinction between the public sphere of politics and the private sphere encompassing most of social, economic, familial, and religious life – which latter is preserved and regulated but not as a rule directly entered into by the state – would harden into one of the basic organizing categories of the liberal moral outlook. If Hobbes's views on the compatibility of the interests of merchants with those of the monarchy were a little naive,[41] the more general assumption on which they rested, while no less naive, was radically innovative and of lasting historical importance.[42]

This negative libertarian view of social life in general, and of the production, exchange, and consumption of wealth in particular, was also of great importance in the subsequent history of the liberal ideology of individual rights. Indispensable as it obviously is to the functioning of a capitalist market, it became deeply embedded in the emerging social system. Hobbes did not intend to justify such a system nor had he any very clear idea of what it was. His negative libertarianism survived and achieved the preeminent status it did in the dominant ideology because of its affinity with these emerging economic and social relations. It provided the conceptual tools for the construction of an ideology that could legitimate these relations. An important consequence of this negative libertarianism was that it provided for the notion of toleration as the basic yardstick for political freedom. This to an extent reflects the historical fact that one of the principal ideological battles of the seventeenth century was for religious toleration, a notion Hobbes openly endorsed. It is most interesting from our point of view, however, because it marks a separation of liberal rights theories from the communalist rights theories of the seventeenth century (such as those of the Levellers) and the radical rights theories of the eighteenth century and beyond, all of which emphasized participation, not toleration, as the central measure of a free society.[43]

A fourth consequence of Hobbes's account is that the class of objects and actions to which there are private individual rights is potentially infinite. There is a basic equation of doing, knowing, and making at the root of Hobbes's creationist or workmanship view of the world which generates the notion that I can own my actions, or be proprietor of them, in the same way as I can own or be proprietor of an object I have

41 On this subject see Thomas (1965:215ff).
42 Its contemporary manifestations will concern us in some detail in Chapters 4 and 5.
43 These issues are taken up in greater detail in Chapter 3.

made. In this way the individual private property right is the conceptual model for rights in general. Hobbes implicitly accepted the growing orthodoxy that the value of objects to which there are rights, of property, is some function of the work required to produce those objects and of the effective demand for them on the market. Since the capacity to demand includes both needs and wants, and since the latter are regarded as intrinsically insatiable, it follows that there are no necessary limits to what there may be private rights *to,* or at least no limits other than those imposed by technological barriers to what can be produced. This was a period in which wealth was seen increasingly as dynamic and continuously expanding, inhering in the capacity to work, not in land or in precious metals. Hobbes never articulated a *theory* of production, but his "making" model of ownership implied such a view. His dynamic account of demand was sufficient to entail that the value of objects to which there might be private rights was intrinsically unlimited and in practice determined on the market, that is, by what people will in fact pay for them. Whatever we believe to be the value of our property, its true value "is no more than it is esteemed by others" (1968:152).

The expansion of this workmanship model of proprietorship to a general model of action entailed that just as there were no intrinsic limits to objects that could be owned, exchanged, and consumed in the private sphere of the market, there were likewise no intrinsic limits to the actions that could be performed. Individuals' freedom of action varies with their capacities. The only sense in which individuals may influence others' actions is via their voluntary interactions in the market. Aside from this constraint, provided they remain within the law, there are no limits to what people may do, and no one to whom they are accountable for their actions. This view had three significant implications.

First, the notion that entitlement is conferred by some combination of making and voluntary exchange forms the basis of market-based conceptions of distributive justice that can, and would, be used to legitimate monumental inequalities, so long as these are worked through the market. Second, the view that individuals own what they make in virtue of their ownership of their actions takes the capacity for individual action as given, as prior to and independent of man's social relationships. It is insensitive, for instance, to the fact that the individual's capacity to work is critically dependent on his or her position in the social division of labor, and that it would be vastly more limited without the existence of that division. We will see that this view of individual capacities was to become one of the central vulnerabilities of the liberal ideology of individual rights, for if the capacity to produce is potentially infinite *because of* the economies of scale inherent in the division of labor, it can hardly be seen as conferring rights that are independent of that division of labor. Third, although Hobbes had a naturalistic theory of needs – one that would be dubbed "paternalistic" by many a contemporary liberal – the fact that he equated indispensable needs with inessential wants in his account of desires as psychological imperatives together with his view that the true nature of these desires is determined behaviorally, by what people actually do, destroyed the possibility for any thoroughgoing distinction between needs and other sorts of desires. Although Hobbes did not propound a theory of revealed preference, his account of desires as inclusive of needs and wants, as subjectively identified, as potentially infinite, and as expressed and valued through the market, was an account that contained all the key elements of the modern individual preference function. This preference function became a standard axiom in classical and neo-classical theories of demand and in liberal theories of distributive justice. While Hobbes's remarks about wants and needs fall short of a full theory of effective demand, we will see in the next chapter that by the later part of the seventeenth century views remarkably like his would be incorporated into the systematic explorations of market behavior by Barbon, Locke, and their contemporaries.

A final ideological consequence of Hobbes's discussion concerns the nature and functions of the state. Although Hobbes conceived of the power of the state as absolute, he regarded the functions that the state will in fact perform as regulative of the private relationships that constitute his negative libertarian society. This is true not only in the economic sphere, where the state performs only those regulative functions necessary for the market to work, but in social life generally where, as we saw, rights have the same structure as private property rights of exclusive dominion. Action in general is considered private, and the sphere of negative liberty, guaranteed by the silence of the law, is expected to comprise the vast majority of social life.

It is often argued that Hobbes's investiture of the state with absolute power is at odds with the liberal view of man's relationship with the state and even that it has strong authoritarian implications. It is true that for Hobbes the power of the state is absolute, but it is important to notice that the powers Hobbes ascribes to the state are basically those which most liberals, too, regard as nonnegotiable: the guarantee of property rights and the rule of law, of territorial integrity and a workable currency system, the enforcement of contract and basic criminal sanctions, and the raising of taxes for these limited purposes. In liberal-capitalist societies the power that the state has to perform *these* functions *is* seen as absolute, as a condition for the civil freedoms liberals cherish. Note that Hobbes regards it as essential for the survival of any society that there *be* a decisive and absolute sovereign power, but this has nothing to do with the conduct of government which may be monarchical, aristocratic, or democratic (1968:239–51). His point is that without the existence of a decisive authoritative power that can enforce the rules and norms essential for social interaction, society will collapse into chaos. "*Take away the Civill Law,*" he tells us, "*and no man knows what is his own, and what another mans*" (1968:296). In a society where negative libertarian economic and social practices are firmly established and have an air of permanence, these powers of the state tend to be latent and invisible, at least until threatened. They are present nonetheless as must be obvious to anyone who reflects on what would happen, in contemporary Britain or America, if the state ceased forthwith to enforce contracts, protect individual property rights, or regard itself as responsible for territorial integrity.

A closely related implication concerns the activities that regulation of a negative libertarian society will entail in prac-

tice. I have already noted that a regulative state is not necessarily minimal in the modern sense of entailing relative inaction. If the state's goal is to regulate a society based on private
relationships, the policies and practices it will have to adopt to
achieve this end will vary greatly with historical circumstances.
The idea of a regulative state would only entail the existence
of a minimal state from liberal premises for the comparatively
brief period between the rise of equilibrium theory and the
definitive discovery by Keynes that there is no tendency toward efficient equilibrium in capitalist markets.[44] Hobbes
wrote in a period of extensive social, economic, and political
dislocation, when national markets in basic commodities such
as land, corn, and labor were still establishing themselves,
when the legal nature of property was in a process of extensive redefinition, when the state had for over a century been
playing a central role in the redistribution of feudal wealth as
transmissible property, when the very existence of private property and of a legally ordered society was seriously threatened
by civil war. In such a period the goal of regulating a negative
libertarian society would require a state that was in many respects interventionist. It would have to create the conditions in
which a negative libertarian society could exist. These facts
were reflected in much contemporary economic and political
writing. Despite the presence of many elements of classical
economic thinking there was no notion that the economy, let
alone the rest of society, could be *self-regulating*, no assumption
that it is a system with inertial self-equilibrating tendencies.
On the contrary, the evidence of the past century would have
suggested to contemporaries that secular, not cyclical, changes
characterized the basic socioeconomic structure, and the evidence of the past several decades suggested to writers like
Hobbes that without decisive social and political authority resting in the hands of the state, chaos and destruction, rather

44 Keynes was not the first to discover this. It had concerned economists in liberal
and radical traditions such as Marx, Hobson, Kalecki, and others, before Keynes
wrote. The idea achieved orthodoxy in the liberal consciousness, however, in
association with Keynes's theory of consumption functions and in particular his
argument that the diminishing marginal propensity to consume creates a permanent tendency toward disequilibrium, or at least an inefficient equilibrium, as a
result of the insufficient aggregate demand it generates.

67

than the harmonious hum of a self-equilibrating social mechanism, would result. The myth of the minimal state could only arise once the social and legal institutions necessary for the functioning of a negative libertarian society had become so deeply entrenched that they would seem to be part of the natural order of things, and thus to function independently of the state. By its inaction the state would then preserve a status quo that its activism in an earlier period had been instrumental in creating.

Seen in this light, Hobbes's rejection, on the one hand, of all feudal definitions of property and right for the modern idea of exclusive dominion and its corresponding "spherical" and negative notion of individual privacy, and his insistence, on the other, that all civil rights, including property rights, are distributed by and exist on sufferance from the state, must be seen as ironically paradoxical. Hobbes *does* embrace a bourgeois conception of property rights, he *does* see all social relationships as essentially private, and he *does* see the role of the state as basically regulative of those private relationships; in short he *does* articulate a negative libertarian view of society. Yet he sees no contradiction between this and advocating a state that has both absolute power and no fixed limits to the extent to which it may intervene in society. On the contrary, he sees such a state as essential to the creation and preservation of this type of society. The key to this apparent paradox lies largely in comprehending it historically, in understanding the imperatives for the institution of a negative libertarian society in mid-seventeenth-century England. Part of the key, however, is logical, and is to be sought in Hobbes's characteristic tendency to pursue any argument to its logical extreme. He saw quite clearly that a society based on negative libertarian relationships, if it was to survive and remain stable, would have to be created and regulated by the state, and that this regulation would require different amounts and kinds of intervention in different historical circumstances. He had no ideological stake in pretending that the state did not perform these constitutive and regulative functions, or in pretending that in the areas decisive for the survival of a negative libertarian society the power of the state was not absolute. The myth of the minimal state would only

68

arise in conjunction with the classical equilibrium model which was not present in the intellectual milieu in which Hobbes wrote, and had no application to his contemporary reality. This model was never very generally applicable, and certainly no-where near as generally as it would be assumed to be in the axioms of classical and neo-classical economics, or in the main-stream of liberal ideology after John Stuart Mill. For this reason Hobbes supplies us with a more accurate and transparent account of the nature and role of the state in a negative libertarian society than do its subsequent defenders.

IV. CONCLUSION

In what sense is it accurate or useful from our point of view to regard Hobbes as a "bourgeois" theorist? Although there is much in the preceding analysis to confirm Macpherson's central contention that we discover at the heart of Hobbes's writing a "conception of the individual as essentially the proprietor of his own person or capacities, owing nothing to society for them" (1962:3), it also seems clear that Macpherson's analysis is seriously inadequate in three different respects. His possessive market model is historically inaccurate as a picture of the socioeconomic structure in England in the early to mid-seventeenth century, the view that Hobbes's account can be reduced to an articulation of the central normative propositions of that model is at best exegetically incomplete and more probably seriously misleading, and, most important from our point of view, Macpherson's simplistic reduction obscures some of the most subtle and important aspects of Hobbes's influence on the subsequent evolution of the liberal ideology of individual rights.

To begin with the historical viability of the model, for Macpherson a possessive market society is one in which there is an absence of an authoritative allocation of work or rewards, a presence of an authoritative enforcement of contracts, assumptions that individuals are rational utility maximizers, that land, natural resources, and labor are individually owned and alienable, that some individuals "want to increase their level of utilities or power," and that there is inequality of energy, skill, or possessions (Macpherson, 1962:53–4). This is contrasted with a "simple market society" which lacks alienable land, resources, and labor, unequal desires for power or utilities, and inequalities in energy, skill, and possessions, and with a "customary or status" society. Macpherson's claim is that

> the model of a possessive market society, and no other, does correspond in essentials to modern competitive market societies, that each of its postulates is required to produce that correspondence, and that that model and no other does meet the essential requirements of Hobbes's society. (Ibid:61)

Passing over various difficulties that have been raised concerning the supposed exhaustiveness of these models and their coherence as distinct models of society,[45] the most serious historical difficulties with the possessive market model concern its inaccuracy as a picture of seventeenth-century England. It is one thing to hold that significant elements of the capitalist organization of society had begun to appear in England by the time of the Civil War, that those elements both influenced contemporary political writers and were causally important in the evolution of capitalist societies and the ideologies they spawned, and that an understanding of these causal connections will be helpful in analyzing the ideologies that prevail in our contemporary world. It is quite another to presume the applicability of this vague model to all "modern competitive market" societies and thereby ignore the vast significant differences between, for example, England in the 1640s and the United States in the late twentieth century. An argument of this generality lacks historical credibility and exposes Macpherson to endless objections from some historians as Hexter, Pocock, and others, who lump "Marxists and Straussians" together for their simplistic division between feudalism or traditionalism and "modernity," and their tendency to identify all that was said or done after about the time of Machiavelli as "contributing to" or "reflecting" either the rise of the bourgeois world or the decline of Western civilization.

Leaving aside the intrinsic difficulties with all such massive historical assertions, it is not at all clear that Macpherson's

45 For discussion of which see Letwin (1972).

model can very usefully be applied to seventeenth-century England. Although my analysis has confirmed the presence in this period of modern notions of contract, a growing wage labor force, and emerging national markets in various commodities, the overall picture is very much one of a society in transition.[46] For Macpherson to make the point that almost half the population of England consisted of wage-laborers invites the obvious retort from Letwin and others that over half did not, which clearly contradicts his assertion that England "approximated closely to a possessive market society in the seventeenth century" (1962:61). It may seem a little tendentious to make these points against Macpherson, especially if one is in sympathy with his general enterprise. His model is intended to be general and schematic, to make a few basic points about economic and social organization. But it is these basic points that are misleading, for they obscure the important transitions that were going on in England in this period. For this reason Macpherson's model provides no useful basis for an *historical* understanding of the political writings of the time.

A final historical weakness in this model is that it fails to take account of the central role played by the state in the transition to a capitalist society in England. Macpherson does acknowledge, elsewhere in his account, that the state played an important role in regulating trade, employment, and investment, and cites Barry Supple's important book on this subject,[47] but he appears to miss the more important point that during this period the state was actively creating many conditions for the functioning of a market society. Not only by its direct participation in the redistribution of feudal land, but also through the massive revolutions in public law, private law, and the relations between the two, the state was centrally in-

46 For a useful discussion of the historical literature, also concluding that seventeenth-century English society is best characterized as transitional between feudalism and capitalism, with certain sectors (notably agriculture) more advanced than others, see Wood (1983:7ff). The view that Hobbes's political theory should be understood in England's transitional socioeconomic context is also argued for by Thomas (1965:185–236), although he defends a more traditionally aristocratic view of Hobbes than that presented here.
47 Macpherson (1962:62); Supple (1959:225–53).

volved in instituting market relations in England. We might say with some plausibility that Macpherson is himself hoodwinked by the myth of the minimal state.[48]

Turning to the usefulness of Macpherson's model as a device for interpreting Hobbes's political theory, although his possessive market model has some affinities with the interpretation I have given, it is clear that Macpherson is plainly wrong on some exegetical questions, and that his discussion is so vague that it misses some of the key respects in which Hobbes articulates a negative libertarian ideology. Macpherson is wrong, for instance, in his discussion of Hobbes on inequality. A defining characteristic of the possessive market model is that there is basic inequality of energy, skill, and possessions (Macpherson, 1962:54). Yet it is a cardinal axiom of Hobbes's whole system that people are by nature equal in faculties of body and mind, that "though there bee found one man sometimes manifestly stronger in body, or of quicker mind then another; yet when all is reckoned together, the difference between man, and man, is not so considerable, as that one man can thereupon claim to himselfe any benefit" (1968:183). It is this basic natural equality that makes all men equally vulnerable in the state of nature and thus motivates their unanimous agreement. Macpherson tries to avoid this difficulty by asserting that, although Hobbes did not postulate any basic inequality, this is nonetheless required by what he takes to be Hobbes's conception of a possessive market society. A possessive market society, he says, requires substantial inequality of command over resources since such a society is divided between employers and employed, causing inequality of insecurity, the class of employed apparently being more insecure than that of employers. This generates the conclusion that Hobbes "failed to allow in his model for the inequality of insecurity which the other attributes of his model necessarily

48 It might be said in Macpherson's defense that since the huge scholarly interest in the role of the state in the transition from feudalism to capitalism occurred after his book was written, he cannot be taken to task for not considering the issues it raises. There is some truth to this, but it is worth pointing out that one of the most subtle and powerful accounts of this matter is still Polanyi's *The Great Transformation*, published in 1944, and that I am more interested in the viability of Macpherson's model than in making any judgment about his scholarship.

imply" (Macpherson, 1962:85). If ever there was a paradigm
case of a non sequitur surely it is this: Macpherson begins by
proposing a model that is held to explain Hobbes's theory;
he then finds Hobbes asserting something in direct contradiction to one of the defining characteristics of his model, and
so concludes by blaming Hobbes because he "failed to allow"
for it.

For Macpherson to berate Hobbes for not having what
amounts to Marx's concept of class is plainly absurd. By 'so
doing he misses what is really most interesting in Hobbes's discussion of equality for the history of the liberal ideology of
individual rights. Hobbes begins from radically egalitarian
premises, produces an argument which appears to treat all men
equally every step of the way, and nonetheless arrives at a conception of the social world that is very largely governed by
market relations, as though such a view flows directly from
man's natural equality. This is a device that would appear again
and again in the subsequent history of liberalism. It turns on
ascribing to presocial individuals a negative-libertarian conception of freedom and gearing social institutions to the preservation of that freedom. This is how a system that can generate
enormous inequalities gets its egalitarian *gloss* and can be justified via an appeal to egalitarian principles. Hobbes was a
theorist of mass, not class, society. This is precisely why the
grammar of his account is more congenial to liberal ideology –
in which social relationships are legitimated in universalist
terms – than to class-based relationships that constitute liberal-
capitalist practice. This appears to be lost on Macpherson in his
eagerness to demonstrate that Hobbes "failed" to conform to
the possessive market model.

Another serious inadequacy of Macpherson's model as an
exegetical device for interpreting Hobbes is his vague assertion
that individuals attempt to maximize "utilities or power." There
are several important roots of utilitarianism in Hobbes's discussion, but this assertion is inaccurate and does not begin to get at
them. Power, for Hobbes, is a relational concept denoting
causal efficacy, a means for achieving goals. Utility, in the modern sense in which Macpherson wants to attribute it to Hobbes,
is a measure of subjective satisfaction. Power may be a means

for maximizing subjective satisfactions, as Hobbes suggests in Chapter 10 of *Leviathan*, but it can be put to many other uses, at least some of them antithetical to this goal. Furthermore, there are other ways to maximize satisfactions than having power — such as living in accordance with the laws of nature. It is false to equate Hobbes's account of the desire for power with the desire to maximize utilities. Although Hobbes's account of the intrinsic insatiability of human desires generates a conception of human motivation that contains many key elements of the idea of a preference function, it is a misleading and unnecessary anachronism to attribute to him the whole utilitarian doctrine of human motivation. His central preoccupation with power and his axiom that man's primary psychological drive is fear mean that our claim about human motivation must be more partial than this if it is to be accurate.

Hobbes provided many of the conceptual tools for the utilitarian theory of human motivation — that people want more rather than less, that they define their own goals which vary across persons and time, and that these goals are conceived of and pursued independently of the activities of others. The vast gulf between his account and modern utilitarian accounts is that for Hobbes none of this is inconsistent with a theory of objective interests explicitly derived from a theory of human nature. It may be true, as intuitionists since G. E. Moore have claimed, that utilitarianism also rests on an implicit naturalism in its identification of utility with a natural human capacity. If this is so, however, it is a different and much weaker sense of naturalism than that implied by Hobbes's theory of objective interests, which rests on a view of ethics as a demonstrable science, perceivable with the absolute certainty of Euclidean geometry. In the context of Hobbes's theory of science [see section II(iii)], it made sense to hold *both* a "subjective" theory of rights, where individuals define their own goals in a kind of proto-emotivist fashion, *and* a theory of "objective" interests held to be unambiguously demonstrable and indubitably certain. What is worth emphasizing here is that the coexistence of these two theories was pegged to a view of science that was not destined to survive the eighteenth century. In the post-Humean era liberals would find themselves compelled to jettison all notions of objective interest, as values were separated from facts and ethics descended into the realm of the merely subjective. Once the view of science that had given Hobbes's theory its broad coherence fell into disrepute, his theory of rights became a basis for attacking the very idea of an objective interest. This development belongs to the era of neo-classical utilitarian theory; it is quite antithetical to Hobbes's view, as is it in fact to early versions of utilitarianism. Macpherson's desire for a model of ideological assumptions that is applicable to all "modern" market societies leads him to project values that he sees around him onto earlier periods for which they are inappropriate, or, perhaps more accurately, in which they were present in partial and embryonic forms. This in turn generates an unhistorical attempt to straitjacket arguments in accordance with his preconceived model, resulting in his stipulative identification of Hobbes's notion of power with subsequent conceptions of utility. Not only does his account lack plausibility as an interpretation of Hobbes, it also misses the more subtle, though nonetheless vital, developments in the history of the ideology he is concerned to analyze.

Macpherson's discussion of Hobbes on human motivation also misses one of the principal roots of modern utilitarianism in Hobbes's thought, one which is vital to the case Macpherson wants to make. This is Hobbes's transformation of the doctrine of natural law into what is essentially a brand of rule-utilitarianism. Hobbes radically transforms the idea of natural law from a system of divine injunctions from which rights are derived to a set of maxims that take rights as given and justified on the grounds that they are demonstrably rational. It is too simple to say that these maxims are reducible to man's "possessive individualism." It is Hobbes's view that if men are left to their own devices, to pursue their individual wants unregulated by law, they will *not* behave rationally. Their selfish pursuit of their passions will produce chaos, war, and death. The maxims embedded in the laws of nature are in principle rationally demonstrable to all and Hobbes takes great pains to demonstrate that they in fact function in the interests of all. This may, however, conflict with what a given individual in a given situation "possessively" regards as his interest. The law is there to force men

75

to behave rationally. For Hobbes, this means according to their true interest. This is the basis of Hobbes's command theory of law, which became central to utilitarianism in its major classical variants. The idea of rationality has been through several metamorphoses in the liberal tradition that have functioned to detach it from theories of objective interest and to identify it instead with simple maximization of exogenously determined goals. The criteria that are seen as relevant to identify a practice as rational have likewise varied, but utilitarian arguments for the legitimacy or illegitimacy of laws invariably resolve into claims that they are rational or irrational. If there is a single move in Hobbes's theory that links his account to that of Bentham and his followers, it is surely this redefinition of the whole epistemological basis for the law.

There are two separate roots of utilitarianism in Hobbes's account of individual rights. The first lies in his pluralist conception of the good according to which individuals identify, attach value to, and pursue their goals in relative isolation from one another, and are proprietors of their actions and thus own what they make or exchange. This is captured by Macpherson's possessive individualism thesis, although it is mistaken to imply that this entails anything like a doctrine of subjectivism. Such a doctrine would arise only in conjunction with the late eighteenth-century separation of facts from values which found its subsequent expression in utilitarianism in the neo-classical denial of the possibility of interpersonal comparisons of utility. The second source of utilitarianism in Hobbes's account is his rationalist theory of law that resolves into a version of rule-utilitarianism.

Macpherson's historically unviable model leads to misinterpretations of Hobbes's theory and prevents him from adducing some of the most effective arguments available in support of the thesis he wants to argue. It also leads him to miss one of Hobbes's most important contributions to the liberal ideology of individual rights which resides in his account of the nature and functions of the state. The anachronistic assumption built into Macpherson's application of his model of Hobbes's England – namely that market relations were already more or less fully established—leads him to ignore statements by Hobbes that seem incompatible with his model but that are pregnant with ideological significance for the early liberal-capitalist state. For Hobbes, the state distributes transmissible private property rights (and so rejects and undercuts feudal land law). It creates and enforces a system of bilateral reciprocal contracts (and is thus by definition in opposition to large areas of medieval private law that still prevailed in Hobbes's England). It grants all individuals equal "negative" freedom where the law is silent (and thereby implies the illegitimacy of the obligations embedded in both feudal private law and absolutist public law, many of which were still in place well after the Civil War). Hobbes thus articulates a conception of the state which, when seen in the actual historical context of the transitions then occurring in English society, must be seen as innovative. None of this is reflected in a model that is derived from and portrays an established market system where the state plays a different role, but there is no reason for us to think that it should be so reflected.

Two aspects of Hobbes's account of the state that are of particular interest to us concern the nature, functions, and limits of its power and the moral justification for its existence. These go to the core of the enigmatic position of the state in the liberal ideological tradition and it will be useful to conclude by summarizing my earlier discussion of them. First, the territorial state is granted power that is absolute, limited at any given time only in ways that the legitimate agent or agents of the state may deem appropriate. The property and other civil rights that it grants, as well as the laws it enacts, are inviolable injunctions applicable equally to all. But if the *power* of the state is absolute, its *purposes* are quite limited and resolve basically into creating and regulating a negative libertarian society and within it a market-based economy. The expansion of the private sphere that followed the Reformation has been much commented on and needs little further discussion. The state divested first the church and then itself of direct responsibility for the spiritual and material well-being of its citizenry, and instead defined its responsibility as indirect, as creating and maintaining a system in which individuals could take care of their own needs and wants, both spiritual and material. A language had been created that made this seem both morally desirable and practically efficient. It could seem morally desirable because it rested on a negative libertarian conception of freedom implied by the separation of right from law and the adoption of the spherical conception of the private rights of individuals as against one another. A merely regulative state could thus appear to be one that maximizes freedom. It could seem to be practically efficient in the context of emerging beliefs about the nature and production of wealth that came increasingly to be regarded as residing in the capacity to produce for exchange.

Although separate, these moral and practical justifications for the regulative state would become importantly related. As Locke was the first of many to point out, mere regulation of private relationships is not a sufficient condition for the preservation of even negatively defined freedom, unless it is accompanied by guarantees that some basic material needs will be filled, and that some of the actions the state is capable of performing can never be justified. The moral justification for the regulative state was shown to rest on factual assumptions about what mere regulation of the private sphere would actually result in. It was a short step from here to basing the moral argument *upon* the practical argument, to arguing that the regulative state is justified *because* it leads to the most efficient method of generating wealth. But this is to anticipate the argument. For the present I merely note that, although this regulative conception absolves the state from direct responsibility for the well-being of its citizens, its indirect responsibility significantly includes doing whatever is necessary for the efficient functioning of the market.

Second, despite the awesome power Hobbes gives to the regulative state, he provides the conceptual tools for perpetual attacks on it. Much of his account reinforces the liberal vision of the state as an intruder on the privacy of the individual. The equation of freedom with toleration and privacy from government rather than participation *in* it, the rejection of both feudal and traditional absolutist conceptions of public law, and the derivation of the legitimate authority of the state from the private-law rights of individuals, all served to make the legal and moral status of the state intrinsically questionable, on the grounds that it threatened the private-law rights whose protection had become its raison d'être.

3
The classical moment

I. INTRODUCTION

One would have to be ignorant, foolish, or both to suppose it now possible to give an entirely novel interpretation of Locke's role in the rise of Anglo-American liberalism. There are three ways, however, in which the account offered here is held to be distinctive. First, I will argue that the theory of rights articulated by Locke contributed to and rested on a conservative liberalism. This is not to invoke the view of Dunn, Tully, and others that Locke was basically a Christian writer, firmly rooted in the values of the sixteenth-century neo-Thomist revival. I think this interpretation, though partly correct, suffers serious inadequacies. Nor do I wish to deny that many of Locke's political and religious arguments, particularly in his later writings, were politically radical in the historical context in which he wrote, so much so that many of his Whig contemporaries distanced themselves from the argument of the *Two Treatises* after 1688. They found Locke's right to resist more radically threatening than had been required to get rid of James II, and certainly more radical than they were prepared to subscribe to thereafter.[1] These facts notwithstanding, I believe Locke's theory shaped the economically and socially conservative nature of liberalism as a political ideology in important and lasting ways, as capitalism began to establish itself and to advance. No text is inherently liberal, radical or conservative – the ideological functions of the same text vary greatly with historical circumstance and reader.[2] It is striking, however, that Locke's arguments provided many of the ideas that would become central to legiti-

---

1 This case is powerfully argued for by Franklin (1978:87–126). See also Ashcraft (1986), especially Chapters 8 and 9.
2 See Shapiro (1982:535–78).

mating capitalist economic practices, not by "transcending" natural law and claiming that the lower classes are incapable of rational behavior, as Macpherson and others have claimed, but by modifying the natural-law tradition to make it consistent with the economic and social practices capitalism would require, and doing this in universalist and egalitarian terms. Locke's radical politics did not generate much in the way of conceptual tools to challenge this emerging liberal capitalist view, in large part because of his central focus on toleration, admittedly the burning issue for radical politics in his day. It was an idea ripe for manipulation in a world in which toleration would increasingly come to connote toleration of capitalist social and economic practices by an attentive but subordinate state. From this point of view what was significantly missing from Locke's political vocabulary was a theory of democratic participation. In the one area where Locke's arguments had potentially more radical longer-term consequences – the labor theory of value and its political implications – his arguments were destined not to have a lasting influence in the liberal tradition.

Second, as with my interpretation of Hobbes, I offer an account of Locke's view of the nature and functions of the state that squares neither with Macpherson's nor with contemporary minimalist interpretations of the kind defended by Robert Nozick. By again taking account of the difference between a regulative and a minimal state, I argue that, although he equivocates a good deal, Locke does in fact sanction significant state intervention. Finally, in contrast to some who hold that Locke's theory was the first modern illustration of the liberal tendency to argue for the priority of the right over the good, and in contrast to others who see his rights as derived from a Thomist view of the good, I argue that Locke's rights rest on a theory of objective interests of a kind not uncommon in English political theory up to the time of Hume. Close attention to his view of the nature of moral knowledge and the possibility of an incontrovertible ethics reveals why Locke saw no contradiction between a theory of objective interests and a "subjective" theory of rights; he regarded these as entailing one another.

81

II. LOCKE'S THEORY OF RIGHTS

Traditionally, Locke, far more than Hobbes, has been regarded as the founder of modern liberal conceptions of individual human rights. He offers an account of natural rights according to which every person, in virtue of the law of nature, is entitled to life, liberty, and property in order that he may survive and thrive. Thus all property owners are entitled to the protection of their property in virtue of their mutual agreement to obey the law. Like Hobbes, Locke believed that the state of nature was an actual historical condition which still prevailed in parts of the world and to which civil societies could, and did, in certain circumstances return,[3] but to Locke its character and political implications were very different. His contract did not generate a command theory of law as did Hobbes's but rather a representational one, and his citizenry retained substantial rights of resistance against the state. Whereas Hobbes's sovereign was never obligated to its subjects because it never contracted with them, emerging instead as a byproduct of the citizens' mutual agreements one with another, government for Locke is bound by a contract with the people. If it violates its fiduciary trust the citizens' natural right to revolution is activated, although just how this process might occur is not entirely clear and has been the subject of much exegetical dispute.[4]

The preceding is a fairly loose statement of Locke's view. As will be seen, such central terms as "property," "owners," "consent," and "resistance" had vitally different meanings in the context in which Locke wrote than do they for us today. To illuminate the full significance of his account for the liberal rights tradition, I now examine his argument in more detail.

i. The subject of rights

Although the state of nature, for Locke, is not necessarily a state of war as it is for Hobbes, and although we do not find in

3 Some commentators have suggested that Locke's state of nature was not conceived of as an actual historical state, but impressive evidence to the contrary is adduced by Ashcraft (1968:898–915; 1986: Chapter 6).
4 For an extensive discussion of this see Ashcraft (1986:Chapter 8).

Locke's writings the same fear of the masses that permeates
Hobbes's, there are several important parallels in their appeals
to the interests of the masses as the ultimate justification for
their political arguments. It is worth stressing that the kind of
threat presented by the masses to the ruling classes was significantly different in Restoration England from that which had
prevailed during the Civil War and Interregnum.[5] After 1660
the landowning class was secure from revolt from below. As
England entered the mercantile revolution that was to open
the way to the industrial revolution of the eighteenth century,
social and economic conflict was more effectively managed
within existing political structures. This was in part because of
general improvement in the standard of living, there being
general agreement among contemporaries by the mid-1670s
that the country was prospering. The abundant harvests after
mid-century reinforced this new social stability, in contrast to
the social unrest generated by the terrible harvests of the
1640s. After a century of decline, real wages were rising and
by the 1690s famine was perceived to be a thing of the past.
The substitution of wheat for rye, the growth of large-scale
market gardening and dairy farming, of intensive crop culti-
vation and stock breeding, all combined to improve living
standards and weaken the pressure on the political system
from below. The Restoration confirmed the defeat of popular
democratic movements in London. By the 1680s industrial
struggles had begun to assume their more modern forms of
strikes, mutinies, and other combinations to secure higher
wages. Although there were incidents of machine-breaking
and rioting, what Hill refers to as the oligarchic political structure was essentially secure and, more important, widely perceived to be so.

The revolution of 1688 was a palace affair and even in their
most radical moments in the early 1680s the Whigs never
conceived of revolt as anything else. Hobbes had, understand-
ably, regarded revolution as synonymous with a return to the
state of nature and civil war. Locke, writing in the early 1680s,
saw it as a return to the social community that stood between

5 The remainder of this paragraph is based on Hill (1961:200–8) and Appleby
(1978:99–102).

the state of war in the state of nature and civil society, for the reestablishment of a government in conformity with the fiduciary trust that the community grants to the legislature (Locke, 1963:417–8).[6] If England's political structure after the Restoration was basically oligarchical, and if the Whig revolutionaries had no intention of altering that structure, it is nonetheless true that Locke like Hobbes, saw it essential to legitimate the state in universalist terms. All men are equally the subjects of natural rights that are both logically and temporally prior to civil society. Each man

is born with a double Right: *First, A Right of Freedom to his Person,* which no other Man has a Power over, but the free Disposal of it lies in himself. *Secondly, A Right,* before any other man, to *inherit,* with his Brethren, his Fathers Goods. (Locke, 1963:441)

When we look for the justification offered by Locke for this generalized individual natural right we find that there are several. Locke tends to shuffle perpetually among arguments from nature, reason and scripture – with important consequences as we will see. Sometimes he seems to regard all these terms as synonymous. Thus in the *Essays on the Laws of Nature,* written in 1660, the law of nature is identified as a decree of the Divine Will that reason does not establish but discovers as a law enacted by a superior power and "written in the hearts of men" (Locke, 1958:141ff). In the *Second Treatise,* however, published in 1690 (though probably written in 1681)[7] the Law of Nature is treated as synonymous with reason itself:

The *State of Nature* has a Law of Nature to govern it, which obliges everyone: And Reason, which is that Law, teaches all Mankind, who will but consult it, that being all equal and independent, no one

6 Whether or not this community is a transitional entity between the state of nature and civil society (so that revolution need not be synonymous with a return to the state of nature) has been much debated by Locke scholars. It is not an issue we need to resolve here. Recent scholarship has inclined to the view that Locke's "positive community" does exist in the state of nature; by definition a return to the former therefore involves a return to the latter. See Tully (1980:96–7, 125–6), Ashcraft (1986:Chapter 8).

7 For a review of the debate on dating Locke's *Second Treatise,* see Ashcraft (1980: 429–85). Ashcraft convincingly concludes that it was probably written in late 1681 or 1682.

ought to harm another in his Life, Health, Liberty, or Possessions. (Locke, 1963:311)[8]

In the *First Treatise* we find several attempts to identify reason with nature. A genuinely impartial observer, Locke argues,

will have little Reverence for the Practices which are in use and credit amongst Men, and will have Reason to think, that the Woods and Forests, where the irrational and untaught Inhabitants keep right by following Nature, are fitter to give us Rules, than Cities and Palaces, where those that call themselves Civil and Rational, go out of their way by Authority of Example. (Locke, 1963:219)

Locke's view is that man's originally sinful passions led him astray, but observation of nature can show him his natural and genuinely rational mode of existence. Two chapters later we find a further identification of nature and reason with scripture in the context of his rejection of Filmer's theory of inheritance:

God having made Man, and planted in him, as in other Animals, a strong desire of Self-preservation, and furnished the World with things fit for Food and Rayment and other Necessaries of Life, Subservient to his design, that Man should live and abide for some time upon the Face of the Earth, and not that so curious and wonderful a piece of Workmanship by its own Negligence, or want of Necessaries, should perish again, presently after a few moments continuance: God, I say . . . directed him by his Senses and Reason, as he did the inferior Animals by their Sense, and Instinct, which he had placed in them to that purpose, to the use of those things, which were serviceable for his Subsistence. (Ibid.:242)

What is natural is rational and is also God's will. Thus in the *First Treatise* Locke is at great pains to establish that Filmer's patriarchial theory of authority depends on misinterpretations of the scriptures *and* on arguments that lead to rational contradictions *and* on false assertions about nature.[9]

In his attempts to establish that all men are equally subjects

---

8 On this point note Dunn's (1969:193) observation that Locke affirmed "the existence of a perfect parallel between the calculus of rationally apprehended moral truths and the divinely furnished system of hedonic sanctions."

9 For attacks on Filmer's religious arguments, see Locke (1963:191–231), his rational arguments (ibid.:237–9), and his arguments from nature (ibid.:218–20).

of natural rights, Locke appeals to all three types of argument. To begin with the argument from reason, Locke, like Hobbes, argues that all men equally have a rational capacity for genuine knowledge and that sound political arguments must appeal to that capacity.[10] Thus at the outset of the *First Treatise* he claims that anyone who will "but think himself" will see the absurdity of Filmer's propositions. He sets himself the task of giving convincing reasons to anyone who is willing to listen, claiming that "[i]f anyone, concerned really for Truth, undertake the Confutation of my Hypothesis, I promise him either to recant my mistake, upon fair Conviction; or to answer his Difficulties." Like Hobbes in his attacks on the arguments from authority and the "insignificant speech" of the Schoolmen, Locke has nothing but contempt for Filmer's "proofs" of Adam's Royal authority, which are nothing but "often repeating it, which among some Men, goes for Argument" (Locke, 1963:176; 172–3; 175; 184. Cf. also 1959, I:37–8). Also reminiscent of Hobbes in this regard, Locke was quick to defuse arguments from authority by appealing to man's natural and unencumbered reasoning capacities. In his discussion of reason in Book IV of the *Essay* he notes:

[T]here are many men that reason exceedingly clear and rightly, who know not how to make a syllogism. He that will look into many parts of Asia and America, will find men reason there perhaps as acutely as himself, who yet never heard of a syllogism, nor can reduce any one argument to those forms. . . . God has not been so sparing to men to make them barely two-legged creatures, and left it to Aristotle to make them rational, i.e. those few of them that he could get so to examine the grounds of syllogisms. . . . God has been more bountiful to mankind than so. He has given them a mind that can reason, without being instructed in methods of syllogizing: the understanding is not taught to reason by these rules; it has a native faculty to perceive the coherence or incoherence of its ideas, and can range them right, without any such perplexing repetitions. (Locke, 1959, II:389–91)

10 I am here taking exception to Macpherson's "differential rationality" hypothesis, according to which the laboring classes were, for Locke, incapable of fully rational behavior and hence of full political membership. See Macpherson (1962:232–8). This issue is taken up in section IV of this chapter. For an extended critique of Macpherson on this point, see Ashcraft (1986:Chapters 7 and 9).

The view that sound political arguments must appeal to the universal innate capacity of human reason also infuses the argument of *A Letter Concerning Toleration*. Princes, Locke argues, may be born superior to other men in power, but in nature they are equal. "Neither the right nor the art of ruling does necessarily carry along with it the certain knowledge of other things" (Locke, 1979:189). As far as genuine knowledge is concerned "[i]t is only light and evidence that can work a change in men's opinions" (ibid.:174). In the *Second Treatise*, Locke avers that the laws of nature are more easily intelligible to men than positive laws, for "[a]s much as Reason is easier to be understood, than the Phansies and intricate Contrivances of Men . . ." In his discussion of the authority of parents, the whole basis of Locke's argument against Filmer is that their authority is temporary *because* all adults are equally capable of rational behavior. Thus are parents to "inform the Mind, and govern the Actions of their yet ignorant Nonage, till Reason shall take its place and ease them of that Trouble" (Locke, 1963:315–6; 348).

Locke's rationalist appeals were directed primarily toward a fairly small educated and reading public. It is doubtful that he gave much thought, in this connection, to the lower classes. What is significant from our point of view is that he framed these appeals in universalist terms, acknowledging an equal rational potential in all men; the differences he discerned among them were attributed to education and social circumstance.[11] Because all men are born equally rational, each had the "right of nature" to enforce the laws of nature in the absence of legitimate civil authority. For this reason civil society must be shown to be in the rational interests of every individual.

The religious argument for man's individual natural rights turns on the creationist view that Locke opposes to Filmer's Adamite theory of property and political authority – to the view, that is, that God gave the world to Adam and his heirs in virtue of their inheritance from him.[12] Filmer argued that par-

11 On this point, see Wood (1983:129–42).
12 This view, and its significance for understanding Locke's contrasting argument, has been discussed in some detail by Tully (1980:35ff) and Ashcraft (1986: Chapters 3 and 4). It is taken up in more detail in sections II(ii), II(iii), III, and IV of this chapter.

ents since Adam had absolute authority over their progeny because they created them. Locke claims that God creates all children and uses their parents for this purpose. Parents do not fashion the child and most commonly do not even intend to create it; they do so as a byproduct of the instinctive desires God has placed in them. The authority parents have over their children is thus provisional; it expires when the children attain the age of reason and therefore provides no legitimating model for patriarchal political authority. The implications of this creationist view will concern us in section II(iii) of this chapter. The central point to note at present is that all men are created equal as the children of God and this is the religious basis for their equal rights vis-à-vis one another in the state of nature (Locke, 1963:215–6, 231, 348).

Finally, to establish man's equal natural rights to self-preservation, Locke invokes arguments based on assertions about nature and human nature. These appeals are not altogether mutually consistent. Nature is at times considered instructive of how man ought to live, as when we are asked to observe the harmonious ways of the animal kingdom (1963:219). At other times Locke cites beast-like behavior as indicative of the depths to which man can fall if he fails to observe the law of nature (1963:307–8; 314–5; 319ff). But the naturalist appeal to how men behave in fact is at times critical to Locke's theory. In his discussion of resistance to prerogative power in the *Second Treatise*, for instance, Locke argues that the decisive test of when the executive has overstepped its rightful limits is when "the Majority *feel it,* and are weary of it, and find a necessity to have it amended," for "God *and Nature* never allowing a Man so to abandon himself, as to neglect his own preservation" must leave him with this final authority (1963: 427, emphases added). In *A Letter Concerning Toleration,* there is a similar descriptive appeal:

[I]f men enter into seditious conspiracies, *it is . . . their sufferings and oppressions* that make them willing to ease themselves. Just and moderate governments are everywhere quiet, everywhere safe; but oppression raises ferments and makes men struggle to cast off an uneasy and tyrannical yoke. . . . [F]rom *the common disposition of all mankind,* who when they groan under any heavy burthen endeavour naturally to shake off the yoke that galls their necks. (Locke, 1979:215, emphasis added)

Despite his quickness to identify instances of the genetic fallacy in Filmer's argument (as when the latter asserts that the existence of such practices as slavery and child-selling in the world indicates their naturalness), and despite his rhetorical use of the argument that "when Fashion hath once Established, what Folly or Craft began, Custom makes it Sacred" (1963:219), Locke is thus not above appealing to what men and animals actually do, or appear to do, as evidence that these practices are both natural and justified, when it suits his purposes – whether these be to show biological grounds for monogamy, or to arrive at the particular view of resistance he wants to sustain (1963:363–4; 1979:215).

Locke's rationalist, naturalist, and religious arguments converge on the proposition that the prepolitical individual is the only legitimate subject of natural rights. Men are naturally equal and in general perceive themselves to be so; their equal rational capacities mark them as fundamentally opposed to traditional and patriarchal systems of political authority and their equality as children of God, their creator, assumes a fundamental moral equality among men. Since for Locke all civil rights arise from the institutions geared to the preservation of man's natural rights, this egalitarian view of the subject infuses his entire political theory.

ii. The substance of rights

What are there rights *to*? Locke answers this very broadly by saying that each man has a right to his life, liberty, and property; that in the state of nature he has a further right to enforce the law of nature for reasons of punishment, prevention of and compensation for injuries done to him, and that although this right to enforcement is renounced on entering civil society, man's other rights are grouped together under the single term property. Thus "no *Political Society* can be, nor subsist without having in it self the Power to preserve the Property..." for "the chief end [of civil society]... is the preservation of Property" (1963:367, 366). Property inheres quite generally in the capacity to do or make. It is in no way restricted to physical objects. We are proprietors of our *actions* and have exclusive rights over the freedoms and objects created as a result of those actions. Thus are slaves excluded from civil society not merely because they have no estates, but because they have "forfeited their Lives, and with it their Liberties." That is, they have given up their property in themselves. By comparable, if not entirely compatible, logic Locke holds, conversely, that absolute monarchy can never be justified because, by alienating their capacity for autonomous action, the subjects become slaves (Locke, 1963:366–8).

Unlike Hobbes, Locke regards the process of the creation of objects of entitlement as independent of government (although he expects government to facilitate and regulate it). He takes the more traditional view that the emergence of property rights is prior to, and, ultimately, served by the institutions of civil society. It is this aspect of his argument that has encouraged the view of Locke's state "as in effect a joint-stock company whose shareholders were the men of property" (Macpherson, 1962: 195). As Macpherson acknowledges, and as Tully, Ashcraft, and others have recently argued at some length, this view does justice neither to Locke's theory of property nor to the view of political authority generated by that theory. It will be useful to look at Tully's argument in some detail.

Tully's central claim is that at least two very different conceptions of right prevailed in seventeenth-century English and European political thought. Following Skinner (1978, II:138ff) and Tuck (1979:22–30, 46–7ff) he argues that on the one hand there was a "private" conception, adopted primarily by Grotius but also subscribed to by Hobbes, Filmer, and Pufendorf, and deriving ultimately from the Ockhamist "subjective" tradition. On the other there was a "common" conception deriving from the Thomist natural-law tradition that viewed individual property rights as functions of the individuation of the common, given by God to man for the preservation of human life, the first dicate of the law of nature.[13] In this tradition natural rights

13 There were differences of some importance among the writers comprising these traditions; Tully describes them in considerable detail (1980:53–94).

are not prior to natural law; on the contrary they are derived from it. Writers adhering to a "broad" conception of property, comprising common and private property, include Suarez, Selden, Cumberland, and Locke (Tully, 1980:64–79ff). The law of nature, for Locke, gives to all a theoretical inclusive use-right to the common – a right, that is, not to be excluded from it by others. The foundation of property is derived from this fact and from two characteristics of human beings. First, each individual is proprietor of his or her own person and, second, no one has a right to it other than that person. The individual qua natural being is God's property since God created us, but the individual qua person – that is, a being capable of intentional action – is not, and it is this latter individual that has the proprietorship of his or her own actions. In Locke's view, when God gave the earth to Adam, He was not giving him private dominion over it, He was giving it to mankind in common. We all therefore have an inclusive right (a right not to be excluded) to the common, but not an exclusive right (which is private dominion from which we can exclude others) to it. The former is *ius ad rem* (right to use a thing), the latter *ius in re* (right to a thing). This is the basic difference between Locke and Filmer on property. In the latter's Adamite conception, God gave Adam an unlimited right to property, passed on via inheritance to his heirs. The notion of use-rights to the common thus never arises. A similar view was held by Grotius, who claimed that all property is by definition private, and by Pufendorf, who embraced the notion of a "negative community" that exists before the introduction of private property and is merely an agreement that all things are free for any taker. Tully emphasizes that these notions all have much more in common with one another and with subsequent liberal conceptions of property than they do with Locke's Thomist conception of a positive community guaranteeing *ius ad rem* to all in common. This view, if correct, stands the conventional wisdom concerning the relationship between individualistic conceptions of property rights and liberal political theory on its head for "[t]he authors who adopt the private concept, Grotius, Filmer and Pufendorf, integrate it into the absolutist theories. The author who ad-

heres to the common concept most emphatically is Locke"
(Tully, 1980:79).[14]

There is no denying the plausibility of Tully's argument as
an account of the different origins of these two types of theories of property. But how significant is it in overturning the
conventional identification of Locke's theory with the classical
liberal view of property rights as individual exclusive dominion
against all takers? First, Locke's notion of positive community is
not, strictly, a theory of common *property* at all. Tully claims that
the "combination of a conditional use right in land, and an
usufruct in the products of one's labor was the standard form
of property" in England and was "available to Locke" as the
basis for his theory of common property, modeled on the English Commons which were "called 'properties' " (ibid.:124–5).
But Locke tells us repeatedly that the origin of property consists in the capacity to work, not in the land. Thus a hunter
owns his catch because in laboring to remove it from the state of
nature "wherein she was common" he "hath *begun a Property*"
(Locke, 1963:331). God gave the world to mankind in common,
but Locke refers to it as his "Waste," for " 'tis *Labour* indeed that
puts the difference of value on every thing" and thus "*Labour,* in
the Beginning, *gave a right of Property.*" Even in gathering food
that has grown wild, "[t]hat labour put a distinciton between
them and the common . . ." and thus became his private right.
Tully himself quotes Locke as holding that if I dig ores from
land that is part of the common, the "labour that was mine,
removing them out of that common state, hath fixed my property in them." The act of removing them from the state of
nature "*begins the property*" (ibid.:337; 338; 341; 330; Tully,
1980:124–5).

Locke is famously vague about the exact contributions of
labor and nature to the *value* of property – although "*labour
makes* the far greater part" (Locke, 1963:338) – but two points
should be noted in this connection. First, the value of property
is quite distinct from its ownership, and on this point Locke is
in no way equivocal, empirically or morally. Second, in being
unsure of how, precisely, to incorporate the value contributed

14 For further discussion of these and other seventeenth-century "inclusive" and
"exclusive" theories, see Tully (1980:53–130).

by nature into a labor theory of value – recognizing that the capacity to work must comprise the vast majority but believing that nature must make some residual contribution – Locke was in the mainstream of the new economic orthodoxy, widespread among economic writers after Petty.[15] That Locke's view differs from Filmer's is undeniable, but it is in no sense a conservative reaffirmation of preabsolutist orthodoxies, as Tully asserts.

In support of his interpretation of Locke on common property Tully also has a good deal to say about the famous Lockean provisos that accumulation must not lead to waste and that "as much and as good" must be available to others in common. For Locke the problem of waste dissolves with the introduction of money which can be accumlated without deteriorating, but what of the "as much and as good" proviso? As Tully points out, every man has an inalienable right to subsistence [see section II(iv): subsistence is defined quite generously]. God gave the world to mankind in common to secure that right, but what does this mean? Remember that for Locke the source of the means of subsistence is almost exclusively the capacity to work, not nature. If this be so, all that is required for the fulfillment of the proviso is that people be enabled to work.[16] It seems most likely that Locke believed that in the kind of society he advocated, violations of the proviso would never in fact arise for precisely this reason, a view supported by his attitude toward enclosure and the unemployed.

Tully disputes Macpherson's claim that after the introduction of money the subsistence proviso of the law of nature became "transcended" because of increases in productivity (Tully, 1980:152; Macpherson, 1962:203; 211). He sees no supporting evidence for Macpherson's claim that accumulation generates increases in productivity which more than makes up for the lack of land available for others.

Locke explicitly states and repeats that, through increasing productivity, less land is used and more is left for others. He also specifies that this inverse ratio between increasing productivity and decreas-

15 See Chapter 2, section II(ii).
16 For further discussion of this point, see Isaac (1986).

ing amounts of land required to provide comfort and support, would ensure that even with double the present world population, appropriation could still take place in the natural manner without "prejudice [to] the rest of Mankind." (Tully, 1980:149)

Tully is confused here, however. Accumulation, in Locke's view, will generate increases in productivity such that in practice no one's subsistence rights will be violated. What Locke says is this:

[H]e who appropriates land to himself by his labour, does not lessen but increase the common stock of mankind. For the provisions serving to the support of humane life, produced by one acre of inclosed and cultivated land, are (to speak much within compasse) ten times more, than those, which are yielded by an acre of Land, of an equal richnesse, lyeing wast in common. And therefor he, that incloses Land and has a greater plenty of the conveniencys of life from ten acres, than he would have from an hundred left to Nature, may truly be said, to give ninety acres to Mankind. . . . I have here rated the improved land very low in making its product but as ten to one, when it is much nearer an hundred to one. (Locke, 1963:336)

It is clear that this justification turns on the increase in productivity of the enclosed land. There is no implication that it is desirable on the grounds that it functions indirectly to preserve other common land, nor does Locke suggest any theoretical or practical limit to the enclosure of land that would otherwise be "lyeing wast in common." Locke believed that the increase in productivity resulting from enclosed land would generate so much more wealth for all that man's natural use rights to the common would become moot. Though this argument may rest on questionable empirical beliefs about distribution and "trickle-down" assumptions that history would prove reluctant to substantiate, it clearly was Locke's view. His advocacy of enclosure for reasons of increased productivity refutes Tully's (1980:130) conclusion that "in the *Two Treatises*, Locke provides a justification, not of private property, but, rather, of the English Common." Locke's thesis about productivity, reminiscent of Petty's, implies that, although common-law rights are not in principle transcended, in practice claims to them will never arise. Once money is instituted unlimited accumulation of *jus in re* is perfectly legitimate.[17] This is supported by Locke's well known view that the able-bodied unemployed should be put to work, since their unemployment was the result of their laziness and moral ineptitude. Although God gave the world to mankind in common "for their benefit, and the greatest Conveniencies of Life they were capable to draw from it," he gave it

to the use of the Industrious and Rational, (and *Labour* was to be *his Title* to it;) not to the Fancy or Covetousness of the Quarrelsome and Contentious. He that has as good left for his Improvement, as was already taken up, needed not to complain, ought not to meddle with what was improved by another's Labour: If he did, 'tis plain he desired the benefit of another's Pains, which he had no right to. (Locke, 1963:333)

What God has given us in common we have no more than a right to "labour on" (ibid.). Locke's natural-law view of common property was thus quite consistent with the view that the able-bodied poor should be put to work.[18] In this, too, he was in the mainstream of economic thinking. Such writers as Petty, Fortrey, Reynell, and many others had criticized the policy of depopulating England through emigration, though they all simultaneously acknowledged the costly problem of high and growing unemployment. The belief that the capacity to work was the source of wealth, buttressed by the equally widespread view that a large population held down wages and encouraged internal trade, reinforced this analysis of the causes of unemployment and of the appropriate remedies (Appleby, 1978: 135–41; Coleman, 1956:280–95; Johnson, 1937:249ff).

This is not to say that Locke's conception of positive com-

---

17 Tully further asserts (1980:149) that Locke could not have been concerned with accumulation of capital because, following Keith Tribe, he holds there was no "independent category" of the "economy" of which land could be a part. My ultimate concern is with the fact that Locke's argument by its very terms could be used to justify capital accumulation (whether he intended this or not), but it is worth pointing out that Joyce Appleby's important (1978) study of seventeenth-century English economic theory and ideology (discussed later) creates a heavy burden of proof for anyone who wishes to adhere to the Tribe–Tully view.

18 For an extended discussion of the implications of these passages, see Isaac (1986).

munity is irrelevant to his theory of rights,[19] but he did have conventional views for his time of the origins of wealth, the desirability of enclosure from the point of view of productivity, and of treatment of the unemployed. He was not primarily interested in defending the English Common. The differences between Locke and his "adversaries" (the term Tully uses to denote Locke's various absolutist opponents, Filmer, Grotius, and Pufendorf)[20] should not obscure the fact that Locke's men create rights of exclusive dominion and that Locke expects these to be perfectly consistent with his natural-law proviso in practice.[21]

Tully is correct, however, in saying that Locke's account of the substance of rights derives from the workmanship metaphor. Although his principal interest is in Locke's theory of property rights, he points out that Locke applies this metaphor quite generally to all acts of doing and making. It is thus central, for instance, to his definition of privacy and his argument for toleration. The individual agent, capable of autonomous intentional action, is entitled to whatever that autonomous action legitimately can create. This idea is not without its ambiguities, but for the present we will restrict our attention to Locke's use of it. Although all men are the workmanship of God, "sent into the world by his order and about his business," in their actions vis-à-vis one another they are autonomous agents and may do as they like, within the limits imposed by the law of nature. Among other things this means that they must respect one another's autonomy qua rational intentional agents, so that no man may "harm another in his Life, Health, Liberty, or Possessions" (Locke, 1963:311). Man is thus born "with a Title to perfect Freedom, and an uncontrouled enjoyment of all the Rights and Privileges of the Law of Nature, equally with any other Man" (ibid.:366–7). For Locke, so long as man is not in violation of the laws of nature, his action is by definition his *own*, his private business. Although Locke is primarily concerned with religious toleration, when he comes to

19 It is discussed further in section II(iv).
20 Although, as Tully notes, on many key particulars the arguments of these writers differed from one another. See Tully (1980:64–80).
21 There is one minor exception to this, relating to the poor who are in "extream want," discussed in section III.

discuss the limits of the power of the magistrate, we find that he views religious action as paradigmatic of private action in general. Thus:

> The care ... of every man's soul belongs unto himself, and is to be left unto himself. But what if he neglects the care of his soul? I answer: what if he neglects the care of his health or of his estate, which things are nearlier related to the government of the magistrate than the other? Will the magistrate provide by an express law that such a one shall not become poor or sick? Laws provide, as much as is possible, that the goods and health of subjects be not injured by the fraud and violence of others; they do not guard them from the negligence or ill-husbandry of the possessors themselves. (Locke, 1979:186–7)

The commonwealth is "a society of men constituted only for the procuring, preserving, and advancing their own civil interests" which are the "life, liberty, health, and indolency of body; and the possession of outward things such as money, lands, houses, furniture, and the like" (ibid.:172). It is the duty of the magistrate to secure these things, but that is all: "[A]ll civil power, right and dominion, is bounded and confined to the only care of promoting these things" (ibid.:172). Locke goes out of his way to make toleration in general not contingent on the truth or falsity of the belief to be tolerated. We are all subject to "the duties of peace and goodwill ... as well towards the erroneous as the orthodox" (ibid.:184).[22]

Locke was well aware that a perfectly unqualified principle of toleration will generate paradoxes, conflicting injunctions, and illiberal conclusions. He therefore imposed three kinds of limits on toleration. The first concerns toleration of practices inimical to the principle of toleration itself; that is, actions which, if tolerated, result in people being forced to do things that they would not otherwise do. "For all force (as has often been said) belongs only to the magistrate, nor ought any private persons at any time to use force, unless it is in self-

22 This exceptionally broad theory of religious toleration, and Locke's view that the ends of civil society are purely secular, are further reasons for questioning the interpretation of Locke as a conservative Thomist. For further discussion of Locke's religious radicalism in his later writings, see Ashcraft (1986:Chapters 1 and 2).

97

defence against unjust violence" (Locke, 1979:179). "Unjust violence" seems to mean direct violation of another's will, a refusal to tolerate another's private actions. Toleration requires intolerance of antitolerant acts: "[F]or who could be free when every other Man's Humor might domineer over him?" (Locke, 1963:348).

Second, in the *First Treatise*, Locke is unequivocal that because all people are bound by the laws of nature (whether these are divine injunctions, natural imperatives, or canons of rationality) they have an absolute liberty to act autonomously, but not a license to do as they please. Thus are children under the authority of parents until they are old enough to understand that law, and thus practices like cannibalism, sale of children, adultery, incest, and sodomy, all of which "cross the main intention of Nature" (ibid.:218–20), cannot be tolerated. Leaving aside how Locke expects us to know what is and is not against the main intention of nature, he clearly expects that the civil law will uphold this law and will not tolerate trangressions against it.

Finally, actions will not be tolerated which are prejudicial to the existence of the commonwealth. Thus atheists ought not to be tolerated, not because of the nature of their beliefs, but because those beliefs are threatening to the commonwealth. "Promises, covenants, and oaths, which are the bonds of human society, can have no hold upon an atheist" (Locke, 1979:212).[23] Papists and "Mahometans" ought not to be tolerated because they are bound to alien civil powers. "That church can have no right to be tolerated by the magistrate which is constituted upon such a bottom that all those who enter into it do thereby *ipso facto* deliver themselves up to the protection and service of another prince" (ibid.:212). It is difficult to know to what extent such beliefs were sincerely held by any writer in the political climate of Restoration and revolutionary England. On the question of atheism, Locke regarded questions about the existence of God as separate from questions about alternative religions. It is clear from the *Essay* that he believed in versions of

23 For an extended account of Locke's views on promising and trust, and their political implications, see Dunn (1984:279–301).

the cosmological proof and the argument from design.[24] In *A Letter Concerning Toleration* he seems to follow Hooker in invoking a version of the argument from common consent.[25] For whatever reason, Locke regarded the existence of God as self-evident and its denial as threatening to the life of the commonwealth. This was sufficient reason, as for those who acknowledge an alien civil power, to deny toleration.

In its essentials Locke's view of toleration was the standard Whig one of the 1680s, though more extreme than was typical. Since the Restoration Charles and James had been attempting to expand toleration of Catholics and nonconformists to undermine the religious and political power of the Anglican clergy. Charles's declaration for toleration in 1662 and his declaration for indulgence a decade later met with insurmountable political opposition, but James had considerably more success with his similar declaration in 1687. James's uneasy alliance with both Catholic and Protestant nonconformists was broken at the Revolution as a result of Anglican promises to tolerate nonconformists in the general interests of Protestantism. This was realized to some extent in the Toleration Act of 1689, although it did little more than exempt some narrowly defined groups of dissenters from some specific penalties. The Act achieved its purposes, however. It split Protestant from Catholic dissenters, the latter being excluded from toleration legislation for the rest of the Stuart period. Henceforth Catholicism could be regarded as treasonable as it was in the Act Against Popery of 1700, aimed at "preventing the further growth of popery and of such treasonable and execrable designs and conspiracies against his Majesty's person and government."[26] Locke's view was thus in the mainstream of Whig thinking on toleration that triumphed at the Revolution, which largely explains its contemporary influence. Its

231836

24 See (1959, II:306–24). For commentary, see Tully (1980:38–43).
25 "All men know and acknowledge that God ought to be publicly worshipped; why otherwise do they compel one another unto the public assemblies? Men, therefore, constituted in this liberty are to enter into some religious society" (1979: 193).
26 The acts referred to in this paragraph are reprinted in Browning (1953:359–410).

influence on the subsequent evolution of the liberal ideology of individual rights derived from the negative libertarian view of the substance of rights that it presumed and sought to justify.

iii. The basis for rights

Locke's theory of natural rights is rooted in the triple appeal to reason, nature, and scripture behind his theory of natural law. If the exact relationships among these various appeals, and between them and his account of natural law, are not entirely clear, neither is the relationship between his natural law and his natural rights. In the *Essays on the Law of Nature* he rejected the traditional scholastic and Christian correlativities between right and law, a striking fact since in his earlier writings he adhered strongly to traditional natural-law views. In the *Essays,* however, we find him embracing the radically untraditional conceptual disjunction that we found in Chapter 14 of *Leviathan.*[27] Locke says:

[Natural Law] ought to be distinguished from natural right: for right is grounded in the fact that we have the free use of a thing, whereas law is what enjoins or forbids the doing of a thing. (Locke, 1958:111)

Right is thus categorially different from law, the former indicating a capacity for autonomous action, the latter externally imposed obligatory constraints. Thus Locke's view is not as easily categorized as Tully (1980:67–8) suggests. As Finnis (1980:206–8) points out, by following Hobbes and Pufendorf in distinguishing law from right in this way, Locke departed from the Thomist tradition, a departure rooted in Grotius's revival of the Roman law concept of a right as one's *suum,* a kind of moral power or *facultas* which every man has. This notion has its conceptual roots, as Skinner (1978, II:117, 176–8) has established, in the writings of Suarez, and ultimately Gerson and the conciliarist tradition. This "subjective" view of natural rights as "essentially something someone *has,* and above

27 For a useful account of the movement in Locke's political and moral thinking over his lifetime, see Ashcraft (1986:Chapter 1) and specifically on his changing conceptions of natural law, see Riley (1982:83–97).

all (or at least paradigmatically) a *power* or *liberty*" involved a shift in perspective that carried the right-holder, and his right, "altogether outside the juridical relationship which is fixed by law (moral or posited) and which establishes *jus* in Aquinas's sense: 'that which is just' [or fair]" (Finnis, 1980:207–8).

The categorial division between right and law required a highly artificial distinction which does not withstand much analysis. It has become a commonplace in the liberal tradition, at least since Kant, that my right to X *is* your obligation to respect that right, even if this is understood in the minimal sense of a Hohfeldian "no-right" to respect my negatively defined liberty. Unless employed in the purely descriptive sense of Hobbes's natural rights, which Locke clearly does not intend, an account of rights entails and is embedded in some notion of law and obligation. Yet Locke's conceptual model requires that natural rights are in some important sense basic and prior to natural laws, a point that should not be lost sight of in the face of recent Locke scholarship emphasizing the centrality of Locke's theology to his politics.[28] Although he equivocates a good deal, it is clear from the *Essay*, the *Second Treatise*, and the *Reasonableness of Christianity*, as well as the early natural-law writings, that Locke conceived of the natural laws which bind human beings as being grounded in God's capacity for autonomous action. They are expressions of His will and are *His* natural rights.

This Cartesian view was theologically controversial and Locke was never entirely comfortable with what he took to be its implications.[29] It made the divine will basic to natural law— and the capacity to will, by analogy, basic to all law as conceived of on this analytical model. This could be argued to entail that there are no immutable laws of nature demonstrable with the certainty of mathematical proofs. Yet the demonstrability of ethics was an obsession that Locke was able neither fully to reconcile with his view of natural law nor to abandon.[30] If natural law was tied to the will of God, it was

---

28 The most important arguments on this point are made by Dunn (1969), Tully (1980), and Ashcraft (1986).
29 For an account of Descartes' views, see Kenny (1979:16–22).
30 For further discussion of this tension in Locke's writings, see Riley (1982:87ff).

presumably alterable by that will, and not necessarily perceivable by human reason alone. Conversely, if natural laws were a body of rules in conformity with the rational nature of things, this could imply that God did not have the power to alter natural law by command, that natural law is binding even on God, or that it would be valid, as Grotius had argued, even if God did not exist.[31] Locke wanted to hold both to his celebrated view that morality and mathematics are parallel in that both are open to conclusive demonstration, and to his doctrine of theological voluntarism which made the will of God, and hence *His* natural right, basic to natural law from which what humans perceive as natural law is derived. Our natural law *is* God's natural right.

This generated profound tension in Locke's view of natural law (which intensified over his lifetime) between his voluntarist theology and theory of action, on the one hand, and his conviction that natural law was part of an immutable natural order on the other. Throughout his writings we find commitments to both these views and attempts to reconcile them. In the seventh *Essay on the Law of Nature* for instance, he argues that "certain duties arise out of necessity and cannot be other than they are." This is not because "nature or God (I should say more correctly) could not have created man differently." Rather the explanation is that

since man has been made such as he is, equipped with reason and his other faculties and destined for this mode of life, there necessarily result from his inborn constitution some definite duties for him, which cannot be other than they are. In fact it seems to me to follow just as necessarily from the nature of man that, if he is a man, he is bound to love and worship God and also to fulfil other things appropriate to the rational nature, i.e. to observe the law of nature, as it follows from the nature of a triangle that, if it is a triangle, its three angles are equal to two right angles, although perhaps very many men are so lazy and so thoughtless that for want of attention they are ignorant of both these truths, which are so manifest and certain that nothing can be plainer. (Locke, 1958:199–201)

31 For further discussion of these disputes, see von Leyden's introduction to Locke (1958:52ff).

It is beyond my immediate purpose to evaluate this and other attempts by Locke to reconcile his voluntarism with his theory of immutable natural law.[32] Ashcraft (1986: Chapter 2) suggests that Locke's resolution lies in holding that God has built into men instincts that make them perceive His intentions as intrinsically rational natural laws. It is possible that Locke believed such resolution followed from his argument from design for the existence of God. What is important is that Locke never abandoned the view that natural law was ultimately a function of the divine will, and the conviction that it could not have the force of *law* without being thus conceived. His theoretical machinations were geared to establishing that his naturalist and rationalist arguments were consistent with this view, but he never abandoned the basic commitment to the voluntarist theory. Locke's confusing and sometimes contradictory utterances on how the content of natural law is revealed to men, discovered by them, held to be synonymous with their rational capacities, or even to be those capacities, continue to be debated.[33] Beyond question, however, is that whatever else it is natural law is an expression of God's will. Locke's frequent appeals, so ably portrayed by Tully (1980:35ff), to metaphors of workmanship and watchmaking in the *Two Treatises* and elsewhere, make it fundamental that men are obliged to God because of his purposes in making them. Men are "the Workmanship of one Omnipotent, and infinitely wise Maker . . . they are his Property, whose Workmanship they are, made to last during his, not one anothers Pleasure." Parents are thus obliged to provide for their children "not as their own Workmanship, but the

---

32 This issue is taken up at the end of the present section. For further discussion the reader is referred to Riley's (1982:63–91) useful analysis.
33 Von Leyden has argued with considerable plausibility that Locke does not supply a consistent account of man's knowledge of the content of natural law. Locke passes from "the recognition that man is rational to the assumption that man's reason, on the basis of sense-experience, leads to the discovery of moral truths, nay, if properly employed, to the discovery of one and the same set of moral truths, i.e. natural law . . . to the belief that the truths discovered are divine commands binding on all men, and hence to the assertion that the validity of such commands can be proved, and even shown to be necessary in the same way as a geometrical proposition" (Locke, 1958:59, see also 43–60).

Workmanship of their own Maker, the Almighty, to whom they were to be accountable for them" (Locke, 1963:311, 347). Like Newton, Locke rejected the Aristotelian view that the world is uncreated, that matter must be eternal, on the grounds that it "denies one and the first great piece of his [God's] workmanship, the creation" (Locke, 1959, II:320).[34] God created the world and the creatures inhabiting it for a purpose, and that purpose is immanent in the fundamental imperatives guiding all human behavior.[35]

In the *Essay* Locke defines divine law as "that law which God has set to the actions of men, – whether promulgated to them by the light of nature, or the voice of revelation" (1959, I:475). Although there is some question as to how divine and natural law are related to one another,[36] as to how divine law is discovered by men or revealed to them as natural law, it is clear that the latter is either dependent on the former or comprises part of it. Natural law cannot bind men unless there is a superior power with the capacity to make that law, and hence the right to obligate them. Law always presupposes a lawmaker for Locke, a view which, once secularized, would be central to Bentham's jurisprudence. "That God has given a rule whereby men should govern themselves, I think there is nobody so brutish as to deny," Locke argues in the *Essay* and elaborates as follows:

He has a *right* to do it; we are his creatures: he has goodness and wisdom to direct our actions to that which is best: and he has power to enforce it by rewards and punishments of infinite weight and duration in another life; for nobody can take us out of his hands. This is the only true touchstone of moral rectitude; and, by comparing them to this law, it is that men judge of the most considerable moral good or evil of their actions. (Locke, 1959, I:475, emphasis added)

Riley is persuasive, then, that "Locke's final opinion appears to be that even a perfectly rational moral principle would not be a real law unless it were willed by a superior being who has a right, by virtue of having created everything, to govern his creation as he sees fit, and that even if reason helps us find

34 For further discussion, see Tully (1980:37).
35 For further discussion, see Dunn (1969:95).
36 See Riley (1982:85).

that law, it does not constitute that law" (1982:86. Cf. also Finnis, 1980:337). Locke did not think in terms of symmetrical correlativities of rights and obligations, but all obligations must nonetheless be grounded in rights, so that natural laws are rooted in what von Leyden sums up as "the natural right which the Creator has over His creation" (Locke, 1958:50), the right of ownership God has over what he makes.

There is a deep tension between the claim that both right and law are grounded in the capacity for autonomous willing (divine or human), and the argument that moral law has immutable moral content which is discoverable by human reason. Why did Locke fail to come to terms with this? Largely because, like Hobbes, he was committed to two incompatible assumptions about action, or, more accurately, to two assumptions that could only be rendered mutually compatible by a view of moral knowledge that was not destined to survive the eighteenth century. He was committed to a theory of interests by which man has certain modes of behavior appropriate to himself, resulting from his objective nature and embedded in the laws of nature. Locke was also committed to an essentially Cartesian idea of the individual human agent as the ultimate foundation of human knowledge and action, both morally and ontologically. There was a deep tension between Hobbes's moral account of man's free will and his psychological determinism. Locke's argument exhibits a different but analogous tension. He was convinced that there are moral imperatives that rational men must choose to live by, but it is indispensable to his ethics that the freedom to choose is theirs. This supplies the basis for his "subjective" view of rights, the view that makes individual consent central to the preservation of rights and to authentic knowledge of individual interests. Subjective certainty is the hallmark of genuine knowledge, and uncoerced individual assent the hallmark of legitimate action. This is the central idea that Locke seeks to capture with his notion of a right. Rights are not mere correlates of extrinsically determined obligations, they reflect the individual's capacity for autonomous intentional action.

Natural law may dictate that man is subject to divine, natural, or rational imperatives to live in certain ways, but two points should be noted in this regard. First, these are clearly conceived of as general negative constraints. Provided men do not violate natural law they may act as they please and create obligations to themselves by their own autonomous actions, ". . . for we are not bound to anything except what a law-maker in some way has made known and proclaimed as his will" (Locke, 1958:187). Where natural law is silent we cannot be bound. It is precisely because God has created man with free will and the capacity for autonomous action that men can create laws and obligations to themselves. If we were not free in this sense, we could not create obligations to ourselves. "[E]very man is put under a necessity, by his constitution as an intelligent being, to be determined in willing by his own thought and judgment what is best for him to do: else he would be under the determination of some other than himself, which is want of liberty" (Locke, 1959, I:346). Within the limits set by the law of nature men may act, as Tully notes, in a Godlike fashion: "[m]an as maker . . . [has] analogous maker's knowledge of, and a natural right in his intentional actions" (Tully, 1980:109–10, 121).

The limits within which men may act autonomously are thus conceived of quite broadly. This is why, *pace* Barker and others, there is no fundamental tension between natural law and contractarianism even for the mature and more radical Locke, as Riley has recently pointed out. Natural law "defines only general moral goods and evils, only moral duties and sins; it cannot point out what is a crime, in the strict legal sense, in a commonwealth" (Riley, 1982:64). On the contrary, since natural law

neither appoints nor removes civil magistrates, neither creates nor pulls down particular political structures, consent and promise and contract must provide this appointing and removing and creating and pulling down. When natural law is used directly in politics, and not simply as a criterion of right, it will be in marginal or exceptional cases, such as those of aliens or of rulers who place themselves in a state of war with their subjects . . . the social contract, for Locke, is necessitated by natural law's inability to be literally "sovereign" on earth, by its incapacity to produce "one society." (Ibid.:69)

This is why men can only be obligated to commonwealths by their own intentional actions. "Nothing can make any Man so [obligated], but his actually entering into it by positive Engagement, and express Promise and Compact" (Locke, 1963:394; cf. also 318). Within the general limitations of the law of nature, man is free to act as he pleases precisely because God has created him with the capacity so to act. In this way Locke manages to ground his negative libertarian view of civil freedom in his voluntarist theology. God makes man, we are told in the *First Treatise*, "*in his own Image after his own Likeness,* makes him an intellectual Creature and so capable of *Dominion.*" We are free agents because God gave us free will, it is His purpose that we should have it. "God having given Man an Understanding to direct his actions, has allowed him a freedom of Will" (Locke, 1963:197, 348). Thus we have a natural obligation to preserve our freedom as individuals, and to preserve mankind as far as possible (ibid.:311; Dunn, 1969:95ff). "The *Liberty of Man, in Society,* is to be under no other Legislative Power, but that established, by consent," and in civil society as outside it, unless there is legitimate law created either by voluntary human action or by God's commands, the negative libertarian view prevails. I have a natural liberty "to follow my own Will in all things, where the Rule prescribes not; and not to be subject to the inconstant, uncertain, unknown, Arbitrary Will of another Man. As *Freedom of Nature* is to be under no other restraint but the Law of Nature" (Locke, 1963:324).

The second point about the asymmetrical relation between law and right concerns its broader historical implications. Natural law, for Locke, is grounded in divine natural right, or God's will, a view that makes natural law derivative and secondary in Locke's system, dependent ultimately on the will and hence existence of God. Since God's natural right is thus basic, Locke was inadvertently opening the way for modern doctrines of the priority of right, though he himself only held this view in an unqualified form as it applied to God's actions, men being free only within the limits imposed by the law of nature or God's natural right. Once God came to be removed from the picture, however, this asymmetrical analytical model of the relationship between right and law imposed no constraints on us except our own autonomous wills. The fact that Locke offered no real argument concerning why the divine will is basic or why making confers ownership, left his view intrinsically open to manipulation. The notion of an autonomous will would become an axiom from which all political arrangements must consistently be derived. We can accept as conclusive much of the revision in Locke interpretation undertaken by Dunn, Tully, Riley, Ashcraft, and others and recognize with them the centrality of Locke's theology to his political writings.[37] The implications of this for Locke's place in the liberal tradition, however, are not so devastating to older conventional wisdom as Tully and others seem to suppose.[38] Although we now know that the "subjective" rights tradition has a genealogy much older than the seventeenth century, Locke is not so decisively separated from it in vocabulary or substance as Tully would have us believe.[39] For Locke, the theory of positive community and common property in the state of nature do not, in practice, prevent the emergence of conventional property rights of exclusive dominion.[40] These are "subjective" in the sense that they supply decisive authority to the right-holder for all significant economic, social, and political purposes. We can now see that this view has its philosophical foundations in Locke's voluntarist theology, and in particular in the theory of authentic action this theology presumed and reinforced. Locke's view of action is at the heart of subsequent liberal commitments to the priority of right over law which lies at the basis of modern doctrines of constitutionalism.[41]

37 Implicit in this reinterpretation is a rejection of Strauss's reading of Locke on natural law. For a good summary and critical discussion of Strauss's view, see Riley (1982:87–91).

38 To be exempted here is Ashcraft (1986). His central argument is that there is a fundamental tension in Locke's writings between a religious and political radicalism and a socioeconomic conservatism, a tension, he contends, fundamental to the liberal tradition of political theory. I do not accept that Locke's political ideas were as radical as Ashcraft claims, but, as further elaborated, the rest of his analysis is substantially compatible with my own.

39 Tully's claim rests in major part on his interpretation of Locke's theory of common property, taken up further in section IV of this chapter.

40 See section II(ii) of this chapter.

41 Contemporary debates concerning the relationship between the right and the good, and right and law, are taken up in Chapters 5 and 6.

At one level what Locke is confronting in his analysis of the relationship between right and law is the paradox of free will in Christianity. God made man in his own image with the capacity to behave in accordance with his will, but also with the freedom to choose not to. (It is never entirely clear how an omnipotent and perfectly good being can create the evil options available for men "freely" to consider.) This Protestant view, usefully summed up by Ryle (1949:159) as the belief that man had to be assumed to know "the moral state of his soul and the wishes of God without the aid of confessors and scholars," led the early Protestants to speak in terms "of the God-given 'light' of private conscience." It was central to the mature Locke's political and religious outlook. In *A Letter Concerning Toleration* he argued that the state may not force religious conformity on anyone, for "every church is orthodox to itself; [and] to others, erroneous or heretical." A church must therefore be a voluntary association of individuals which the magistrate both safeguards and limits, but may not try to regulate internally. "[T]he care of souls is not committed to the civil magistrate." His power consists in "outward force," but "true and saving religion consists in the inward persuasion of the mind" (Locke, 1979:181, 172, 173). Individual natural rights mark this capacity for individual persuasion.

The issue, however, is much larger than the question of free religious will. It goes to the heart of the tensions among Locke's arguments from nature, reason, and scripture. As with Hobbes, there is, prima facie, no conflict for Locke between the "subjective" theory of rights and the theory of objective interests embodied in the laws of nature, because he adheres to a view of knowledge by which moral truths can be known and demonstrated with certainty. The documentation of this fact is perhaps the most important contribution of Tully's book.[42] Overturning Laslett's view that the argument of the *Essay* is irrelevant to the *Two Treatises*, Tully points out that, like Grotius, Pufendorf, Cumberland, and Vico, Locke was convinced of the supremacy of the moral over the natural sciences. Locke made a basic distinction between "ec-

42 Although Tully does not accept that Locke had a "subjective" conception. See the discussion of common property in sections II(ii) and IV of this chapter.

type" and "archetype" ideas, the former being "[g]eneral ideas of substances" and the latter "in some sense, constructed by man" (Tully, 1980:9–12ff). This generated a radical disjunction between natural and conventional knowledge, underpinned by Locke's distinction between nominal and real essences. In substances that depend on the external world for their existence, only nominal essences can be known to man: the real essence is available only to the maker of the substance, God. In the case of archetypes, however, nominal and real essences are synonymous, so that real essences can by definition be known to man. Since social practices are always a function of archetype ideas, it follows that real social essences can be known to man, that he can have incontrovertible knowledge of his civil interests (ibid.:16–22). This kind of "maker's" or "constitution" theory of knowledge is identical to that of Hobbes.[43] Locke saw no difficulty in reconciling his "subjective" theory of rights with his account of objective interest. He thought he could demonstrate the latter with the kind of certainty that must command universal assent from rational beings. People might in fact be ignorant of the truths of morality or mathematics, but this is a function of their lack of education, laziness, or inattention – not a difficulty intrinsic to the discovery of such knowledge. At the outset of the *Essay* Locke makes this clear in his rejection of Descartes' epistemology. He plans to establish that men, "barely by the use of their natural faculties, may attain to all the knowledge they have, without the help of any innate impressions; and may arrive at certainty, without any such notions or principles [as innate ideas]" (Locke, 1959, I:38).

Locke's "maker's" view of knowledge, however, glosses over important ambiguities in his account of the basis for rights. The problem for Locke is twofold. He runs into difficulties concerning actions that men may take within the limits set by the law of nature, as well as when they violate, or are alleged to violate, fundamental natural law constraints. In the first and arguably less important case, it is clear that Locke's negative libertarian account of the substance of rights, and the voluntarist model of

43 See Chapter 2, section II(iii).

action derived from his theology, both presume and require that there are at least some significant areas of social and political life wherein natural law will either be silent or be consistent with alternative possible courses of action. Thus people might disagree over what to do in a particular case and not be helped by natural law. This must be true for his account of free human will to have any meaningful content whatsoever. Moreover, it is not an answer to this difficulty to say that here we are entering the realm of what Locke conceived of as prudential or practical knowledge, which is provisional and corrigible, gained primarily from the study of history, and more of the character of experiential generalizations than transcendental natural laws.[44] Locke's argument that we are free moral agents must entail the possibility of autonomous choice about moral questions, and hence the possibility of genuine moral disagreement. To this it might be responded that it is true but trivial, a possibility of which Locke took obvious account. The machinery of government Locke defends in the *Second Treatise,* with its emphasis on separation of powers and mechanisms of majority rule – as well as the individual rights defended from majoritarian and governmental tyranny in the letter on toleration – was designed with precisely this possibility in mind: that some moral disagreement is inevitable in society and political institutions must accommodate this fact. If Locke's natural law theory is interpreted in this way, however, an important implication is that natural law will be silent on – or indifferent to – many of the issues of distributive justice and social and political organization that have preoccupied writers in the liberal tradition since Locke, and that continue to dominate debates in contemporary liberal theory.

Locke's difficulty is more serious. It extends to the boundaries of legitimate political disagreement, to situations where there are alleged or actual transgressions of natural law. If natural laws are conceived of as divine commands implanted in us so that we feel them as instinctive imperatives, how are men to resolve disagreements about the content of natural law in particular cases? Locke's descriptive naturalism is neither

44 For analysis of these two types of knowledge and their respective roles in Locke's political theory, see Ashcraft (1986:Chapter 2).

internally consistent nor helpful in this regard, since the ways
of the animal kingdom are sometimes appealed to as examples
of what to do and at others they illustrate practices that men
as higher creatures should avoid.[45] Locke's only alternative is
to appeal to the rationality of natural law, and to man's alleged
capacity to comprehend it and act on his comprehension of it.
It is characteristic of man's natural condition that he has the
capacity for free choice. Men differ from animals precisely in
that they can suspend their instinctive desires and think critically about them before acting on them. "[D]uring this suspension of any desire, before the will be determined to action, and
the action (which follows that determination) done, we have
the opportunity to examine, view, and judge of the good or
evil of what we are going to do . . . and it is not a fault, but a
perfection of our nature, to desire, will, and act according to
the last result of a fair examination" (Locke, 1959, I:345). Yet
Locke was certainly aware that rational deliberation could result in conflicting judgments about the content of natural law.
Part of Locke's critique of Filmer in the *First Treatise*, as Ashcraft (1986: Chapter 3) has pointed out, turns on the hermeneutical claim that because more than one interpretation of
the Scriptures is sometimes possible, there can be no authoritative interpretation by ecclesiastical authorities. Individuals
must rely on their commonsense and rational capacities to
choose among contending interpretations. The tension is present here too, however, because Locke does not appear to
doubt that there is a correct interpretation that reasonable
people will rationally arrive at. He does not doubt that he can
convince people that his literal reading of the Scriptures is
consistent with their commonsense interpretations. Although
God speaks with more truth and certainty than men, "when he
vouchsafes to speak to Men [through the Scriptures], I do not
think, he speaks differently from them, in crossing the Rules
of language in use amongst them. This would not be to conde-
scend to their Capacities, when he humbles himself to speak to
them, but to lose his design in speaking, what thus spoken,
they could not understand" (Locke, 1963:208–9). Common-

45 See section II(i) of this chapter.

sense readings of the Scriptures must, therefore, reveal their true meaning.[46]

Locke's assumption that people can always be brought to agree on fundamental moral and political questions was obviously at variance with his own political experience. He acknowledged this in the most Hobbesian of terms: "For though the Law of Nature be plain and intelligible to all rational Creatures," he tells us in his discussion of the aims of political society in the *Second Treatise*, "yet Men being biased by their Interest, as well as ignorant for want of study of it, are not apt to allow of it as a Law binding to them. . . . Men being partial to themselves, Passion and Revenge is very apt to carry them too far, and with too much heat, in their own Cases" (ibid.:396). It seems, here, that man's natural freedom is the problem, causing the inconveniences of the state of nature and necessitating the formation of civil society. For Hobbes this view could generate a command theory of law to force men to be rational; for Rousseau it would generate a Lawgiver to manipulate men to be "genuinely" free. Locke, however, takes the idea of individual consent too seriously to make an analogous move and he equivocates as a result. This is perhaps best illustrated by his discussion of prerogative power, the natural right of resistance, and the dissolution of government in the closing chapters of the *Second Treatise*.

The right of resistance defended in the *Second Treatise* was politically radical in England in the late 1680s. Locke placed himself at odds with the Whig establishment in 1689 by maintaining the Lawsonian view that when James left the throne what resulted was an entire dissolution of government. In violating the fiduciary trust placed in him James had, in Locke's view, created a situation in which he was in a direct state of war with the people. They thus had the right to resist him and to remove him as king.[47] The standard Whig view, in contrast, was that the Convention Parliament discovered that the throne had been vacated. The Whigs were unwilling to accept

---

46 For an extensive analysis of Locke's hermeneutical and methodological critique of Filmer's reading of the Scriptures in the *First Treatise,* on which I draw in this paragraph, see Ashcraft (1986:Chapter 3).

47 For an excellent discussion of Tory and Whig attitudes to resistance, and how they differed from Locke's view, see Franklin (1978:98–123) on which I rely here. See also Ashcraft (1986:Chapter 8).

that the indirect consequence of James's forfeiture was dissolution of the government, which would leave Parliament without the legal authority to install William and Mary on the
throne. It was not clear why such forfeiture should not be
seen as constructive abdication, as the Tories argued, in which
case James's daughter Mary would immediately succeed, assuming his infant son could be shown to have no legal claim.
Most Whigs accepted as part of the doctrine of a mixed constitution that the power of the monarchy was independent of
Parliament. Even if the crown might be shown to derive its
initial grant of authority from Parliament, this could not entail
a right by Parliament to tamper with the royal succession. The
Whigs, however, fearful of the radical consequences of the
Lockean position, held fast to their position that there had
been no general dissolution of government *and* that Parliament had inherent power to supply a royal vacancy.[48] The
Lockean view would entail not only that the king had been
justly removed from office, but also that the rule of law and
the legal authority of Parliament had been ended, necessitating a return of power to the general community. For fear of
these radical implications the Whigs paid a heavy price in
terms of logical consistency as Franklin (1978:116–7) has
noted and it may be true, as he claims, that the principal
reason Locke maintained the radical view was that he saw the
alternative as theoretically hopeless.

Whatever the reason, Locke's view was not without difficulties of its own. The most important concerns how and by
whom circumstances where resistance is justified are to be
determined. As Filmer had maintained against arguments for
limited and mixed monarchy alike, once the proposition is
granted that there is no final and authoritative judge within
the constitution, if the king is charged with tyranny neither

48 Since Locke kept his views and authorship of the *Second Treatise* secret, this was
not widely identified as his position. As Franklin (1978:87–126) has shown, however, the Whigs openly confronted and rejected this position while Locke was
revising the final chapters of the *Second Treatise*, for it was argued in several tracts
then in public currency. Franklin argues with considerable plausibility that this
view of the basis of political authority and its concomitant account of resistance
and dissolution was first formulated by George Lawson, and that Locke took it
over from him.

Parliament nor any court may settle the dispute. Locke tacitly accepted this position, as Franklin (1978:94–5) notes, but he never fully answered Filmer's charge that this would be an open invitation for continual resistance and even attempted revolution by anarchic individuals and groups disaffected by the actions of king or Parliament. It was precisely this consequence that the Whigs wanted to avoid. Locke tried to downplay these radical implications by holding that not every illegal act by the king justified revolution, "[i]t being safer for the Body, that some few private Men should be sometimes in danger to suffer, than that the head of the Republick should be easily, and upon slight occasions exposed." Unless a ruler actively places himself "into a State of War with his People, dissolve the Government, and leave them to that defence, which belongs to everyone in the State of Nature" he may not legitimately be resisted (Locke, 1963:450; Franklin, 1978:95). In the chapter on prerogative power Locke goes so far as to maintain that the independence of the ruler is such that there may be circumstances in which he may act where there is no law, and even in some cases "against the direct Letter of the Law" (Locke, 1963:424), provided this is for the public good. Wise and good princes will use this power well; others will misuse it. When Locke considers how to establish when prerogative power is being abused, he has no real answer:

Between an Executive Power in being, with such a Prerogative, and a Legislative that depends upon his will for their convening, there can be no *Judge on Earth*. As there can be none, between the Legislative, and the People, should either the Executive, or the Legislative, when they have got the Power in their hands, design, or go about to enslave, or destroy them. The People have no other remedy in this, as in all other cases when they have no Judge on Earth, but to *appeal to Heaven*. (Ibid.:425–6)

The appeal to heaven implies a resort to force, but this takes Locke uncomfortably close to the Hobbesian position that although a person cannot be blamed in certain circumstances for resisting legitimate authority, such resistance is not itself legitimate, and the person must hope that it will be recognized as valid in the life to come.

115

Locke clearly assumes that genuine cases of a prince's violation of his fiduciary trust will be obvious, but the only specific elaboration in this regard is an appeal to majority opinion in the community. The right to resist is held not to lay "a perpetual foundation for Disorder" on the grounds that it "operates not, till the Inconvenience is so great, that the Majority feel it, and are weary of it, and find a necessity to have it amended" (ibid.:427). Locke has no institutional mechanism for dealing with what would come to be known to nineteenth-century liberals as tyrannous majorities, or for preventing the systematic violation of the rights of minorities by the king or his magistrates. In such circumstances all these groups can do is resort to (presumably unsuccessful) force; in so doing the moral status of their actions remains deeply ambiguous. Locke maintains that in cases of alleged tyranny the people shall be the judge, but he gives no account of how their opinions will be consulted or their wills implemented, beyond this ill-defined appeal to majority rule. Given the supreme importance he attaches to personal consent as the final legitimating mark of all political action and institutions, questions concerning whether, and how, majority rule succeeds or fails in representing the personal assent or dissent of every individual necessarily force themselves onto the theoretical agenda.[49] Considering the sensitivity to these issues Locke exhibits in *A Letter Concerning Toleration*, it is somewhat surprising that he says so little on the subject of dealing institutionally with minority opinions. He fails entirely to confront the (presumably typical) case where there is strong disagreement over whether or not the ruler has betrayed his fiduciary trust. Locke *predicts* that people will be slow to resist in fact, that the right to resist, even in circumstances of manifestly tyrannous acts, will frequently not be exercised.

For if it reach no farther than some private Mens Cases, though they have a right to defend themselves, and to recover by force, what by unlawful force is taken from them; yet the Right to do so, will not easily ingage them in a Contest, wherein they are sure to perish; it

---

49 For a useful discussion of the weaknesses in Locke's account of majority rule as a mechanism for representing personal consent, see Riley (1982:93–7).

being as impossible for one or a few oppressed Men to *disturb the
Government*, where the Body of the People do not think themselves
concerned in it, as for a raving mad Man, or heady Male-content to
overturn a well-settled State; the People being as little apt to follow
the one, as the other. (ibid.:452)

But as even Franklin (1978:96) – who is concerned to establish
the case for Locke's political radicalism – admits, this amounts
to considerably less than an argument. It is clear that Locke's
conception of the political community was at best "tepidly republican." Both Lawson and Locke thought of political membership in terms of the forty-shilling freehold as it then existed. It is true, as Franklin claims, that "their conception of
the social compact, especially in Locke's more abstract presen-
tation, is egalitarian in format, and could easily be interpreted
more generously . . . to justify the right of the people to recon-
struct the representative in order to make it more responsive"
(ibid.:125). Two points should be kept in mind, however.

First, Locke's central question is *when is resistance to government justified* – the clear implication being that except in truly
exceptional cases it is not. Second, there is nothing in Locke's
writings remotely approaching a doctrine of democratic participation. He thought of individual rights primarily in terms
of toleration, of the spheres of people's lives in which they
may be left alone, of what limits should be imposed on what
can be done to them. There is no notion of the people partici-
pating in government as being intrinsically good or right, as
there was to be for Rousseau. This is a decisive limit to the
radicalism of Locke's ideas in the longer historical term. His
doctrine of toleration was comparatively broad, and Franklin,
Ashcraft, and others are correct to emphasize that his account
of the right to resist seemed terrifyingly radical to his Whig
contemporaries. When issues of religious toleration and conformity moved off the centerstage of political controversy,
however, the negative libertarian view of freedom Locke embraced had vastly different and more conservative ideological
implications.

A final point concerning the basis of Locke's rights relates
to the structure of his moral reasoning. The very fact that
Locke supplies an ahistorical logical account of how political

associations come into being and why they might, in certain circumstances, be dismantled, gave a special place to the individual as limited by his personal interpretation of natural law. Locke's doctrine of dissolution presumed that public law is wholly dependent on and derived from private law, a conclusion Hobbes reached by different reasoning.[50] For Locke (also as for Hobbes) public law derives its validity from the moral acts of individual consent that comprise it, not the historical existence of the law. Whether we interpret Locke as holding that the law is valid because people in fact consent to it, because they must rationally consent to it, or because they tacitly consent to it, these are all a far cry from the common-law case as argued by many of his contemporaries. Pocock claims (1957:236ff) that Locke's lack of interest in historical arguments about English law places him at odds with the mainstream of English political thought of his time. Locke exercised long-term influence, however, because he was able to make an antiabsolutist case without appealing to arguments for an Ancient Constitution that were becoming increasingly difficult to sustain.

iv. *The purposes of rights*

Locke's rights, natural and civil, were geared primarily to the preservation of individual life, and by extension, to the life of mankind. Locke conceived of preservation much more broadly than did Hobbes, partly by arguing that if the right to life is inalienable the means to the preservation of that right must be available to all, and partly by defining the purposes of social cooperation much more generously. Hobbes held that any kind of stable government is preferable to the state of nature. Locke argues that some governments make it even more difficult for individuals to realize their purposes than does life in the state of nature, and that they should therefore be opposed. Locke also defines the individual preservation that motivates the formation of civil society more generously: he seldom mentions preservation, subsistence, or the satisfaction of needs without a parenthetical reference to wants, conveniences, or desires.

50 Chapter 2, section II(iii).

Thus, although Locke argues in the *First Treatise* that man's basic natural right is to self-preservation, this generates an entitlement for every individual to the "necessaries *and conveniencies* of Life" (1963:248, emphasis added). In his rejection of Adamite theories of property we find a similar broad conception. Everyone has

a Right to the use of the Creatures [of nature], being founded Originally in the Right a Man has *to subsist and enjoy the conveniences of Life*, and the natural Right Children have to inherit the Goods of their Parents, *being founded in the Right they have to the same Subsistence and Commodities of Life*, out of the Stock of their Parents. (Ibid.:250, emphases added)

In *A Letter Concerning Toleration* the purposes of civil society are likewise expansively defined:

[T]he pravity of mankind being such that they had rather injuriously prey upon the fruits of other men's labours than take pains to provide for themselves, the necessity of preserving men in the possession of *what honest industry has already acquired, and also of preserving their liberty and strength, whereby they may acquire what they farther want*, obliges men to enter into society. (1979:207, emphasis added)

The satisfaction of wants beyond subsistence needs is thus built into the rationale for the contract from the outset. It is true, as Ashcraft (1986:Chapter 6) contends, that ultimately needs have a different moral status for Locke, deriving from man's use-rights to the common in the state of nature. In the *First Treatise* Locke maintains that in situations of dire need people do have a moral claim on "another's Plenty," although this is a requirement of charity. He contrasts this with the requirement of justice that "every Man [has] a Title to the product of his honest Industry, and the fair Acquisitions of his Ancestors descended to him" (1963:205–6). It is thus not clear that this moral claim has any legal force. It would, however, be inconsistent with the account of positive community in the state of nature for Locke not to acknowledge the moral priority of man's natural right to self-preservation over the conventional rights established following the institution of money. In his discussion in the *Second Treatise* of a rightful conqueror's reparations following a conquest, Locke notes that, although the conqueror has a title to "Reparation for Damages received," this cannot extend so far as to make it impossible for the women and children in the conquered nation to survive, for the wife cannot be held responsible for the actions of her husband and thus forfeit her property, and the children, too, have a title to their fathers' possessions. The law of nature requires that "all, as much as may be, should be preserved." It follows that "if there be not enough fully to *satisfy* both, *viz.* for the *Conqueror's Losses,* and Childrens Maintenance, he that hath, and to spare, must remit something of his full Satisfaction, and give way to the pressing and preferable Title of those, who are in danger to perish without it" (ibid.:437–8).

If this is conclusive evidence that Macpherson (1962:203–20) is incorrect in claiming that man's natural law rights to satisfy his needs can be "transcended," its implications should not be overstated. The one case that Locke takes seriously as distributively zero-sum is the devastating situation faced by a defeated nation following a war. We saw earlier[51] that Locke fully expected the normal case to be one where subsistence needs are easily met for all and that even in the state of nature God intends men to satisfy many of their wants as well as their needs from the common. Locke conjoins these two terms in so many places, that, although he ultimately assumes a naturalist account of "basic" needs, he thought it largely irrelevant for social and economic life in practice; he conceived of preservation in terms more generous than the sheer requirements of physical survival. In the *Second Treatise* he argued that "[t]he Earth, and all that is therein, is given to Men for the *Support and Comfort* of their being" (ibid.:328, emphasis added). Precisely because of this broad conception of preservation unlimited inequalities are permissible provided Locke's provisos are not violated:

Men have agreed to disproportionate and unequal Possession of the Earth, they having by a tacit and voluntary consent found out a way, how a man *may fairly possess more land than he himself can use the product of,* by receiving in exchange for the overplus, Gold and Silver, which may be hoarded up without injury to any one. (Ibid.:344, emphasis added)

51 Section II(ii) of this chapter.

As we saw in section II(ii) above, in his argument in support of enclosure Locke claimed that individuals who attempt to maximize their wealth do mankind a service because of the productivity effects of their actions for the rest of society.

This practical identification of needs with wants also infuses Locke's economic writings. In the discussion of value in *Considerations of the Consequences of Lowering Interest* he claims again that "the intrinsic, natural worth of anything, consists in its fitness to supply the necessities, *or serve the conveniences* of human life; and the more necessary it is to our being, *or the more it contributes to our well-being*, the greater is its worth" (Locke, 1824, IV:42, emphasis added). Locke thus articulates, like Hobbes, a conception of the good that is essentially pluralist and utilitarian, although also as for Hobbes, this is ultimately limited by his theory of objective interests. Not only does Locke define man's private-law rights so broadly as to be potentially infinite in scope, but he also makes the primary purpose of social cooperation the preservation and expansion of those private-law rights. Political power, in Locke's view, is nothing but the right "of making Laws with Penalties of Death, and consequently all less Penalties, for the Regulating and Preserving of Property, and of employing the force of the Community in the Execution of such Laws" (1963:308).

It would be a mistake, however, to conclude that Locke conceived of social cooperation exclusively in atomistic terms. He thought of men as naturally sociable, and able to develop and flourish individually only in a society which fostered their sociality. "God, having designed man for a sociable creature," he avers at the outset of Book III of the *Essay,* he placed him "under a necessity to have fellowship with those on his own kind" and furnished him with a natural capacity to use language "which was to be the great instrument and common tie of society" (1959, II:3).[52] Locke thought social intercourse inevitable and his goal was to organize it along lines demonstrably rational. He believed that such organization could foster this sociality by providing for men's individual capacities for authentic action, by generating a productive system that would

52 For a useful discussion of Locke's views on man's natural sociability, see Wood (1983:109–48).

create plenty for all, by preserving, through toleration, freedom
from political tyranny, and by encouraging self-development as
the disciplined pursuit of happiness through hard individual
work – a kind of proto-Protestant ethic of self-development as a
condition for the fulfillment of man's social capacities and
responsibilities.[53] Rather than attribute to Locke an Aristotelian
view of community, which he clearly did not hold, it would perhaps be more accurate to equate his view of man's social condition with Oakeshott's conception of *societas:* an association of
agents who "by choice or circumstance, are related to one
another" and mutually bound not by "engagement in an enterprise to pursue a common substantive purpose or to promote a
common interest," but by "loyalty to one another, the conditions
of which may achieve the formality denoted by the kindred word
'legality'." It is "a formal relationship in terms of rules, not a
substantive relationship in terms of common action . . . each
[person] pursuing his own interests or even joined with some
others in seeking common satisfactions, but related to one
another in the continuous acknowledgement of the authority of
rules of conduct indifferent to the pursuit or the achievement of
any purpose" (Oakeshott, 1975:201–2, 245ff). Although there
are tensions in Locke's view of the relation between men's individual drives and the demands of sociability, these were sub-
merged in his rationalist account of natural law and his empirical
belief that the system he advocated, and the plenty it would generate, could allow for the general development of the needs and
wants of all. If Oakeshott's *societas* constitutes a midpoint between the radical social atomism we associate with modern libertarian writers, on the one hand, and substantive communitarian
ideals on the other, it seems best to capture the kind of negative
libertarian society Locke envisaged.

III. IDEOLOGICAL CONSEQUENCES OF LOCKE'S ARGUMENT

Locke believed, as did Hobbes, that the autonomous individual is the subject of all legitimate rights. He or she is the

53 For a useful discussion of this view of human nature as it emerges from the *Essay,*
see Wood (1983:121–74).

subject of all natural rights and all civil rights must ultimately be a function of his or her personal assent. Thus are churches and other religious bodies voluntary associations of individuals with no more substantial powers than the constituting members confer upon them. Thus, ultimately, is the private individual the author of the system of public law and the state itself. The "pride of private judgement" that Hobbes feared, and acknowledged ambivalently as the paradigmatic basis of the politics of the future, was endorsed and even ennobled by Locke in his egalitarian view of reason as the basis for political life and as intrinsically available to all. Locke thought, with Hobbes, that all men have decisive epistemic and moral authority over their actions, but he was not a subjectivist in our sense. His "subjective" theory of rights was held to be compatible with – and indeed derived from – a theory of objective interests. For Hobbes this theory of interests was an egoistic psychology knowable with the certainty of geometry because rooted in intentional action. For Locke its roots are more ambiguous, the appeal being sometimes to nature, sometimes to reason, sometimes to scripture, and usually to some combination of these. Whether or not one of these appeals can ultimately be shown to be basic in that the others are derivable from it, it is certain that Locke, like Hobbes, thought the moral sciences superior to the natural sciences in that they depended on the constitutive intentional action invoked in the workmanship metaphor.

It is admittedly a substantial leap from this to Locke's intersubjective theory of objective interests, which requires not only that all men reason alike, but also that they will reason to the same substantive conclusions about how their interests can best be realized and preserved in civil society. This made sense only in terms of a view of scientific knowledge in which ethics was regarded much as analytical logic came to be regarded in the Western philosophical tradition from Kant to Quine: as proceeding from self-evident premises via incontrovertible chains of reasoning to apodictic conclusions. Locke believed that self-evident truths about human nature, perceivable by reflection, observation, and revelation, generate interests that can be known with certainty and therefore must rationally

123

govern man's intentional actions. We might sum up the tension internal to this claim by saying that for Locke men are free to choose to live according to the laws of nature, or – in secular terms – that Locke has no doubt as to what course rational men, on sound reflection, must inevitably choose. This view made sense only so long as the hallmark of genuine knowledge was subjective certainty of essences, and all people were regarded as having the same essences of which to be subjectively certain.

A second important ideological move was Locke's adoption of the Hobbesian tactic of separating rights from obligations, although Locke derived his view from his quite different voluntarist theology, which made God's will the fundamental natural right, basic to natural law. More than any other single factor this separates Locke's from traditional Christian discussions of right and law. Locke was never entirely clear about the exact status of his natural laws. It might be argued that his voluntarist theology presupposed a moral theory of why making confers ownership, an implicit moral theory in which God's natural right must ultimately be rooted. There are, however, two important respects in which Locke's account differed from the traditional Thomist one. First, Locke did not derive his rights from his view of natural law but regarded them instead as descriptive of man's capacity for autonomous intentional action, modeled on, if limited by, God's identical capacity. Second, although Locke identified natural law with the divine will, from the point of view of man's actions in civil society he much more crucially identified it with man's rational capacities. Locke failed, ultimately, to give a satisfactory account of how men are to know their rational interests in practice, or of how they are to resolve disagreements concerning the content of natural law and its application in concrete cases. His view nonetheless had significant implications for the utilitarian strand of the liberal tradition. Hobbes's natural laws became prudential and essentially utilitarian maxims for the realization of individual interests in the social world. Locke, too, saw reason, which in some of his formulations is identified with natural law and in others is a medium by which we discover its content, as enabling the individual most effectively to realize his private goals in the social world. Thus the requirement that positive law be comfortable to natural law was basically a requirement that it be rational, or, more accurately, that it appear to men to be rational, in the best interests of every individual subjectively understood. It was this rationalist formulation which could be secularized and which, ultimately, would lie at the heart of liberal doctrines of constitutionalism. Once it achieved centrality it brought to the theoretical foreground the concept of unanimity. The weaknesses already present in Locke's majoritarianism became increasingly and painfully evident.[54]

There is potential for powerful conflict between this rationalist view of law and a "subjective" view of rights, when individuals do not believe that the law is in their rational interest. Bentham evades this question by allowing only those rights that are consistent with and derived from his theory of positive law (thus subordinating the subjective theory of rights to the theory of law). Hobbes denies that such a conflict can arise by definition. Locke equivocates because of his genuine commitment to a concept of free human agency. He wants to hold that if the civil law in fact operates in the rational interests of all this type of conflict will not arise. As he acknowledges, however, whether or not this will be so may not always be entirely clear and at least at times will be in dispute. Although he never fully resolved these issues, in general he thought that illegitimate actions by some or all of the government would be manifest. For Locke this belief had ultimately to rest on the leap of faith that we perceive God's intentions as rational imperatives because He has constituted us so to perceive them, a position unavailable to the liberal establishment that subsequently appropriated his doctrine.

It is worth stressing that Locke believed such fundamental disagreement would be the exceptional case which need not, and typically would not, arise; in general the rule of law would be supreme. He has no real answer for the potential problems of tyrannous majorities, or for the situations wherein the law might systematically be manipulated to violate the rights of

54 Contemporary liberal preoccupation with the idea of unanimity will concern us in subsequent chapters.

minorities, or even of majorities, all of which might be sanctioned by his argument. He benevolently assumed that it is possible for the law to function impartially in the interests of all and expected that this would typically be the case. The ideological implications of this were substantial, for in it we find the beginnings of liberalism's attempt to disguise a limited moral and political pluralism as a very broad skepticism or relativism about people's moral and political values and goals. The law is presented as ideologically neutral, as guaranteeing those things that are in the rational interests of all even as it protects, and encourages by enclosure, the creation of a system of property ownership that dispossesses the vast majority. The law is presented as a neutral mechanism even as it denies toleration to those who would challenge the unjust practices of the law, and as it rules out various other practices – cannibalism, sale of children, slavery, sodomy, atheism, and Catholicism – which, because of prevailing mores and political imperatives, Locke regarded as rationally in the interest of all to prohibit. As the last three of these examples starkly illustrate today, such claims are intrinsically vulnerable to the charge that they are biased to a particular contestible conception of the good. Locke never embraced a doctrine of moral relativism or neutralism, but if his religious theory of natural law is abandoned and his rationalist jurisprudence retained, the impetus to take such positions seriously is difficult to escape. Once Locke's view of moral knowledge could no longer be sustained, liberal rights theorists would have to seek more opaque and surreptitious devices for constraining the freedoms of individuals to avoid the more obvious paradoxes of overdetermination that would otherwise result, and to produce the kind of economic and social organization they desired.

A third major consequence of Locke's argument concerns the definition of the substance of rights in terms of negative freedom. "Laws provide, as much as is possible, that the goods and health of subjects be not injured by the fraud and violence of others; they do not guard them from the negligence or ill-husbandry of the possessors themselves. No man can be forced to be rich or healthful whether he will or no" (Locke, 1979:187). We saw in section II(ii) that the origins of ownership in the waste of God notwithstanding, the paradigmatic form of action is private, inhering in the individual capacity for intentional agency. Locke grants everyone the right to the means of subsistence, but, contrary to appearances, the proviso functions as a negative libertarian constraint, because his generous definition of subsistence includes wants and needs. We are not required to care for others except in the exceptional cases of people suffering in extreme want or following the devastating effects of war. In normal circumstances the right to subsistence merely requires that a situation prevail where all can exercise their own private-law rights of dominion over themselves, their actions, and possessions, ideologically a very different proposition. This is all that the law must or may ensure. Note also that Locke believed the dispossessed should be put to work by the state, not given charity, and that he expected workers to live at physical subsistence. In the *Considerations of the Consequences of Lowering Interest* it is clear that he regards as perfectly natural a state of affairs wherein

the labourers, living generally but from hand to mouth; and, indeed, considered as labourers in order to trade, may well enough carry on their part, if they have but money enough to buy victuals, clothes, and tools: all which may very well be provided, without any great sum of money lying still in their hands. (Locke, 1824, IV:23–4)

Locke's proviso, therefore, does not generate a right to anything more than a negative libertarian constraint. The massive inequalities this view obviously sanctioned were acceptable to Locke because of his empirical belief that the productivity effects of enclosure and accumulation would be so great that violations of the proviso would not in fact arise. He believed it sufficient that everyone be enabled to preserve himself, and this is all the law must make possible. By making property rights and even rights of inheritance prior to and independent of the law (though the law must defend them), Locke sanctioned not only vast inequality, but the transmission of this inequality through generations and the cumulative destructive social and political impact of the division of labor on the laborers themselves.[55] Hobbes had charged the state with responsi-

55 This last was to become an important preoccupation of Adam Smith's (1937:733ff).

bility for creating a negative libertarian society. Locke treated it as part of the natural order of things.

An important political consequence of Locke's negative libertarianism was that it made the central ideal of a just polity toleration, not participation. Perhaps more than any other single factor, this gave the emerging ideology of individual rights its conservative political form. Hobbes spoke of freedom in terms of the residual of sovereign power, thus embracing this concept in an embryonic form. Locke turned the ideal of toleration into the centerpiece of his theology and his politics. By making all action by definition private and gearing the law to the protection of that action, Locke affirmed the paradigmatic liberal view of "genuine" freedom as freedom *from* politics: diversity is to be tolerated so long as it does not affect the basic structure and operation of political institutions. Historically this was reflected in the increasing conservatism of the Whig establishment after the compromise of 1688 and their opposition, after 1694, to anything that could plausibly be called a democratic politics. Once they had rid themselves of James and achieved supremacy within the oligarchic state, the Whig aristocracy began to strengthen, not restrict, monarchical authority, by opposing reduction of the standing army, supporting the Act of Union with Scotland, reducing the democratic franchise in London, and forcing through the Septennial Act (Goodwin, 1979:35ff).[56] Even Locke's more radical account of the right to resist provided nothing close to the kind of appeal to democratic participation and mass political education characteristic of radical leaders in the eighteenth century, the so-called "friends of liberty" of whom Albert Goodwin (1979:25ff) has so eloquently written. Locke occasionally spoke of law in terms of enabling conditions rather than mere restraints on natural freedom,[57] but in these pas-

56 For an account of the retreat of the Whigs from radical politics after 1688 see Dickinson (1976:28–45).
57 As in Chapter VI of the *Second Treatise* where he says that "[t]he end of law is not to abolish or restrain, but to preserve and enlarge freedom: for in all states of created beings capable of laws, where there is no law there is no freedom. For liberty is to be free from restraint and violence from others, which cannot be, where there is no law" (1963:347–8).

sages he was clearly arguing that the law should enlarge the private freedoms of the individual, to make sure that he is not " . . . subject to the arbitrary Will of another, but freely follow his own" (Locke, 1963:348). The egalitarianism in the liberal rights tradition was thus from its inception a gloss. It rationalized an oligarchic state and was never intended to have what we should recognize as substantive democratic consequences.

A fourth ideological consequence of Locke's discussion derived from his treatment of human desires. As we saw in section II(iv), Locke's broad definition of subsistence rested on an identification of wants with needs similar to that embodied in Hobbes's account of human desires. For Locke, as for Hobbes, this generated the proposition that the class of objects and actions to which there are private rights is potentially infinite. Hobbes and Locke thus supplied a theoretical foundation for the idea of effective demand that was coming to dominate contemporary economic thinking. There had been a number of implicit references to a postulate of demand during the sixteenth century, in, for example, the quantity theories of money formulated by Copernicus in the 1520s and Navarus in the 1550s,[58] but it was not until the seventeenth century that writers consciously concerned themselves with the phenomenon of effective demand. We find isolated references to this notion in the early seventeenth-century literature on trade – Misselden (1623:98), for example, asserts that while prices are determined by the "goodness" of money, they fluctuate "according to the occasions of both parties" – but it is in the literature on usury and wages that the concept first presents itself as a candidate for serious investigation.

The Ancient Hebraic and Aristotelian abhorrence of usury was affirmed in the Just Wage and Price doctrines of such Scholastic writers as Aquinas and Duns Scotus, and by Dante in *The Inferno* equated morally with blasphemy and sodomy. In the seventeenth century, however, discussions of usury began to center on the most desirable rate of interest for the economy rather than on the moral desirability or otherwise of usury as

58 For discussion of Copernicus' and Navarrus' theories, see Spiegel (1971:86–9).

such.[59] This general trend toward instrumental thinking about economic questions is manifestly the central concern of Locke's considerations on interest and money (Routh, 1975:29–30; Appleby, 1978:63–72). Appleby points out that, although much of the fifteenth- and sixteenth-century literature on usury had concentrated on the barrenness of money, the evident success of money-as-capital in generating increased agricultural productivity made criticisms of usury directed at its purported effects – such as the idleness of living off unearned income – less plausible. Some writers, such as Filmer, emphasized the difference between idleness and usury; some, such as Mun, defended the latter for its effects on productivity. "How many Merchants and Shop-keepers," asked Mun, "have begun with little or nothing of their own, and yet are grown very rich by trading with other men's money?" Usury is the means by which the rich and established merchants supply the opportunity for younger and poorer ones to establish themselves: "to the performance whereof, if they want means of their own, they may, and do, take it up at interest: so that our money lies not dead, it is still traded." Mun concluded that "contrary to those who affirm, that Trade decreaseth as Usury encreaseth . . . *they rise and fall together*" (Mun, 1954 [1623]:178–9).

Once economic writers began to concern themselves with the effects of usury on productivity, a series of related questions about money, value, and prices began to force their way to the top of the theoretical agenda. Writers became increasingly concerned with the determinants of the rate of interest, the cost of money on foreign exchanges, and the determinants of prices in general. None of these questions could be addressed without the articulation of a notion of effective demand, as can be seen, for example, in Petty's attempt to formulate a theory of prices. He argued that:

59 Tawney (1961:49) writes of the Scholastic accounts of usury: "These doctrines sprang as much from the popular consciousness of the plain facts of the economic situation as from the theorists who expounded them. The innumerable fables of the usurer who was prematurely carried to hell, or whose money turned to withered leaves in his strong box, or who (as the scrupulous recorder remarks) 'about the year 1240,' on entering a church to be married, was crushed by a stone figure falling from the porch, which proved by the grace of God to be a carving of another usurer and his money-bags being carried off by the devil, are more illuminating than the refinements of lawyers."

[F]orasmuch as almost all Commodities have their Substitutes or Succedanea, and that almost all uses may be answered several wayes; and for that novelty, surprize, example of Superiours, and opinion of unexaminable effects do adde or take away from the price of things, we must adde these contingent Causes to the permanent Causes [land and labor] abovementioned, in the judicious foresight and computation whereof lies the excellency of a Merchant. (Petty, 1899 [1672], I:90)

Petty is here trying to formulate a concept of effective demand by recognizing that, from the point of view of their economic effects, peoples' beliefs about their wants and needs are operationally equivalent to those wants and needs; that demand is an inherently subjective notion that nonetheless has objective effects. In *The Political Anatomy of Ireland* he applied this notion:

if a Picture-maker, suppose, make Pictures at 5L each; but then, find that more Persons would employ him at that rate than his time would extend to serve them in, it will certainly come to pass that this Artist will consider whether as many of those who apply to him at 5L each Picture, will give 6L as will take up his whole time to accommodate; and upon this Computation he pitcheth the Rate of his Work. (Petty, 1899 [1672], I:182)

For this reason "we make an Equation between Art and Opinion" (ibid.).

Petty's endeavor to grapple with the effect of demand on prices was followed by a series of more systematic attempts by Barbon, Houghton, Law, North, and Locke, all of whom rejected the notion of a "fixt price" holding that the value of commodities depended on their usefulness,[60] or, as Barbon (1690:20) put it, "things are worth just so much as they can be sold for."[61]

The debate on the determinants of interest rates and their effects on prices continued throughout the latter part of the

60 For discussion of these authors see Roll (1974:112–7) and Appleby (1978: 179–83).
61 Gregory King went further and formulated a demand law for the price of wheat which referred to deviations from an assumed norm and states that if the harvest falls below this norm by 1, 2, 3, 4, or 5 tenths the price will rise above its "constant" by 3, 8, 16, 28, or 445 tenths (Yule, 1915:296).

seventeenth century, continually bringing writers back to the elusive idea of effective demand. In their attempts to specify the role of demand in price formation, a number of these writers confronted the conundrum of reconciling the evident relevance of demand to price with their labor theories of value. None of them arrived at the classical (Smithean) solution, that demand determines long-run output and has only short-term effects on market price, which fluctuates around the "natural" price determined by labor. Barbon (1690:19–20) offered two ways of calculating prices: one from the costs of production and one from the price that would clear the market. Locke defended a theory of prices based on a law sensitive to different rates of elasticity of demand for different commodities:

By the like proportions, of increase and decrease, does the value of things, more or less convenient, rise and fall, in respect of money; only with this difference, that things absolutely necessary for life must be had at any rate; but things convenient will be had only as they stand in preference with other conveniences: and therefore in any one of these commodities, the value rises only as its quantity is less, and vent greater, which depends on its being preferred to other things, in its consumption. (Locke 1824, IV:31)

He thus defended his quantity theory of money against the mercantilist view that associated low interest rates with high prices. Regarding the demand theory of price he argued that the prices of all commodities, including money, were determined by the amount of money in circulation:

All things, that are bought and sold, raise and fall their price, in proportion as there are more buyers or sellers. Where there are a great many sellers to a few buyers, there use what art you will, the thing to be sold will be cheap. On the other side, turn the tables, and raise up a great many buyers for a few sellers, and the same thing will immediately grow dear. (Ibid.:39)

Another issue that led economic writers to pay closer attention to effective demand was wages. Although most seventeenth-century mercantilist writers favored low wages, there was a dissenting group of high-wages advocates who propounded the "Keynesian" (Wiles, 1968:113–26) view that high

wages and a more equitable distribution of income are conducive to increased domestic trade and stimulate production.
John Cary (1765 [1696]:96–102), for example, opposed low
wages on the grounds that they would reduce the price of
exports and cause workers to spend less on food, thereby reducing the income of landlords. Davenant and Defoe argued
similarly defending a more equal distribution of income to the
same end.[62] Many of Locke's contemporaries remarked that
high wages were an indicator of a nation's prosperity and low
wages of its opposite. Thomas Manley (1669:19) held this
view, claiming that high wages could stimulate trade through
their effect on demand. Similar assertions were made by Josiah Child (1693:ix), Davenant (1942 [1696]:72), and William
Hodges (1696:20).[63] This type of reasoning is a direct consequence of viewing wealth as a capacity to produce rather than
in intrinsic terms; once the matter is seen in this way attention
must of necessity be directed toward the capacity to consume,
hence the notion of effective demand. Distribution can be
thought of as a positive-sum game because demand is perceived to be elastic and the "stock of the nation" is potentially
infinite.

In addition to attacking the role of demand in the functioning of the economy, seventeenth-century writers began to
treat the concept of demand itself in a more analytical way. In
particular, they were confronted with the fact that once they
were thinking of potentially infinite capacities for production
and consumption, it was no longer possible to analyze production merely in terms of subsistence needs. From the functional
point of view to which they found themselves increasingly attracted, needs and wants became synonymous terms. Petty
had begun to equate these in his attempt to formulate a notion
of effective demand, and as we saw Locke was able to assert
that "the intrinsic, natural worth of any thing, consists in its
fitness to supply the necessities, *or serve the conveniences* of human life; and the more necessary it is to our being, *or the more*

---

62 Grampp (1965, I:62–3) points out that the commitment to high wages conflicted
with the general mercantilist predisposition toward high prices, often held to
stimulate employment.
63 For detailed discussion of the "Keynesian" theorists, see Wiles (1968:113–26).

it contributes to our well-being, the greater is its worth" (Locke, 1824, IV:42, emphasis added).[64]

An important consequence of this assimilation of needs and wants was that it implied a new, utilitarian, theory of human psychology for the analysis of economic behavior. Writers concerned with sustaining demand as a means of stimulating production began to extol the virtues of prodigality and accumulation. Appleby (1978:190–1) notes that in contrast to much of the political writing in Restoration England, economic writers gave open endorsement to the Hobbist maxims of an infinite capacity for desire and the relentless pursuit of self-interest. Some, such as Josiah Child, actually cited Hobbes as an authority in this regard. The psychological thesis behind this was most systematically spelled out by Barbon in his *Discourse on Trade* (1690:13–15):

The Use of Things are to supply the Wants and Necessities of Man: There are Two General Wants that Mankind is born with; the Wants of the Body and the Wants of the Mind. . . . Wares that have their Value for supplying the wants of the Mind, are all such things that can satisfy Desire; Desire implies Want. It is the Appetite of the Soul, and is as natural to the Soul, as Hunger to the body. The Wants of the Mind are infinite, Man naturally Aspires, and as the Mind is elevated, his sense grow more refined, and more capable of Delight; his Desires are inlarged, and the Wants increase with his Wishes, which is for every thing that is rare, can gratify his Senses, adorn his Body, and provide the Ease, Pleasure, and Pomp of Life.

In *A Discourse Concerning Coining* (1696:1–3) Barbon repeats this argument, adding that "the greatest Number of them [commodities] have their value from supplying the wants of the mind," which leads him eventually to a theory of prices based on the relation between scarcity and effective demand (ibid.:3–11). Such theories required a philosophical identification of needs with wants of decisive importance for

---

64 Barbon employed the same reasoning to argue that the market is the best judge of value and Pufendorf (1710 [1672]:681–3) echoed this assimilation in his discussion of value in his *De Jure Natural et Gentium Libri* wherein he asserted that the "foundation of price in itself is the aptitude of a thing or action, by which it can either mediately or immediately contribute to the necessity of human life, *or to making it more advantageous or pleasant*" (emphasis added). For detailed discussion of this point, see Bowley (1963:128–34).

the subsequent evolution of the liberal ideology of individual rights, and lying at the heart of the modern doctrine of revealed preference. In identifying these two ideas and operationalizing them as effective demand, Locke and his contemporaries were – no doubt unwittingly – destroying the basis for the argument that the market might be satisfying the wants of some without satisfying the needs of others, let alone at the systematic expense of those needs. A necessary concomitant of attributing to man an infinite capacity to desire was the postulate of scarcity that would become axiomatized in classical political economy after the time of Say, and that was central to the neo-classical tradition that followed. If a man's capacity to consume is intrinsically insatiable, no matter how much can be produced there will still be scarcity in the technical sense that if people had the resources they would consume more, although, as Bentham and his successors argued, at a steadily diminishing rate. This new economic logic had no place for a concept of satiation.

A final ideological consequence of Locke's argument concerns his account of the economic functions of the state. In Chapter 2 we saw the importance of distinguishing a state geared to the regulation of the market from the modern idea of the minimal state. Locke's state is less interventionist than Hobbes's and Locke regarded property rights as prior to the state. Nevertheless Locke, like Hobbes, regarded regulation of the market by the state as involving active intervention. None of these writers had the concept of equilibrium or of the market as *self*-regulating, a concept first proposed by Mandeville at the turn of the eighteenth century and not systematically championed before Smith. Perhaps the clearest indication that Locke believed the state should regulate the market is in his *Considerations of the Consequences of Lowering Interest*. The thrust of his argument is that the state should enforce an interest rate conducive to expanded trade and manufacturing. In practice the state cannot enforce an artificial interest rate at variance with the rate dictated by the supply of and demand for money. Therefore, he argues, any attempt by the state to reduce the prevailing interest rate to four percent will fail, but this does not preclude the state from enforcing *a* rate of interest. In Locke's view, if this is not done serious consequences will follow for the market:

[I]n the present current of running cash, which now takes its course almost all to London, and is engrossed by a very few hands in comparison, young men, and those in want, might not too easily be exposed to extortion and oppression: and the dexterous and combining money-jobbers not have too great and unbounded a power, to prey upon the ignorance and necessity of borrowers. There would not be much danger of this, if money were more equally distributed into the several quarters of England, and into a greater number of hands, according to the exigencies of trade . . . But, when a kind of monopoly, by consent, has put this general commodity into a few hands, it may need regulation, though what the stated rate of interest should be, in the constant change of affairs, and flux of money, is hard to determine. (Locke, 1824, IV:64)

The point of Locke's quantity theory of money, and of the tortuous computations he thought it entailed, was to establish the *best* rate for the market which the state should then enforce:

[I]t should be within such bounds, as should not, on the one side, quite eat up the merchant's and tradesman's profit, and discourage their industry; nor, on the other hand, so low, as should hinder men from risquing their money in other men's hands, and so rather choose to keep it out of trade, than venture it upon so small profit. When it is too high, it so hinders the merchant's gain, that he will not borrow; when too low, it so hinders the monied-man's profit, that he will not lend; and both these ways it is an hinderance to trade. (Ibid.)

Locke's objection to a lowering of the interest rate is that it will not meet this criterion, not that the state should not regulate the rate of interest. The rate should be what is best for the market, but Locke has no belief that the market will necessarily generate and sustain that rate. This an unambiguous indication that, although he believed in the desirability of well functioning markets, he had no sense of the market as self-equilibrating. This is only one of several areas in which Locke favored active state regulation of market institutions. He also expected the state to regulate labor markets by forcing the able-bodied poor to work at subsistence and to support the extension of a market in land by legislating enclosures. The modern idea of the minimal state has therefore been incorrectly read into, and seen as justified by, Locke's argument, which rested on a recognition of the necessity for state intervention as and when required.

IV. CONCLUSION

Macpherson's interpretation of Locke is without question less problematical than his reading of Hobbes, but there are important difficulties with it analogous to those discussed in the preceding chapter. First, national market relations were more fully established, at least in some basic commodities, by Locke's time than when Hobbes wrote,[65] but the questions previously raised concerning the historical viability of Macpherson's excessively general interpretive model still raise serious issues. Second, Macpherson's central claim that Locke's entire argument presumes the existence of, and is intended to justify, a class-based organization of society is misleading. Macpherson avers that Locke's background assumption of a "class" society allows him to defend a state consisting of property owners and politically excluding the working class. The working class is presumed to be devoid of both property and rationality, incapable of consent and hence of full political membership (Macpherson, 1962:248–52; 232–3). Although laborers lived from hand to mouth Locke did not believe they were in principle less capable than others of rational behavior, as Macpherson claims, or that they did not own their capacities for autonomous action (ibid.:230).[66]

Neal Wood has recently attempted to revive a modified version of Macpherson's differential rationality thesis. It merits brief attention because it goes to the heart of the confusion attending accounts of the significance of Locke's argument for

---

65 For a useful account of the growth of markets in different commodities, see Thirsk (1978:158ff)
66 For an extended critique of Macpherson on this point, see Ashcraft (1986:Chapters 7 and 9).

bourgeois modes of thought. Wood distinguishes "moral" from "naturalistic" rationality in Locke's writing, holding that only the former is distributed universally, the latter being distributed along class lines. However, he finds (1983:115) no explicit textual basis for this claim and he qualifies it so heavily that it is difficult to discern any substantive content to it. He acknowledges that for Locke all men are born with equal rational potential, and that "differences in rationality among them stem largely from environment and education." Locke explicitly invoked an egalitarian theory of natural mental capacities in attacking the notion that American Indians have genetically inferior intellects to Europeans, arguing that primitive peoples are no less well endowed naturally than are civilized peoples (ibid.:116, 113–4). Given these qualifications it is hard to see in what sense this supposed differential rationality has a *natural* basis for Locke. Wood's broader argument, that we find at the heart of Locke's philosophy the ideal of a bourgeois man, a "self-directed individualist with a work ethic," in contrast to the traditional "war ethic" and its "gentlemanly" values, so that in Locke's vocabulary "labor, industry, perseverance, sobriety, and usefulness replaced aristocratic honor, pride, dignity, spirit and the non-utilitarian" (ibid.:121, 123, 148), seems to be at odds with the "natural" differential rationality thesis. It is surely because Locke presupposed and articulated this bourgeois conception (which Wood so ably documents) in universalist terms that he is a significant figure in the evolution of liberal ideology. The fact that Locke did hold that *all* men are the proprietors of their capacities, and intrinsically capable of rational judgment concerning their use made it possible to conceive of labor power as an alienable capacity exchangeable for any other in a voluntary transaction.

The whole issue of differential rationality that Macpherson raised is reminiscent of the confusion generated by his discussion of the senses in which Hobbes is supposed to have been a "bourgeois" thinker. Macpherson claimed that Locke was unaware of the "contradictions" deriving from Locke's alleged attempt to state in "universal (non-class) terms, rights and obligations which necessarily had a class content" (1962:251). It is difficult to see why Macpherson or Wood, if they so believed, should expect Locke to hold the assumptions about differential rationality that they attribute to him, and to charge Locke with a "contradiction" here seems absurd. If Macpherson wanted to establish that Locke did not have Marx's concept of class, so be it. It is hard to see why anyone would suppose that he did or be surprised that Marx's theories contradicted Locke's. Macpherson's underlying point, that Locke's account of rights contributed to the liberal egalitarian gloss of inegalitarian social relationships is valid. It requires, however, no differential rationality exegetical hypothesis (quite the contrary), and no anachronistic accusation of unperceived "contradictions."

A second aspect of Macpherson's thesis of interest to us concerns his claim that Locke regarded wage-labor relations as natural, that he "took it for granted, throughout his justification of the natural right to property, that labour was naturally a commodity and that the wage relationship which gives me the right to appropriate the produce of another's labour was a part of the natural order" (1962:220). This claim has drawn heavy fire from Locke commentators and Macpherson overstates it when he argues that Locke "was not confused about the class structure of his own England," which Macpherson suggests Locke intended to justify (ibid.:216). But my analysis establishes that the claim is fundamentally sound. One of the most comprehensive attempts to overturn Macpherson on this point, recently attempted by Tully, confirms this.

The famous "turfs" passage on which debate on this issue has focused, and on which Tully bases his argument, reads as follows:

[T]he Grass my Horse has bit; the turfs my Servant has cut; and the Ore I have digg'd in any place where I have a right to them in common with others, become my *Property*, without the assignation or consent of any body. The *labour* that was mine, removing them out of that common state they were in, hath *fixed* my *Property* in them. (Locke, 1963:330)

The issue is the sense in which my servant's labor is mine. Tully (1980:137) denies that Locke is concerned with the wage-labor relationship, claiming, "[s]ince it is a free man that makes himself a servant, the agreement must presuppose that the choice not to become a servant is available to him." This condition, Tully claims, is fulfilled by the availability of spontaneous products of labor and utilizable land on the English common, an institution that for Locke is inviolable: it is guaranteed in natural law. God gave the earth to men in common to ensure their subsistence. Each individual therefore has a right to live from the common, at least to meet his subsistence needs. Since he cannot be forced into a wage-labor relationship in order to meet these needs, Locke cannot be discussing such a relationship in the turfs passage. In support of this Tully cites the following passage from the *First Treatise:*

[A] man can no more justly make use of another's necessity, to force him to become his Vassal, by with-holding that Relief, God requires him to afford to the wants of his Brother, than he that has more strength can seize upon a weaker, master him to his Obedience, and with a Dagger at his Throat offer him Death for Slavery. (Locke, 1963:206)

According to Tully (1980:137–8) this makes it impossible for the capitalist to appear in Locke's theory: Locke actually stigmatizes the capitalist wage-labor relationship that Macpherson attributes to him. A final argument adduced by Tully is that Locke could not have been concerned with capitalist wage-labor relationships because they did not exist. "A social division of labour, in which a laborer is hired to do a complete service, was the dominant and non-capitalist mode of production in England until at least the late eighteenth century" (ibid.:140–2).

There are several difficulties with this view. First, exegetically Tully stretches our credulity in claiming that the turfs passage refers to a mode of production in which the laborer sold an entire craft. In support of this he cites the following passage:

[A] Free man makes himself a Servant to another, by selling him for a certain time, the Service he undertakes to do, in exchange for Wages he is to receive: And though this commonly puts him into the Family of his Master, and under the ordinary Discipline thereof; yet it gives the Master but a Temporary Power over him, and no greater, than what is contained in the *Contract* between 'em. (Locke, 1963:365–6)

This is taken as evidence that the capitalist wage-labor relationship does not concern Locke. If this be true of this passage (which is difficult to accept given the assumptions about time it obviously rests on, and the lack of any reference to the "complete service" to be performed during the period of employment), it is hard to see how it can be true of the turfs passage (which is what the argument is about) because in *that* passage no craft is being sold: a turf is being cut. A second difficulty for Tully concerns the voluntary character of the relationship between master and servant–"since it is a free man that makes himself a servant, the agreement must presuppose that the choice not to become a servant is available to him." This can be interpreted at two levels, a juridical one and a material one. If the claim is that the servant is legally free not to be a servant, it is wholly unconvincing as a criticism of the view that we are dealing with a capitalist relationship. Juridical freedom of this type is precisely characteristic of the capitalist wage-labor relationship.[67] Tully apparently wants to convince us that Locke did not have Marx's concept of wage-labor, but in attacking the straw man Macpherson created he is plainly missing the point. The claim must surely be that Locke had a view of wage-labor roughly akin to that of the classical economists of the eighteenth century–to which the ideology of the voluntary transaction between employer and employee was central, a conception subject to Marx's unrelenting scorn.[68] If it is Tully's claim, however, that the dictate of the law of nature to preserve mankind never allows us to force someone to work for another on pain of starvation, this re-

67 For further discussion of this point, see Isaac (1986).
68 To take one of a host of poignant illustrations, at the end of his analysis of exchange in volume 1 of *Capital*, Marx quips contemptuously: "This sphere that we are deserting [exchange], within those boundaries the sale and purchase of labour-power goes on, is in fact a very Eden of the innate rights of man. There alone rule Freedom, Equality, Property and Bentham. Freedom, because both buyer and seller of a commodity, say of labour-power, are constrained only by their own free will. . . . Equality, because . . . they exchange equivalent for equivalent. Property, because each disposes only of what is his own. And Bentham, because each looks only to himself. The only force that brings them together . . . is the selfishness, the gain and the private interests of each. Each looks to himself only, and no one troubles himself about the rest, and just because they do so, do they all, in accordance with the pre-established harmony of things, or under the auspices of an all-shrewd providence, work together to their mutual advantage, for the common weal and for the interest of all" (Marx, 1970, I:172).

solves into Locke's discussion of charity. The only obligation on those with plenty is to maintain those unemployables who are in "extream want" (and it is not clear that such a person has a right to anything more than work). Beyond this, as we saw in section II(ii) above, no obligations are entailed by natural-law rights to the common.[69]

We turn now to Tully's historical argument that Locke could not have been concerned with the wage-labor relationship of capitalism because such relationships did not exist. Tully cites a brace of authorities from (one side of) the transition debate and a passage from Marx's *Grundrisse* referring to a transitional organization of work that is "still half artistic, half end-in-itself etc., Mastery" (Marx, 1973:497), but offers no evidence in support of his claim that capitalist relations of production were absent until the late eighteenth century. This is a notoriously complex question, turning on how we differentiate the agrarian, commercial, industrial, and capitalist revolutions from one another. If we restrict our attention to the issue of wage-labor, however, it is clear from my review of the evidence in the last chapter that by mid-century wage-laborers constituted a very considerable proportion of the population. Locke was unquestionably writing in an environment in which wage-labor existed in significant quantities.

However we finally evaluate Locke's intentions in writing the "turfs" and "freeman" passages, preoccupation with internal analysis of the texts should not blind us to the fact that Locke is articulating a view of labor in which (1) x freely contracts (2) a capacity that becomes (3) y's for (4) a limited period of time to (5) perform a specified function that (6) creates wealth which (7) belongs to y. He thus states all the central ideas of the classical conception of wage-labor, whatever he subjectively intended. This formation undeniably contributed to the creation and reproduction of an ideology in which the

69 Thus while Dunn (1969:216) notes that Macpherson is incorrect in claiming that Locke *favored* unlimited accumulation, he also observes that "[t]here is every reason to believe that Locke supposed that a man in a non-political situation had a right to the whole produce of his labour. . . . There is every reason to suppose that he believed that the relations of capitalist production and monetary exchange provided the basis for the emergence of vast but altogether just differentials in the ownership of property."

commodification of individuals could appear both rational and desirable. It is in this sense that the spirit of Macpherson's argument is vindicated, albeit against a good deal of the letter of his own formulations.

Macpherson's account suffers from an additional inadequacy. His attempt to straitjacket Locke's argument to conform to his "possessive individualist" model leads him to miss some aspects of it significant for the subsequent history of liberalism. He misses the subtle way in which Locke gave the liberal ideology of individual rights its conservative flavor. No implicit denial of the rationality of the working class excluded that class from the political system. The double move of first charging the state with the responsibility of sustaining a negative libertarian society, and, second, of translating the ideal of liberty into the practice of toleration, a substantial (but by no means isolated) departure in the religious and political conflicts of Restoration England, effectively functioned in the long term to defuse the potentially much more radical idea of participatory democracy.[70] This negative libertarian view had the additional consequence of making it possible to conceive of all activities relating to the production, reproduction, and consumption of wealth as fundamentally private, engaged in for individual benefit, but with beneficial social consequences for all.

Macpherson's anachronistic model makes him insensitive to the special role played by the state in the commercial and early industrial revolutions, in fostering market practices at home and abroad, which Locke and his contemporaries took for granted. The full significance of this will become evident in Chapters 4 and 5, where we consider in more detail some of the changing realities behind the myth of the minimal state.

Macpherson, in his quickness to impute contradictions to Locke's argument without making an attempt to recover the intellectual context in which it was written, fails to perceive why Locke saw no contradiction between a rationalist theory of objective interests and a "subjective" theory of rights. These were reconciled, as for Hobbes, by a creationist view of

70 For an account of radical democratic movements in the Civil War and after, see Hill (1972).

knowledge pregnant with ideological significance. Once negative libertarian relationships have been portrayed as natural,
embodied in and dictated by the laws of nature, a theory of
objective interests requiring that the state be comfortable to
those laws amounted to a rational imperative for the state to
foster and maintain those social relationships. Locke, therefore, provided no less than a natural-law justification for a
capitalist state.

Thus far I have sought to show in some detail the emergence and early consolidation of the liberal ideology of individual rights at the hands of the seventeenth-century English
contract theorists. In examining the core components of their
accounts of rights, I have tried to show how these ideas arose
and what their consequences were for the emerging liberal
rights tradition. They were yet to go through several metamorphoses, some of which we will examine, and other new
ideas were yet to be incorporated. Much of this core, however,
would prove to be very hardy and would shape the language
of liberal politics of the future. It has been customary to argue
that at the heart of this discourse was the idea of possessive
individualism deriving from the innovative view of man as the
proprietor of his capacities embodied in the workmanship metaphor. My analaysis has confirmed a modified version of this,
although it is only a part of the story: it refers mainly to the
substance of the rights defended by these writers. By way of
summing up I conclude with some observations about the
other three terms at the core of this political ideology.

There is an important respect in which the subject of rights,
the idea of a person, embraced by these writers is a Cartesian
idea. Since Hobbes and Locke were, for different reasons,
hostile to substantial components of Descartes' philosophy,
and since we are all taught as freshman philosophers that
there is a basic division between the empiricism of Locke,
Berkeley, and Hume and the rationalism of Descartes, Leib-
niz, and Spinoza, it will be necessary to specify this with some
care. These writers' accounts are basically Cartesian in the
commitment to the beliefs that the individual's will is the cause
of his actions, and that every individual has decisive authority
over his will because he has privileged access to the contents of

his own mind. The metaphor of "the ghost in the machine," attacked by Gilbert Ryle in *The Concept of Mind*, is an undeniable part of Locke's theory of rational individual reflection. Despite his mechanistic behaviorism and his opposition to Cartesian essentialism, Hobbes, too, embraced the Cartesian view of the subject of rights, as Ryle observed.[71] The model of action became intentional action and only the agent could be said to know his intentions with absolute certainty. Absolute certainty was the hallmark of genuine knowledge, an idea that also originates with Descartes.[72] Hobbes and Locke embraced this notion of the subject of rights for different reasons. Hobbes feared the masses and recognized that any viable political system would have to appeal to the interests of the "overmighty subject" who was to be the stuff of the politics of the future.[73] Such appeals could only be successful, however, if each individual could be convinced that the Leviathan would preserve his or her individual interests. For Locke the idea of privileged access has two sources. First there is his Protestant view of the relationship between man and God, which makes individual assent the defining characteristic of authentic religious experience. Hence the core of every man's soul "belongs unto himself" and "true and saving religion consists in the inward persuasion of the mind" (Locke, 1979:186–7; 173). Second, there is Locke's broader rationalist appeal to all to consent to his political arguments, on the grounds that these are rationally compelling. Thus, if anyone can reveal errors in his reasoning, "I promise him either to Recant my mistake, upon fair conviction; or to answer his Difficulties" (Locke, 1963:173ff).

Thus, for very different reasons, Hobbes and Locke defended egalitarian conceptions of rationality, generating contempt for authority and making the individual sovereign over

71 On Locke's absorption of the Cartesian view of the self, see Ryle (1949:159). For his account of the failure of Hobbes's argument to transcend the view of the mind as an internal theater inside the body, see ibid.(327–30).
72 For an account of the influence of these Cartesian ideas on early Enlightenment thought, see Rorty (1979:136ff).
73 In this regard it is interesting to note, with Tuck (1979:139–42), that despite Descartes' un-Hobbesian political psychology, several influential Dutch Cartesians adopted substantial elements of his political philosophy, and saw it as consistent with their radically voluntarist conceptions of free will.

his knowledge and actions. This view, with the workmanship model, gives individual rights their distinctively modern and secular character. It opens the way to retaining the basic workmanship metaphor that confers asymmetrical rights on the agent or maker, and shedding God from the picture. So long as rights were ultimately derived from man's relationship with God this could not be done. Once they became a function of intentional action, and it was additionally held that man is autonomously capable of such action, God became superfluous to the argument. Even for Locke the legitimacy of religious institutions was a function of the voluntary actions of individuals.

Although the consequences of this secularization were not worrisome to Hobbes, we saw that they were to Locke, who felt it necessary to place some limitations on the autonomy of individual action. This generated the proscription of various activities via the distinction between liberty and license, a deeply problematical move, reducing ultimately to an undefended assertion about man's rational natural interests. Locke wanted to say that man is free to act autonomously and so create entitlements for himself within the limits set by the law of nature or will of God. As God's creation, man cannot violate His intentions. Deciding what these are in practice, however, is arbitrary. Locke argues against Filmer in the *First Treatise*, for instance, that a father does not own his son because in the act of procreation it is God's intention that is critical – He merely uses adult human beings to achieve His ends. Yet in the act of making inanimate objects it is man's intention that is critical, conferring rights of exclusive dominion on the maker. This kind of assertion cannot withstand serious analysis. Obviously both procreation and, say, cutting turfs, can be done with varying degrees of intentionality. Locke argues that a father does not fashion the intricacies of the child, but simply acts out the sexual desire implanted in him by God, but it might equally be argued that in a complex division of labor any given agent, in making something, will employ tools and materials he did not and typically could not make himself. Some are the "waste" of God; others are made by other people with their specialized capacities and abilities. It is thus arbitrary to say that in this latter case the last

146

human maker has a right of exclusive dominion but in the case of procreating he does not. One could easily construct an argument of the kind Locke constructs against Filmer's claim that parents own their children, showing that we do not in fact make the commodities we seem to make because our making them presumes the actions of others in the social division of labor. This is the standard socialist objection to liberal theories of individual ownership, a point worth noticing parenthetically. The principle "from each according to his ability to each according to his work" does not question the view that making confers ownership: it rests on a competing analysis of who "really" makes.[74] This may be one reason why the labor theory of value could not survive in its classical form in the mainstream of the liberal rights tradition. It made that tradition intrinsically vulnerable to immanent attack. Leaving aside Locke's arbitrary limitations to the making principle, Hobbes and Locke both clearly embrace it and regard the extra-political individual as the "basic unit of making" in all significant matters relating to wealth and politics in civil society. This view would become axiomatic to virtually all liberal rights talk in the future.

Hobbes and Locke also made decisively innovative moves as far as the basis for rights is concerned. Whatever else natural law is for them both, we have seen that it has a strong utilitarian component, generating maxims for the rational realization of exogenous goals by private individuals. In both their arguments law sheds its historical character (again, for very different reasons) and becomes a kind of prudential calculus for civil interaction. In my view, that classical utilitarianism has its roots in the seventeenth-century rights tradition in this way is the most important and perhaps least noticed argument in Macpherson's book, though he does misidentify its precise roots in their writings.

Both Hobbes and Locke rest their theories of the purposes of rights on a view of human desires which importantly equates wants with needs into an operational concept of effective demand. This provides the conceptual basis for a plural-

---

74 This is not true of Marx's vision of a utopian communist society that would function by the principle from each according to his ability to each according to his *need*.

ism of goals, but not a relativism of goals of the type prevailing in liberal ideology since the late eighteenth century. The former could only be transformed into the latter after shedding the theory of objective interest embedded in early empiricist views of moral science, thus facilitating the rise of emotivism and the decline of subjective theories of rights into "mere" subjectivism.

Part III
The modern arguments

4
The neo-classical moment

I. INTRODUCTION

John Rawls and Robert Nozick have been so discoursed upon that one might reasonably wonder whether everything worth saying about them has not been said. What justification can be offered for here devoting two chapters to their arguments? It is of considerable interest, however, that they have achieved such prominence in the liberal tradition. A major part of our enterprise is to understand the tenacity of the liberal ideology of individual rights, to explain its historical persistence despite the intellectual difficulties critics have found in its various formulations. If it is true that the arguments of Rawls and Nozick face serious difficulties that have long been known to attend rights-based contract theories, the question arises as to why they have been so influential. Not only have they provoked a massive secondary literature that has worked over virtually every aspect of their arguments, not only have they acted as catalysts for the propounding of alternative liberal theories of right and justice by Galston, Dworkin, Ackerman, Barry, Walzer, and many others, but both have been influential outside the academy on both sides of the Atlantic – a rare achievement for a living philosopher in any age. Rawls's theory is frequently invoked in jurisprudential argument[1] and Nozick has been hailed as the principal philosophical protagonist for conservative libertarianism.[2]

---

1 See, for instance, Parker (1979:269–95), and, for a comprehensive annotated bibliography of writings by and about Rawls, Wellbank et al. (1982). This has some 2511 entries covering all fields and gives brief summaries of the contents of each entry.
2 For examples of his influence outside the academy, see "The Inquisitive Robert Nozick," interview by Robert Asahina, *New York Times* (September 20, 1981), section 7; "If Inequality is Inevitable what can be Done About It?" Interview of Nozick, Bell, and Tobin by Anthony Lewis, *New York Times* (January 3, 1982), section 4; and

Although others, such as Friedrich Hayek, have for several decades advanced arguments similar to Nozick's on many particulars,[3] he has formulated a defense of this view unparalleled in its foundational comprehensiveness.

The novelty with which Rawls and Nozick formulate their arguments accounts to some extent for their influence. We will see, however, that many aspects of their claims are neither especially novel nor lucidly argued. (It is worth pointing out parenthetically that many brilliant works of political philosophy go unnoticed for centuries and some, presumably, forever.) The explanation I offer for their influence is that, Kantian arguments notwithstanding, their two theories lock into, make use of, and function to legitimate the two dominant socioeconomic views of our time. Nozick falls squarely into the tradition of neo-classical economics, which is traceable, via Adam Smith, to the English political and economic writers of the seventeenth century, but which takes on its modern form with the rise of marginalism and in particular Pareto's *Manual of Political Economy*. Nozick's ideological impact, I will argue, derives mainly from the fact that it appeals to, and offers what appears to be a cogent philosophical justification for, this tradition. The situation with Rawls is more complex and can be summed up by saying that his is the natural response of a liberal who has read Pigou and Keynes seriously. He appeals to those who believe in the desirability, efficiency, and justice of capitalist markets, recognize they may not always function well and may generate serious inequities for some, and want to find efficient ways of addressing those inequities without altering the essential nature of the system. The ambiguous moral status of Keynesianism and welfare economics has always inhered in the fact that they appeal to the short-term interests of the disadvantaged (such as unemployed workers and firms on the verge of bankruptcy

"Why R. Nozick is doing much better than K. Marx," *The Times* (London, January 25, 1978). Rawls and Nozick have been interviewed or discussed in many popular and semipopular weeklies including the *New York Review of Books*, the *New York Times Book Review*, the *Times Literary Supplement*, *The Economist*, the *Spectator*, *The Nation*, *New Republic*, *The Listener*, the *Washington Post*, *The Observer*, and many others. For these and further references see Daniels (1975:xi–xxxiv) and Paul (1981).

3 See, for instance, Hayek (1960).

during recessions) by ensuring subsistence, creating employment, and expanding credit, yet these policies are geared in the medium term to sustaining the system which generates those very disadvantages – hence the ironic force of Joan Robinson's quip that the one thing worse than being exploited is not being exploited at all.

The Keynesian and neo-classical views of the world share major elements in common, but they also exhibit striking differences. In common they share their origins in classical political economy, large components of which were already present in embryonic form in the intellectual context in which Hobbes wrote. Both are thus grounded in the liberal tradition broadly conceived and make extensive use of much of its economic, political, and moral vocabulary. Both also have similar long-term prescriptive goals in that they are geared toward well functioning capitalist markets, taken certainly to be desirable and often to be inevitable. Keynesian macroeconomics and Pigouvian welfare economics diverged from the mainstream of neo-classical economics over how to achieve these goals. The Keynesian consumption function entailed that "rational" individual economic behavior must generate permanent inertial tendencies toward weak demand and disequilibrium[4] for the system as a whole. Pigou based his challenge to the neo-classical orthodoxy on a distinction between private and social product. He argued that individually "rational" economic behavior would have by-products or "externalities," incidentally felicitous or infelicitous to others; thus the collective results of competitive individual self-interested behavior may not, and often will not, be socially optimal. Private enterprise, "even when it operates under conditions of simple competition, often leads to a distribution of resources less favorable to the national dividend than some other possible distributions" (Pigou, 1960:381).[5]

---

4 I avoid the issue of whether or not Keynes held there could be equilibria below full employment. For our purposes it is sufficient that he held there could not be full employment equilibrium.
5 For a useful discussion of the rise of welfare economics in opposition to neo-classical price theory, and the subsequent rise of modern public choice theory in opposition to welfare economics, see Furniss (1978:399–410). For a more detailed discussion of Pigou's argument, see Blaug (1978:409–10).

Both Keynesian macroeconomics and Pigouvian welfare economics were thus born of an acceptance of the goals of neoclassical equilibrium theory but a rejection (for different reasons) of its axiomatic assumption that competitive individual behavior would produce Pareto-optimal collective results in practice.[6] The claims of these newer orthodoxies seemed to many to be vindicated by the events of the Depression, the persistence of poverty with growth, and the seemingly congenital tendency toward periodic recession – the "boom-bust" model of growth – that appeared to prevail throughout the capitalist world between the wars. Furthermore, the counter-cyclical prescriptions of Keynesian macroeconomics seemed to work. The New Deal and Keynesian eras ushered in astonishing levels of growth that did not begin seriously to slow until the late 1960s. Beliefs that indicative management and "fine-tuning" could produce a permanent state of balanced growth abounded – beliefs that would not seriously be questioned until the 1970s brought serious economic stagnation throughout the advanced industrial world.

Keynesian demand management also brought renewed political optimism based on a new social-democratic consensus, because this new "managed capitalism" had a human face. A by-product of its fiscal policies was the welfare state and its safety net that redressed the worst diseconomies and externalities of capitalist competition. Thus the mixed economy with an active state, attentive but subordinte to the needs of the market, could seem to many to be morally desirable and practically efficient, to effect the rights-utility synthesis in the face of market failure. Rawls's argument naturally falls into this broadly Keynesian vision, which explains its inspirational appeal to so many liberals and the belief among many who perceive difficulties with his particular formulations, that something like it must nonetheless be true and salvageable.

The New Right that has emerged on both sides of the Atlantic in recent years embraces much of the philosophy Nozick espouses in opposition to these Keynesian orthodoxies. Although Nozick's book was written after *A Theory of Justice*, and

6 For a useful discussion of the Keynesian revolution and the impact of Pigouvian economics on that revolution, see Blaug (1978:665–96).

was in part a response to it, his argument is both historically and logically prior. It is historically prior in that the neo-classical tradition to which it appeals and which it seeks to render philosophically coherent is older than the one in which Rawls's argument is best located. It is logically prior in that the Keynesian tradition resulted from a reaction against the perceived inadequacies of neo-classical equilibrium theory, and sought to achieve its goals by alternative institutional mechanisms. It will therefore be heuristically useful to examine *Anarchy State and Utopia* first.

II. NOZICK'S THEORY OF RIGHTS

The fundamental project of *Anarchy State and Utopia* is to describe a form of government that can win the uncoerced assent of every person in society. In tackling this problem Nozick revives the idea of the state of nature employed by Locke, rejecting the utilitarian and legal positivist traditions that have dominated much Anglo-American moral and political philosophy in the nineteenth and twentieth centuries. His core argument is that individuals in a Lockean state of nature would form what he refers to as a minimal state, the "night-watchman state of classical liberal theory, limited to the functions of protecting all its citizens against violence, theft, and fraud, and the enforcement of contracts" (1974:26). This would be accomplished without violating the rights of any individual: it represents the most extensive state that can command the unanimous assent of the citizenry. Locke employed the working assumption that government is legitimate until a majority comes to feel it has violated its fiduciary trust. Nozick, however, begins with a paramount assumption that every individual has and retains inviolable rights of exclusive dominion, which can in no circumstances be breached without his consent. Thus all political institutions, conceived of as coercive by definition, must command the unanimous assent of the governed, or – what amounts to the same thing analytically for Nozick – they must be brought into existence purely by voluntary transactions. From this standpoint a theory of unanimous consent must form the bedrock of a political philosophy.

At the theoretical center of Nozick's argument is a modified version of Locke's account of the state of nature. Nozick argues that its inherent inconveniences, which he paradigmatically understands to be the costs to individuals of continually enforcing their own rights, would lead them to form "mutual protection associations" to function like insurance companies to protect and enforce their clients' rights. The force these associations must employ is such that, considered as a commodity, it is a natural monopoly. One of the associations would therefore eventually become dominant, as the result of an "invisible hand" process depending on wholly voluntary transactions. The only exceptions to this are "independents" who do not choose to join any protective association, preferring instead to fend for themselves. The independents would be forced to join the dominant protective association and would be fully compensated for the rights violations this entailed. No more extensive state than this would emerge by either voluntary or legitimate compensatory means. "Out of anarchy," Nozick argues, "pressed by spontaneous groupings, mutual-protection associations, division of labor, market pressures, economies of scale, and rational self-interest there arises something very much resembling a minimal state or a group of geographically distinct minimal states" (ibid.:16–17). Nozick conceives of this as the unique solution to the problem of legitimate government and his account is intended to have both causal-explanatory and moral force. The minimal state is the only state that would arise in such circumstances and the only one that can be morally justified. To this extent his voluntarist claim could be argued to rest on a naturalist foundation, although the hypothetical character of his argument militates against any very thoroughgoing naturalism.

The minimal state is not merely a satisficing solution to the problem of reconciling the existence of government with the preservation of individual rights. Nozick conceives of the kind of society that would result, were it fully implemented, as the utopian best of all possible worlds. Hence his impassioned conclusion: "How *dare* any state or group of individuals do more [than the minimal state]. Or less" (ibid.:334).

i. The subject of rights

Who are these individuals and what is their natural condition such that they must form the minimal state? In order to understand why Nozick describes them and their agreements as he does, we must first attend to his account of the state of nature. The principal reason Nozick finds Locke's state of nature to be heuristically useful is that it is relatively benign, differing—as it does—from Hobbes's treatment of it as synonymous with the state of war. Although inconvenient because each has the right and need to enforce his own rights (necessitating many ineconomies of smallness and unnecessary transactions costs) it is a situation in which "people generally satisfy moral constraints and generally act as they ought" (Nozick, 1974:5). This analytical move enables Nozick to present what is really an argument against extensive government as though it were an argument against anarchism. By starting from "the best anarchic situation one reasonably could hope for" without being "wildly optimistic" (ibid.) he builds into his premises a view of life without government as inherently desirable. This lends credence to the subsequent claim that the less government there is the more closely will this idyllic situation be replicated in civil society.

There are, however, several respects in which Nozick's state-of-nature explanation differs markedly from Locke's. To begin with it is a *hypothetical* explanation. Although Nozick claims that the process he conjectures "might have arisen if native Americans had not been forced off their land and if some had refused to affiliate with the surrounding society of the settlers" (ibid.:54), it is clearly not intended to have straightforward historical-descriptive force. It is what Nozick refers to as a "fundamental potential explanation." In *Anarchy State and Utopia* and in *Philosophical Explanations* Nozick argues that an explanation of a realm of reality can be genuinely illuminating, though false, providing it could in principle be true; it is in this sense that his explanation is a "potential" one (ibid.: 6–9, 18–22; 1981:571ff). An explanation is "fundamental" for Nozick if it makes use of explanatory variables beyond the realm of what is to be explained; a paradigm case would be the type of invisible hand explanation employed by Adam Smith. Such explanations are contrasted with "straightforward" explanations that do not venture outside this realm — such as hidden hand explanations like conspiracy theories. Fundamental explanations are "more satisfactory" since they yield "greater understanding" of the realm in question. Nozick regards his own state of nature explanation as fundamental in the relevant sense because it makes use of an invisible hand process to explain the emergence of political society in terms of "nonpolitical factors." As he elaborates:

The more fundamental the starting point (the more it picks out basic, important, and inescapable features of the human situation) and the less close it is or seems to its result (the less political or statelike it looks), the better. (Nozick, 1974:19, 6–7)

The idea of a "potential" explanation is taken over from Hempel as "what would be the correct explanation if everything mentioned in it were true and operated" (ibid.:7), but even if not true it can be useful: a fundamental potential explanation can be defective in three different ways and still be useful. It can be law-defective, where the explanatory model employed does not correspond to reality as it should; it can be fact-defective, where the initial conditions it assumes are false but could have been true; or it can be process-defective, where the "fundamental" process (the particular invisible hand process described, for instance) could have but did not occur. "State-of-nature explanations of the political realm *are* fundamental potential explanations of this realm and pack explanatory punch and illumination even if incorrect. We learn much by seeing how the state could have arisen, even if it didn't arise that way" (ibid.:7–9).

Although he does not say this, presumably Nozick assumes his explanation to be defective in all three respects: that the model was never instantiated, the initial conditions did not obtain, and the process did not occur. It is a purely hypothetical explanation of what might have happened (but did not) to people who might have been (but were not) via a process that could have occurred (but did not). Note too, that the realm to be "explained," the society governed by the minimal state, is also a hypothetical entity. This is an important, if unacknowledged, difference between Adam Smith's invisible hand explanation, or such explanations when employed, for instance, in biology, and his own account of the evolution of the minimal state. The former are explanations of actual entities (markets and organisms) which the scientist is trying to understand causally. Nozick's potential explanation is, however, of a potential entity as well. His interest is not in understanding how the actual American state or any other historical state developed, and there is thus a deep circularity to it. To say that state *S* would have arisen out of process *P* had it occurred, and then to describe process *P* as generating state *S* is to say nothing beyond the potential realm at all. Thus Nozick's state of nature has a very different ontological status than Locke's. Locke's was held to have been a condition that had existed historically, and to which men could return. This is not a surprising difference if we bear in mind the historical contexts in which these theories were constructed. Locke wrote at a time when the entire legal and political apparatus had collapsed once in his lifetime, was successfully declared to be illegal, and shaken from top to bottom a second time. In that context to consider a state of nature as an actual entity, relevant to understanding the political world, made a certain amount of sense. Developments of that political order are not on the agenda in the capitalist democracies in the late twentieth century, however. It is hardly surprising that the idea of the state of nature can only plausibly be revived in this hypothetical form.

If Nozick's state of nature is radically different from Locke's, so are the individuals who inhabit it. Nozick does not explain the emergence of individual property rights of exclusive dominion (which Locke derived from his labor theory of value and theory of positive community in the state of nature, both unavailable to Nozick). He takes these as axiomatic in his description of the state of nature as a flourishing (if comparatively inefficient) negative libertarian society, with a market-based division of labor, money, entrepreneurs, and businesses. Thus "[s]ome people will be *hired* to perform protective functions, and some entrepreneurs will go into the business of selling protective services" (ibid.:13). Nozick even takes Locke to task for claiming that any agreement was necessary for the institution of money (ibid.:18).

Isolated individuals in this state of nature are thus the subjects of all legitimate rights for Nozick. Isolated individuals are the subjects of all meaningful moral predicates:

[T]here is no *social entity* with a good that undergoes some sacrifice for its own good. There are only individual people, different individual people, with their own individual lives. Using one of these people for the benefit of others, uses him and benefits the others. Nothing more. (Ibid.:32–3)

Nozick acknowledges the inherently problematical status of natural law in traditional natural rights arguments and is cognizant of the difficulties attending the separation of right from law that we examined in Chapters 2 and 3. He nonetheless adopts a radical version of the negative libertarian view of rights as spheres surrounding individuals. "A line (or hyperplane) circumscribes an area in moral space around an individual" (ibid.:10, 56, 57), he argues, and there are no circumstances in which this line can be breached without the relevant individual's consent. This is his view of rights as "side constraints" on actions, as contrasted with the "end-state" or "patterned" conceptions embodied in conventional utilitarianism, all brands of egalitarianism, Rawls's difference principle, and the standard distributive principles employed in welfare economics. Any principle that declares some distribution in advance to be desirable is patterned in Nozick's sense, and such patterns can be – and typically will be – upset by the voluntary actions of individuals.[7] Patterns can thus only be implemented and sustained via redistributive actions that violate individual rights. Taxation, for instance, is illegitimate – it is a form of forced labor. Nozick's rights as side-constraints are held to be unique in that they specify no pattern or outcome and hence involve no redistribution and no rights-violations in any conceivable circumstances:

7 As in the Wilt Chamberlain example (ibid.:161–4).

The moral side constraints upon what we may do, I claim, reflect the fact of our separate existences . . . that no moral balancing act can take place among us; there is no moral outweighing of one of our lives by others so as to lead to a greater overall *social* good. There is no justified sacrifice of some of us for others. This root idea . . . underlies the existence of moral side constraints. (Ibid.:33)

Nozick rejects out of hand as "gimmicky" all possible attempts to restate his side-constraint view in end-state terms (ibid.:29n), although this claim is vulnerable in its own terms. The end-state formulation of Nozick's principle is that the class of distributions produced by voluntary transactions is the finite class of "legitimate" distributions. More strictly, given a distributive status quo *A*, distributions that are Pareto-indifferent, Pareto-superior or Pareto-optimal with respect to *A* are legitimate; distributions that are Pareto-undecidable or Pareto-inferior with respect to *A* are illegitimate. Without this "end-state" assumption his principles of compensation, retribution, and rectification of past injustices could not even be stated, because by definition they involve a move from a distribution not indifferent to or northeast of *A* to a distribution that is. Some implications of this will concern us in more detail when we examine Nozick's conception of free action in section II(iii) of this chapter. For the present note that, unlike Locke, Nozick offers no account of how and why these exclusive private rights exist. The question therefore arises as to why they should be conceived of in this way. On this point Nozick makes an intuitive appeal to a version of Kant's categorical imperative, claiming that his own view of rights as side-constraints is the only political principle that treats persons as ends rather than means (1974:30ff).

There are several difficulties with this and Nozick is clearly aware of some of them. It is not clear, to begin with, that his rights as side-constraints do preserve the categorical imperative.[8] There are many possible actions that do not violate Noz-

8 As has often been argued in relation to Rawls (see, for example, Wolff, 1977:112ff), it may be that no substantive political principle can be shown never to violate the categorical imperative. The implications of this more general point are taken up in Chapters 5 and 6.

ick's injunction but do violate any reasonable interpretation of Kant's dictum. The case Nozick considers is sexual leering. "In getting pleasure from seeing an attractive person go by," he asks rhetorically, "does one use that other solely as a means? Does someone so use an object of sexual fantasies?" (ibid.:32). There are some circumstances in which the answer would be affirmative, but to this possibility Nozick responds that it may not even be clear who is using whom (ibid.:337n3). This does not, however, bear on the question of whether or not violation of Nozick's injunction is a nonnecessary but sufficient condition for the violation of the categorical imperative, the most plausible reconstruction of his claim. His solution is to claim that "[t]hese and related questions raise very interesting issues for moral philosophy; but not, I think, for political philosophy. . . . Political philosophy is concerned only with *certain* ways that persons may not use others; primarily physically aggressing against them" (ibid.). It can be argued that such activities as sexual leering are intensely political, that they express and reinforce whole systems of power relationships that place women in subservient roles. In refusing to consider this sort of argument Nozick is adopting an exceedingly narrow implied definition of politics. Physical coercion is monopolized by the state and political activities are thus seen as those activities performed by or mediated through the state. Consequently, for Nozick, there can be no political relationships in the state of nature or in civil society beyond the legitimate purview of the state. Hence the "fundamental question of political philosophy . . . is whether there should be any state at all" (ibid.:4). All forms of economic and social and cultural coercion that are not the direct result of the repressive political apparatus of the state are assumed to be irrelevant to political theory. Even in the case where state action is at issue, it appears that only state actions, not failures to act, can be genuinely coercive to individuals. If the categorical imperative were to be taken seriously as a basis for a political theory, it would have to account for those political relationships exercised outside of—as well as through—the state, and for coercive powers exercised as a result of the state's failure to act in certain circumstances.

If politics is conceived this broadly, a principle like the categorical imperative, as Nozick interprets it, could not consistently be applied to political life. It is not obvious that we should therefore revise our conception of politics rather than abandon the categorical imperative. The categorical imperative is problematical for Nozick even within the limits of his own conception of politics. If political authority, unless assented to, is conceived of as violating individual autonomy by definition, it would seem to follow, as Robert Paul Wolff argues in *In Defense of Anarchism,* that no form of institutionalized political authority can be justified because it will inevitably violate the autonomy of some. Wolff contends that in principle unanimous direct democracy, wherein "every member of the society wills freely every law which is actually passed" (1970:22ff), is a solution to the conflict between authority and autonomy. This argument may appear to be similar in structure to Nozick's with the difference that Nozick could claim that every member of the society would "will freely" the institutions comprising the minimal state (leaving aside, for the present, the issue of how he might set about establishing this). Closer inspection of Wolff's formulation, however, reveals that a unanimity rule for passing legislation does not insure the Kantian autonomy of all will be preserved. On the contrary, it guarantees that the autonomy of some will be violated unless there is unanimous agreement among all members of society on every political issue. If a unanimous direct democracy were divided on whether or not to provide welfare payments to the indigent, for instance, in circumstances where the status quo is such that no welfare is provided, unanimity could not be respected. Once the welfare proposal was voted on, revealing the community's division, the unanimity rule would require that the proposal be rejected. This, too, however, violates unanimity because, as the vote has just indicated, there is no unanimity for not providing welfare either. This is a perfectly general result, in principle applicable no less to the writing of constitutions than to the provision of welfare or to any other legislation. Only by adopting a notion of "passing legislating" arbitrarily biased toward the status quo can Wolff, Buchanan and Tullock (1962), Nozick, and the other libertarian defenders of unanimity argue that it preserves individual autonomy. Unanimity *as a decision rule* has no unique properties as far as preserving Kantian autonomy is concerned, except under highly artificial assumptions about the difference between action and inaction. Moreover, these various libertarian formulations do clear violence to Kant's original argument. The categorical imperative does not hold that we should never use a person as a means (Kant rightly saw that we inevitably must). His "Formula of the End in Itself" reads: "[a]ct in such a way that you always treat humanity, whether in your own person or in the person of any other, never simply as a means, but always at the same time as an end" (Kant, 1948:96). We must never treat a person *exclusively* as a means, but always remember that he or she has an autonomous will—which is something quite different. It entails neither Nozick's thesis nor Wolff's claim that no political (or other power-wielding) institutions can be justified.

Nozick nonetheless holds that his version of the principle precludes treating peoples' abilities and talents as resources for others (1974:28–33ff). Why this injunction is held to capture the genuine character of human freedom and ought to be respected is not entirely clear and will be considered in detail in section II(iii) of this chapter. Nor is it clear that the means by which individuals attain their abilities and talents are not relevant to deciding on the senses in which they might legitimately own them. There is no sense in Nozick that individuals' capacities might be functions of the social division of labor, and even if they are, he would consider this morally irrelevant. The individual is proprietor of his capacities and hence the subject of asymmetrical rights of exclusive dominion, as he is for Locke, once society has advanced beyond subsistence and money has been introduced. Nozick's man, however, is not a possession as Locke's man is God's possession. Consequently, it is difficult to see how Nozick's men are constrained by any exogenous moral requirements, why they should, as Nozick claims, "satisfy moral constraints and generally act as they ought" (1974:5). From Nozick's premises, we should expect Hobbesian, not Lockean, natural men—at best indifferent to others and more likely hostile to them, bound by nothing except their own wills and desires.

ii. The substance of rights

In contrast to defenders of "patterned" conceptions of distributive justice, Nozick refuses to place any limitations other than Pareto superiority on distributive outcomes. The former are used to evaluate end-states, whereas he describes his own as historical: if the initial conditions are just and the procedures voluntary, the outcome is just by definition:

What each person gets, he gets from others who give it to him in exchange for something, or as a gift. In a free society, diverse persons control different resources, and new holdings arise out of the voluntary exchanges and actions of persons. There is no more a distributing or distribution of shares than there is a distributing of mates in a society in which persons choose whom they shall marry.... Whatever arises from a just situation by just steps is itself just. (Ibid.:149–51)

The intuitive idea behind this, familiar enough in the neo-classical tradition, is appealing because it appears to reconcile deontological considerations of right with utilitarian efficiency. Each individual's autonomy is preserved because his consent is necessary for every transaction involving his resources. The outcomes are held to be efficient on the grounds that people will engage in voluntary transactions with one another until a Pareto-optimal situation, where mutual benefits are no longer possible through exchange, has been reached.

Nozick divides his account of justice in holdings into three parts: an account of the original acquisition of holdings, a principle of justice in transfer, and a principle of rectification of injustice in holdings. A satisfactory account, he persuasively argues, must deal with all three of these.[9] He explicitly claims not to have developed a fully worked-out account of justice in holdings. He nonetheless has much to say concerning it that illuminates his core assumptions about the substance of rights.

On the subject of acquisition he returns to Locke's state of nature. Nozick is obviously uncomfortable with any labor the-

9 In any theory the third will in significant essentials be determined by the first two. Nozick's account of it (which generates ingenious ruminations about punishment and retribution) need not, therefore, detain us here.

ory of value and he has some fun at the expense of what he considers Locke's formulation of it (Nozick, 1974:174–5). He opts instead for what is actually a Grotian view of acquisition in a negative community in the state of nature, where everything in common is open to all takers. He nonetheless tacks on Locke's (second) proviso that there be enough and as good left in common for others, although it is not clear what basis he has for doing this once the remainder of Locke's theory of acquisition has been jettisoned. Nozick's (incorrect) interpretation of the proviso is that appropriation of an unowned object should not worsen the situation of others (ibid.:175).[10] As we saw in Chapter 3, Locke's second proviso requires only that no one actually starve. People may be made worse off in absolute or relative terms without the proviso being violated. In defining the proviso more robustly, and simultaneously maintaining that a market system will preclude its violation following the institution of conventional property, Nozick is making more extensive assumptions about the benign distributive effects of market exchanges than did Locke.

Nozick takes his formulation of the proviso as axiomatic. He acknowledges (ibid.:175–8) that establishing whether or not the proviso has been violated will involve (probably unverifiable) counterfactuals, but this in no way leads him to qualify his view that the road to its nonviolation is through unregulated markets:

Is the situation of persons who are unable to appropriate (there being no more accessible and useful unowned objects) worsened by a system allowing appropriation and permanent property? Here enter the various familiar social considerations favoring private property: it increases the social produce by putting means of production in the hands of those who can use them most efficiently (profitably); experimentation is encouraged, because with separate persons controlling resources, there is no one person or small group whom someone with a new idea must convince to try it out; private property enables people to decide on the pattern and types of risks they wish to bear, leading to specialized types of risk bearing; private property protects future persons by leading some to hold back re-

10 For a discussion of Nozick's misinterpretation of Locke's theory of property in general and of the proviso in particular, see Drury (1982:28–41).

sources from current consumption for future markets; it provides alternative sources of employment for unpopular persons who don't have to convince any one person or small group to hire them, and so on. (Ibid.:177)

This entire account of justice in acquisition rests on the empirical belief that the operation of capitalist markets is a sufficient condition for legitimate appropriation. "I believe that the free operation of a market system will not actually run afoul of the Lockean proviso. . . . Indeed, were it not for the effects of previous *illegitimate* state action, people would not think the possibility of the proviso's being violated as of more interest than any other logical possibility" (ibid.:182). Nozick acknowledges this to be an empirical claim, but does not appear to perceive this as entailing any need to present arguments or evidence in its defense. Thus we see that the benign assumptions about the productivity effects of private accumulation implicit in Locke's discussion of the substance of rights become explicit in Nozick's. Locke acknowledged the need to offer arguments and evidence in defense of the empirical views he held (the validity of his arguments being another matter). Nozick treats them as self-evident.

Nozick's account of "fundamental" explanations[11] arouses skepticism toward this standard neo-classical view, both as it relates to the preservation of individual rights and as it relates to efficient outcomes. Nozick's account of justice in holdings is what he referred to as a "straightforward" explanation (ibid.:18–22). By his own reasoning one might reasonably question whether there is not a "fundamental" explanation which would yield "greater understanding" of the realm of voluntary exchange. One might notice, for instance, that the voluntary actions of individuals can have consequences malicious for themselves, of which they may be unaware and which they may be unable to foresee. Individuals may inadvertently create a monopoly in a commodity for which there is high inelasticity of demand by buying, in the short term, only from the most efficient firm. Once this monopoly is established it may increase prices, and because capital-intensity in

---

11 Nozick (1974:6ff). This view is discussed in section II(i) of this chapter.

the relevant industry may well have increased to the point where entry costs are prohibitive, no other firm can enter the market. (Other exogenous factors could easily be imagined that would produce a comparable result.) A more "fundamental" and "satisfying" account would refer not merely to the voluntary decisions of individuals to buy the best product at the cheapest price in the initial situation; it would look "beyond the realm" being explained, in Nozick's terminology, at the process as a whole and the broader structural result, and evaluate that in terms of the initial situation – in this case the inadvertently frustrated goals of the original consumers. Presumably Nozick finds it unnecessary to consider this type of case because he believes that in practice unregulated markets do not generate monopolies. In his discussion of the monopoly of force necessary for the formation of the minimal state he argues that this commodity is unique in that the nature of the good requires that it be a monopoly. In other circumstances monopoly would not arise "without the government intervention that . . . creates and maintains it" (ibid.:17). This large assumption, contradicted by much empirical work on industrial concentration throughout the capitalist world,[12] reflects Nozick's benign assumption that unregulated capitalist markets function efficiently and in equilibrium. His empirical beliefs lead him to offer a "straightforward" explanation and to presume there is no more "fundamental" explanation that might lead us to question the justice in holdings achieved under the single constraint of voluntary exchange.

Nozick's account of justice in transfer is complicated because he must sanction a compensation principle that both gets the independents into the dominant protective association and ensures that no more extensive state than the minimal state can arise. Several commentators have observed it is dubious that Nozick achieves either of these goals and certain that he does not achieve both. His compensation argument inevitably involves an implicit interpersonal comparison of utilities (a

---

12 For a good review of the evidence on concentration in Western Europe, Japan, and the United States, see the recent report of the Committee of Experts on Restrictive Business Practices for the OECD (OECD, 1979). See also Shapiro and Kane (1983:13–19).

"paternalistic" judgment in violation of his side constraints). If we pass over this problem and grant the compensation principle, there is no compelling reason why it cannot be employed in defense of a considerably more extensive state than Nozick desires.[13] His quite elaborate discussion nonetheless merits a closer look, for it reveals much about his assumptions of interest from our point of view.

To begin with, why does the compensation principle concern Nozick? Why must he take the "independents" so seriously and thus make his whole argument evidently vulnerable? We have seen that the paradigm case of justice in transfer for Nozick is the (unanimous and voluntary) Pareto-superior exchange. He regards people in the state of nature as exclusive proprietors of their capacities and assets, as bearers of Lockean asymmetrical rights of exclusive proprietorship, without the natural-law constraints that for Locke both limited the scope of those rights and generated rational imperatives for the formation of civil society. An individual whose side constraints are overstepped thus requires consent. Nozick must therefore commit himself to a radical version of Pareto's noncomparable ordinal utilities.[14] Because his whole defense of the minimal state against a more extensive one turns on this view of free action, Nozick must take the independents seriously. He must show that they can be compensated into the dominant protective association, that they can be induced or otherwise made to join it without violations of their rights.

Nozick does not give a single exposition of his compensation argument, or indeed even a single argument. He offers several different arguments intended collectively to demonstrate that his view of compensation can be sustained.

The transactions costs argument. In Nozick's consideration of whether some apparent rights violations might be permissible on practical grounds he asks:

13 See for example Wolff (1981:77–104) and Holmes (1981:57–67).
14 It is true that Nozick says that his principle "uses measurement of utility on an interval scale" (1974:58), but he does not explain this. Presumably his rationale is that interval scales admit performance of arithmetic functions that he believes will be useful in his theory of punishment and might somehow be used to compare functions among individuals, but he nowhere explains how this can be done.

Shouldn't those who have not gotten their victim's prior consent (usually by purchase) [for a rights violation] be punished? The complication is that some factor may prevent obtaining this prior consent or make it impossible to do so. (Some factor other than the victim's refusing to agree.) It might be known who the victim will be, and exactly what will happen to him, but it might be temporarily impossible to communicate with him. Or it might be known that some person or other will be the victim of an act, but it might be impossible to find out which person. In each of these cases, no agreement gaining the victim's permission to do the act can be negotiated in advance. In some other cases it might be very costly, though not impossible, to negotiate an agreement. The known victim *can* be communicated with, but only by first performing a brain operation on him, or finding him in an African jungle, or getting him to cut short his six-month sojourn in a monastery where he has taken a vow of silence and abstinence from business affairs, and so on; all very costly. (Nozick, 1974:71–2)

Since unanimity is so critical for Nozick he must find a way around these issues. One would sometimes sanction violation with compensation, he argues, when communication with the relevant victim is impossible, because of "the great benefits of the act; it is worthwhile, ought to be done, and can pay its way." In the case where communication is not impossible but very costly, "the transaction costs of reaching a prior agreement" may be greater "than the costs of the posterior compensation process." Negotiated consent is unwise because it is inefficient: "Prohibiting such unconsented to acts would entail forgoing their benefits . . . [t]he most efficient policy forgoes the fewest net beneficial acts" (ibid.:72–3). The questions must necessarily present themselves: benefits for whom? Worthwhile for whom? Ought to be done for whom? Can pay its way at what price determined by whom? Nozick cannot appeal to the interests of society as a whole, for he has rejected the idea of an "overall social good," claiming without qualification that "no moral balancing act can take place . . . [t]here is no justified sacrifice of some of us for others" (ibid.:33). Efficient can only mean on at least as high an indifference curve for each party in the narrow Paretian sense. That cannot be determined, however, if one of the agents is not present. The doctrine of revealed preference cannot be applied if one of the agents does not even know he or she is making an exchange, or if the other does not even know who he or she is. Nozick apparently presumes there *must be* rational solutions to these transactions-costs problems. It may well be that unanimity principles generate them willy nilly – that the problem is not the man in the jungle but the principle of unanimity itself.[15] It is a characteristic trait of contemporary deontological liberals to believe that a just society is at least in principle possible, that there has to be a theoretical solution to the problem of reconciling legitimate political authority with freedom or autonomy as they understand it.[16]

The argument concerning productive and unproductive exchanges. Nozick needs to distinguish compensation (unproductive) from normal (productive) forms of exchange. He is most concerned with the individual who, by prior negotiation of the rights violation might actually have raised his position on his utility function somewhat, whereas if compensated without such negotiations need only be restored to his original position. Let us say the state, to build a road, compulsorily purchases my house for $80,000,[17] the minimal sum necessary to make me at least as well off without the house. Had I known these developments were imminent I might have negotiated a sale for $85,000. In such cases the state should only pay $80,000, Nozick argues, presumably to avoid the enormous problems about counterfactuals he would otherwise confront concerning what someone might have been able to do if he were not moved down his utility function by the rights violation. Even if granted, however, this argument leaves unresolved all the critical questions that arose in relation to the transaction costs argument as to how and by whom compensa-

15 Additional problems about unanimity are taken up in section II(iii) of this chapter.
16 For an excellent illustration of this assumption at work, see Wolff (1970:77–8). We will see the same presumption at work in Rawls's argument in Chapter 5, and we will subject it to critical scrutiny in Chapter 6.
17 My example, not Nozick's.

tion is to be assessed. This distinction between productive and unproductive exchange is not without further difficulties.[18] Nozick believes a productive exchange is one wherein there is mutual gain or "market compensation;" an unproductive exchange leaves one party indifferent between the new situation and the old status quo and the other better off ("full compensation"). If *A* is planning a building that will block *B*'s view and *B* bribes him not to build it, that is a productive exchange, but if *A* merely pretends to plan the building in order to be bribed, it is unproductive. If a researcher discovers information harmful to another and is bribed not to publish it, this is unproductive and he "may not charge the best price he could get . . . [for] his silence" unless he happens to be someone "who *delights* in revealing secrets" in which case he "may charge differently" (ibid.:85–6n). Unless Nozick places some constraint on compensation he may face infinite demands from independents. There would be, however, immense difficulties in distinguishing the above cases from one another (he offers no procedure). Nor is the basic problem resolved of how to decide, and by what criteria, how much worse off the victim has been made and what would be required to restore him to his initial position.

The arguments from risk and fear. Nozick attempts, as a third strategy, to build an inertial bias toward compensation into his initial conditions by arguing that if the independents are *not* forced to join the dominant protective association, its members will pay a price in fear of the independents harming them or their property. If this argument is sustained, whatever other problems the compensation theory faces it would seem to be legitimate, for exogenous reasons, for the dominant protective association to force the independents to become members. Nozick argues:

Private wrongs are those where only the injured party need be compensated; persons who know they will be compensated fully do not

18 The history of classical and Marxian political economy from Smith down through the present is littered with unsuccessful attempts to distinguish productive from unproductive forms of economic activity. For useful, historically based accounts see Schumpeter (1978:628ff, and Dobb, 1973:42–43, 59ff, 60–61, 145).

fear them. Public wrongs are those people are fearful of, even though they know they may be compensated fully if and when the wrongs occur. Even under the strongest compensation proposal which compensates victims for their fear, some people (the nonvictims) will not be compensated for *their* fear. Therefore there is a legitimate public interest in eliminating these border-crossing acts. (Ibid.:67)

This argument shifts attention from the action performed by the dominant protective association in forcing the independent to join, with compensation, to the action performed by the independent in not joining. Its underlying logic requires some overriding public interest in not being fearful of independents, legitimating their forcible inclusion. The notion of uncompensated-for fear could otherwise quickly entail forcing people to do an infinite variety of things, once this negative definition of an action as not doing something that somebody else wants you to do is accepted. There can be no notion for Nozick of something being in the public interest unless it commands simple unanimity. He has already ruled out all theories of social entity and interest and clearly no principle of majority rule can be sanctioned by his rights-as-side-constraints. Unanimity is not at issue in this situation, however, where there is by definition at least one independent. In thus claiming that independents should forcibly be included Nozick is appealing to the concept of externality, which has far-reaching deleterious consequences for his argument. The idea that actions have external harmful consequences for others is unexceptionable, but it is impossible to argue from Nozick's neo-classical premises that the state should become involved in their mitigation, unless he gives up much else crucial for him to maintain. Elsewhere he explicitly rejects such appeals,[19] which cannot be surprising: the idea of externality requires not only interpersonal comparisons, but once appealed to it is

19 As in the section entitled "Having a say over what affects you" where it is explicitly claimed that "[o]thers have no right to a say in those decisions which importantly affect them that someone else . . . has the right to make," and that once such actions as stealing and physically assaulting others are excluded "[i]t is not clear that there are *any* decisions remaining about which even to raise the question of whether I have a right to a say in those that importantly affect me" (Nozick, 1974:270).

impossible either to hold that unregulated markets are by definition efficient, or to place merely "minimal" limits on the actions of the state. The extent of the state's redistributive actions will depend on the nature and extent of the real externalities it seeks to counteract. Pigou, for example, in adopting this notion in his *Economics of Welfare*, not only made utility comparisons to distinguish his private from social costs (the corollary of Nozick's private and public wrongs), but his analysis of "external" diseconomies resulted in injunctions for considerable redistribution via taxation and subsidies, to increase wage levels and employment.[20] Pigou's particular empirical analysis and the theory of social value on which it rested are not necessarily correct. However, if Nozick enters the realm of externalities in search of a workable theory of compensation, he is playing a different game by different rules and must give up much of the rest of his theory. Not only must he accept explicit interpersonal comparisons, he must also embrace all the troublesome implications of the view that unregulated markets do not produce Pareto-optimal outcomes. As it is, Nozick's selective use of the externality argument undermines many of his later empirical claims about the efficiency of unregulated markets.

The natural monopoly of force argument. Nozick attempts to justify compensation on the grounds that the commodity sold by the dominant protective agencies is a unique natural monopoly:

The worth of the product purchased, protection against others, is *relative*: it depends upon how strong the others are. Yet unlike other goods that are comparatively evaluated, maximal competing protective services cannot coexist; the nature of the service brings different agencies not only into competition for customers' patronage, but also into violent conflict with each other. Also, since the worth of the less than maximal product declines disproportionately with the number who purchase the maximal product, customers will not stably settle for the lesser good, and competing companies are caught in a declining spiral. (Nozick, 1974:17)

20 For discussion, see Blaug (1978:635ff).

The claim seems to be that the demand curve for purchasing protection is something like a step-function: unless everyone buys it from one company it has negligible value, but if they do, it suddenly becomes more valuable to those who value it. This also involves not only assumptions about the utility functions of all individuals being identical with respect to this good, but an additional "paternalistic" assumption that it is a good for everyone. It is presumably precisely this, however, that the hard-boiled anarchist, whom Nozick claims as his real protagonist, denies.[21] If it was a contingent truth that protection was both a natural monopoly and universally desired, this would raise a host of troublesome issues for Nozick concerning free riding. If everyone knew the contingent nature of this good, there would be massive incentives for not buying it, knowing full well that one could expect to be given it and paid into the bargain (at what price?). Nozick's few remarks about the free rider problem do not begin to address this issue.[22] It is difficult to see what he could say about it except that posturing and misrepresenting one's preferences are dishonest, and that people in the state of nature generally act as they ought. If this was the claim he would need a moral theory to back it up, which he does not supply. Nor is it intuitively evident that such a theory would mesh with the neo-classical theory of revealed preference via market transactions that Nozick invokes time and again against "paternalistic" theories.[23] The natural monopoly argument is thus self-defeating in that it requires interpersonal comparisons and raises a whole nest of problems related to the possibilities of free riding. It cannot therefore generate the kind of compensation argument Nozick requires.

Nozick recognizes that his various formulations of the compensation argument are less than watertight. In this connection he remarks that "we need not . . . state the principle exactly. We need only state the correctness of some principles,

---

21 For defense of this view against Nozick, see Holmes (1981:57–67).
22 These remarks (Nozick, 1974:94, 266–8) do not deal with the issue of compensation of independents.
23 I argue further, in section II(iv) of this chapter, that the theory of objective goods outlined in *Philosophical Explanations* cannot be used to this end either.

such as the principle of compensation" (ibid.:87). The question therefore arises whether there is perhaps some different compensation principle that *would* generate the result he requires.

Theories of compensation are of two principal kinds: those deriving from Paretian welfare economics that attempt to work only with ordinal utilities, and those deriving from Pigouvian welfare economics that explicitly employ intercomparable scales and distinctions between public and private costs and benefits. The first consists of a formidable series of theoretical attempts from Kaldor and Hicks to Samuelson to produce a principle that neither is self-contradictory nor introduces a hidden assumption of comparability. There is now a very wide consensus among welfare economists that this is not possible,[24] but we need not enter these thickets here. There is a clinching reason why, even if it could be done, it would not help Nozick. The issue addressed by the principles of Kaldor and Hicks, Scitovsky, and their progeny concerns hypothetical compensation. Their problem involved finding a way of discussing Pareto-undecidable outcomes that increased overall welfare. Intuitively: if an exchange occurs between A and B whereby A loses and B gains, but the gain to B is greater than the loss to A, it seemed plausible to say that the overall social product or welfare had increased. They wanted to do this, however, without invoking the whole Benthamite system of comparable additive utilities and its radically redistributive implications.[25] This felt need generated the claim that if B could compensate A for A's loss and still be better off than before the exchange, the total product had increased, even though no actual compensation occurred (otherwise we would be dealing with the normal case of productive exchange

24 An up-to-date and accessible discussion of these issues can be found in the chapter on general equilibrium and welfare economics in Blaug (1978:602–44).
25 If we commit both to comparability and to the principle of diminishing marginal utility, efficiency dictates radical downward distribution to absolute equality (Rae et al., 1981:136ff). Since it is basic to the entire neo-classical theory of marginal cost pricing that the principle of diminishing marginal utility be true, the only way out of this is to deny comparability. Other arguments against downward redistribution have been based on investment incentives, but these are notoriously difficult to apply and are, in any case, irrelevant to Nozick's argument for reasons that will be discussed.

covered by the Pareto principle). Now as Little and others have observed,[26] it is a curious notion of welfare that holds that if I take your assets, provided I could in principle (but do not in practice) pay you for them and still be better off, the welfare of both of us has increased. This is not a solution to Nozick's problem, since he requires that the independents actually receive "full compensation" (1974:84). Ordinalist welfare arguments are hypothetical by definition and cannot generate a theory of actual compensation. If Nozick went the whole way with the ordinalists he would have to embrace and justify this deeply implausible notion of welfare, as well as confront the formidable arguments of many economists showing that ordinalist compensation arguments do not work.

This leaves the Pigouvian theories that explicitly embrace some kind of cardinal scale. Whatever their theoretical difficulties and inevitable and explicit value-ladenness, it may be impossible for organized social and political life to proceed without them, as Furniss (1978:406–9) has persuasively argued. For Nozick, however, embracing the assumptions behind the Pigouvian notion of real external diseconomy would involve abandoning his account of rights-as-side-constraints, the centerpiece of his entire political theory. Once the Pigouvian notion is embraced there is no logical reason for stopping with the minimal state. A much more activist state than Nozick envisages could be justified on precisely the same grounds. Nozick needs something like Pigouvian conclusions from something like Paretian premises but the former are not entailed by the latter.

Nozick's account of justice in transfer, based on (strict neoclassical) productive exchange, undercuts his compensation argument and thus his invisible hand explanation of the rise of the minimal state.[27] Instead of confronting these difficulties and dealing with their implications, Nozick banks on the enormous prestige enjoyed by neo-classical microeconomics as the only "real" or "hard" social science. He can make it appear

26 Little (1950:84–116); Fishkin (1979:91–6).
27 It is worth adding here that none of these issues is addressed in *Philosophical Explanations*, and that in discussing his theory of punishment there he again invokes the notion of compensation, remarking parenthetically that the "details of the theory of compensation are not our concern here" (Nozick, 1981:363).

plausible to outline a rough argument and claim that the economists out there will sort out the details. Nozick embraces a radical version of the view of the substance of rights as the exclusive dominion of individuals. He fails to supply an account of compensation consistent both with his rights-as-side-constraints and the rise of the minimal state. The fact that he devotes so much theoretical energy to trying to render these diverse commitments mutually compatible underscores the extent of his commitment to the negative libertarian view. Nozick treats this view as axiomatic. In this he differs markedly from Locke. Locke's theory of conventional property presupposed a theory of positive community in the state of nature, a labor theory of value, and a theory of natural law. None of these is available to Nozick.

iii. The basis for rights

Nozick's rights, as were Locke's, are grounded in a conception of free action. Nozick recognizes, however, that in the absence of a doctrine of natural law, an ethics and politics based on the concept of freedom requires some account of its nature. Formulating a coherent account of the concept of free will must be a central task for Nozick. He remarks in *Philosophical Explanations* that he has "spent more time thinking about the problem of free will . . . than about any other philosophical topic except perhaps the foundations of ethics" (1981:293). The project of that work is largely devoted to rescuing the concept of free will from the various determinisms – evolutionary, sociobiological, physical, and psychological – that seem to Nozick most seriously to threaten it.[28] Nozick's conception of "the problem" of free will is itself revealing from our point of view. His concern is to rescue the idea of individual freedom from its "enemies" who "think it important to deny, for instance,

---

28 I do not claim to do full justice to all the intricacies of this very dense book; my attention is restricted to those arguments that shed light on his theory of rights. It is worth recording, however, that Nozick refers in it to *Anarchy State and Utopia* but does not reject or qualify any of the central arguments made there. He clearly intends his discussions of free will and the foundations of ethics to provide the moral foundations of his political theory, although he acknowledges that he has not made the connections explicit and that there might be some difficulties in trying to do so (Nozick, 1981:498–9n).

that we have free will, that we can do something because it is right, that we know reality, that we are anything other than a congery of physiochemical processes and properties" (ibid.: 444). Nozick defines an action as "an intentional doing arising out of a process of choice among alternatives" (ibid.: 304). His central question about freedom of action, which he repeats many times, is: how can a person freely perform an action "if his doing it was causally determined, eventually by factors originating before his birth, and hence outside his control?" (ibid.:291). He solves this problem by embracing an antireductionist view of explanation grounded in the claim that, just as the truth or falsity of a proposition is not itself a function of the causes which lead it to be asserted, so the fact that there may be true causal explanations of the genesis of our capacity to choose does not in itself entail that we cannot make genuinely free choices:

The question is not whether there will be evolutionary explanations of how consciousness, language, and self-consciousness arise and are selected for. The question is whether once these do arise by a blind process, they then operate and lead to some things unblindly. (Do percepts with concepts *stay* blind?) That there is an invisible hand explanation of our having our cognitive capacities does not mean there is an invisible hand explanation of my writing the contents of this book. (Ibid.:347)

The advent of consciousness opens up new possibilities in Nozick's view. It introduces the possibility that we may be able to comprehend the causal mechanisms that lead us to act as we do, and make decisions based on this knowledge as a result. This is reminiscent of Locke's claim, in Book 2, Chapter 11, of the *Essay*, that man's freedom lies in his capacity to suspend desire before the performance of an action, and that "during this suspension of any desire, before the will be determined to action, and the action . . . done, we have opportunity to examine, view, and judge of the good or evil of what we are going to do." For Locke "it is not a fault, but a perfection of our nature, to desire, will and act according to the last result of a fair examination" (1959, I:345). For Nozick, too, a free action "withstands knowledge of its own causes" (1981:349).

These considerations lead Nozick to a definition of free action in terms of self-conscious choice:

Let us say an act is in disequilibrium for a person if (a) he does (or wants to do) it, yet (b) if he knew the causes of his doing or wanting to do it, this knowledge would lead him not to do it, or not to want to. . . . When condition *a* is satisfied but *b* is not, the act is in equilibrium. . . . [I]f he knew the causes of his doing or wanting to do the act then he still would (want to) do it as much. (Ibid.:349)

Notice, however, that Nozick limits this account of free action severely by his narrow definition of an action as an intentional choice among alternatives. Leaving aside the many conceptual difficulties attaching to such notions of action,[29] in focusing exclusively on actions as choices among alternatives Nozick is bypassing the one kind of determinism he most needs to deal with. Those with misgivings about his view that free actions are best realized in capitalist markets, are not really concerned that a sociobiological explanation might show why a particular consumer made a particular choice q out of the class of options $\{p, q\}$. What is pregnant politically about the freedom or unfreedom of the choice is whether there might be some realistic alternative arrangement of society where his class of options in the relevantly similar situation might be $\{p, q, r, s\}$ such that he would, say, choose r over q. The agent might well know all this (as well as much other relevant causal information) and still want to pick q over p. His choice of q would satisfy Nozick's subjunctive condition for acting in equilibrium, but we may well (and so may the relevant agent) want to say that he did not choose q freely. Presumably this is the logic we have in mind when we wonder if an unemployed black who chooses a job as a bus-boy for half the minimum wage is really acting freely.[30] Hence a (non-trivial) unfree act may well "withstand knowledge of its causes."

It is undeniable that all meaningful choices are among options (it is doubtful that we can even make sense of the idea of

29 See, for instance, my discussion in Shapiro (1982:542–63).
30 Of course there are many additional complexities here concerning what counts as a realistic alternative array of options, whether *A* is aware of all his possible options, and if not, why not (and if so, why), and so on. But these are different issues.

choosing without reference to options). If Nozick's goal is to produce an account of free choice for a *political philosophy* this is a trivial observation; it begs the more fundamental questions concerning the ways in which the options among which people choose are themselves structured and determined. It is trivially true that any organism in adapting to its environment alters the environment as well as itself, but in Nozick's account of knowledge humans differ. They can attempt to understand and alter their environment consciously, not simply react to it as isolated entities. His whole discussion of "the problem" of determinism, however, focuses on causal descriptions of motives for choices among options by individuals, on how we can blame and punish individuals for crimes, and on how we go about bestowing weights in ordering our options.

Nozick's underlying view of the environment in which people choose is thus at least neutral with respect to their actions, probably benign, and certainly not malicious. In an early essay on coercion (1972:101–35), wherein he comes closest to grappling directly with those issues, this is quite explicit. In trying to delineate a concept of free action he confronts the conundrum of how to distinguish threats, offers, and warnings from one another in difficult cases, as where an employer states that if his workers unionize he will close his factory, or where an employee is offered higher pay to change jobs. Nozick's solution to these types of questions is to appeal to what "would have been in the normal and expected course of events" had the relevant statement not been made (ibid.:112). This raises the question, as he fully realizes, whether the normal or expected course of events can itself be coercive. To this he offers two purported answers. In some cases, he argues, the normal and morally expected courses of events diverge. Thus if a slave owner offers not to beat his slave (which is his usual practice) if the slave does *x*, this is a threat not an offer because the normally expected event is not morally expected. The difficulty with this formulation is that it offers no account of how the "morally expected course of events" is arrived at. The logic of Nozick's example presumes that the master and slave will have conflicting moral expectations (ibid.:115–16). In the other case he deals with the normal and moral expectations do not diverge, but we might still want to regard the status quo as coercive. "Aren't some people coerced into not stealing by the legal apparatus?" he asks (ibid.:117). He responds to this with a consequentialist claim that it depends on what the situation would be like without this prohibition. And *this*, he argues, requires too many counterfactuals to be workable.

> But who knows what the world would be like if there was no punishment for crimes? It might well be that things would be so bad that the institution of punishing crimes would improve the consequences of almost all actions, and hence count . . . as making offers to people. (Ibid.:117)

Realizing we have no nonarbitrary reason for saying this is so, he concludes:

> An alternative procedure seems more reasonable; namely, to consider the normal and expected course of events, if Q does A, without P's particular act or without the particular consequence P will bring about, and against this background assess whether P's statement that if Q does A he will do a particular act or bring about a particular consequence constitutes a threat (i.e. whether P's statement, if carried out, makes Q's A worse than it would be in *this* new course of events). . . . There remain some problems about knowing what the course of events would be without this act, but these seem manageable. (Ibid.)

This may involve less complex counterfactuals, but it still involves them. It is morally quite arbitrary, for it assumes that *this* normal and expected course of events is benign or at least neutral. This procedure exemplifies the neo-classical tendency to work always from a status quo as given, and to analyze all distributive changes with reference to that starting point, without subjecting it to critical evaluative scrutiny. Although Nozick acknowledges the need for a theory of "justice in acquisition" for a political account of distributive justice, we saw in section II(ii) that Locke's account, requiring both the theory of positive community in the state of nature and the labor theory of value, is not available to him, and that he offers no alternative account.[31] Nozick apparently assumes that because any general

---

31 Nozick's interpretation and uses of Locke's second proviso in defense of market appropriation is discussed in section II(ii) of this chapter.

definitions of "freedom" and "coercion" involve counterfactual reasoning when applied to specific instances, he can legitimately choose the one that suits his purposes, since competing views will face comparable difficulties. This is true only if we seek such general definitions to begin with, a point taken up in section III of this chapter. Without the assumption that the normal course of events is not itself coercive Nozick's rightsas-side-constraints cannot get off the ground. It amounts to less than an argument to hold this, however, on the grounds that it is too complicated to show it is not true, not least when it appears from the same premises it is equally too complicated to show it is.[32]

If this is Nozick's account of freedom, how might it give rise to the individual rights he defends? For Nozick, one necessary condition for attaining the good for humans, or "tracking bestness," is acting in equilibrium. The other major necessary condition for any organism or entity is maximizing its "degree of organic unity," discussion of which is deferred to the next section. The notion of acting in equilibrium leads to accounts of "ethical push" and "ethical pull" that take account of man's capacity to act in equilibrium, to be a "self-choosing being." This is intended to generate an account having the force of the categorical imperative, if a somewhat different content. Because each person is a "value-seeking I" (that is, each person individually wants to track bestness by acting in equilibrium), the fundamental ethical principle is: "Treat someone (who is a value-seeking I) as a value-seeking I" (1981:462). More fully:

The theory of the moral pull and the moral push come together in this way. Someone else's basic moral characteristic, being a value-seeking I, exerts a pull on me, a moral claim. I am to treat him as a value-seeking I, cueing and shaping my behavior to his being one, thereby responding to him qua value-seeking I. However, the only way I can respond to his basic moral characteristic in this way is by exercising my own. Responding to his characteristic and to the moral pull it exerts, draws upon my being a value-seeking I and the capacities associated with this. Lower capacities just cannot do an adequately subtle and nuanced job of response. (Nozick, 1981:517–8)

32 For more general discussion of related difficulties about status quo assumptions in public choice and welfare economics, see Rae (1975a).

For Nozick this "value-seeking I" is the unique solution to the tension between free will and objectively valid ethical judgments. Nozick's difficulty with Kant's deontology is that if genuine freedom consists in acting only out of reverence for the moral law, it is not clear in what sense our actions can really be free. " . . . [W]hy doesn't reverence for the moral law also show us to be passively bound? If because it reflects or encapsulates our nature, cannot that too bind us? In any case, couldn't one act equally autonomously from another motive?" (ibid.:355). Thus even if the moral law reflects our true nature, since we may not like our nature, or may not for other reasons want to act from it, observing the categorical imperative is inconsistent with genuine free choice.[33]

Nozick nonetheless argues that free will is objectively desirable and ought to be preserved. Thus the

moral law must not only be given to ourselves and so chosen, it must be given by something that itself is chosen. Only what arises from a chosen essence will not bind. But if that essence is chosen, in what way is it inescapable? Can we have our cake and choose it too? There is one essence that would not bind: being a self-chooser. The fullest autonomy is had only by a being whose essense is self-choosing. (Ibid.:355)

A value-seeking I is someone who chooses to be self-choosing. Nozick avers that we must choose *this* with the force of a categorical imperative if we are *really* to be free. He makes the Sartrean point that since choosing not to choose is itself a choice, everyone chooses willy nilly to be a self-choosing being: we cannot escape our freedom because trying to do so is another manifestation of its presence.

Can this argument do the theoretical work Nozick requires of it? That we are constrained to choose does not necessarily entail that we should maximize this capacity, acknowledge it in others, or turn it into the basis of political organization. Nozick claims this is part of what being a self must require, for a "self-choosing being," he argues, "would choose to be a self" (ibid.:359). A genuinely self-choosing being, in Nozick's sense,

---

33 This seems to me to miss the force that the injunction "ought entails can" is intended to have in Kant's argument, but I cannot pursue this here.

however, might choose a whole range of things (otherwise it would not be capable of genuine choice), and, specifically, it might or might not choose to acknowledge others in any particular way. That we are constrained to make choices does not, by itself, entail *any* moral and political principles or program, or even that choosing is valuable. Sartre struggled with this problem for most of his life. Nozick offers some independent reasons why choosing is inherently valuable that are considered in section II(iv) of this chapter. For the present I concentrate on how this neo-Kantian view might generate Nozick's rights.

The connection between this ethics and the side-constraint theory of rights apparently inheres in the claim that a "constraint on treating everything in accordance with its value is your own value" (ibid.:523). Realizing that this will involve conflicts, Nozick adds that a "due sense of proportion" is to be maintained. Thus:

I do not think others should be taxed to support my research, and hence do not apply for or accept government research funds; I do not want to participate in this system, even as a way of receiving back unjustly taken tax payments. Yet I do not try to disengage myself completely from all government activities that I wish would not take place, such as mail delivery and public transportation. I am not required to sacrifice a normal life or normal activities in order to avoid all contact with illegitimate activities. (Ibid.)

The "normal and expected course of events" rears its head once more. Although Nozick remarks that "each of us will judge others by where they draw the lines" (ibid.) he fails to confront the fact that people's capacities to draw different lines frequently differ for reasons not of their own choosing; that no "normal life of normal activities" for an individual can be specified independently of the reasons why he or she has the capacities to live the life he or she does.

In another attempt to resolve this issue Nozick remarks that the domain of individual autonomy "must include a range of important and significant choices (such as religious practice, place of residence, choice of mate and lifestyle, choice of occupation), as well as a vast range of trivial choices which go to make up the daily texture of our lives" (ibid.:501). Nozick does not explain why these particular activities are so central (rather than, for instance, being assured of employment and a living wage) except to say "[t]he choices that are viewed as significant and central to a person's life and self-definition may vary from culture to culture . . . the domain of autonomy might [in a different culture] be demarcated differently" (ibid.:501–2). But this is a version of the Austinian fallacy, supposing that what is taken to be legitimate "by a culture" is for that reason legitimate. This view ignores the (presumably typical) case in a culture where different people have different views of what constitutes the legitimate domain, and of what that entails in practice. It is difficult to see a way out of this for Nozick except through an appeal to the market; this is in fact his fundamental appeal, as we will now see.

Because Nozick believes there are objective goods that can be known, he must take seriously the claim that sometimes people do not strive for them. Otherwise this assertion would be empty. He cannot therefore accept the doctrine of revealed preference as a sufficient condition for an agent's having performed a good/desirable action, since agents may do bad/undesirable things in their voluntary transactions one with another. Hence:

The mechanism of the market lures one to serve the wants of others, but does not lure one to serve their highest capacities or their harmonious hierarchical development, except insofar as others express their desire for this within the market. Nor need working in the market draw directly upon our own highest capacities and motivations . . . [T]he market mechanism does not especially reward us for satisfying those desires. (Nozick, 1981:514)

Although a market is not a sufficient condition for "tracking bestness"[34] it is necessary, because a necessary condition of tracking bestness, for Nozick, is obeying his subjunctive condition to act in equilibrium. This, he believes, can only be achieved via a market. Thus the fact that the market satisfies mere wants "is not a criticism of the market our fellows can

34 This is a modification of Nozick's position in *Anarchy State and Utopia*, where his discussion of markets implies that it is sufficient (Nozick, 1974:17, 248–50).

make; the market serves them no worse than they choose to be served" (ibid.). Any other mechanism might also satisfy our desires, "whatever they happen to be . . . [but] such a mechanism sometimes would lower us even as it got to raise others, and it would merely reinforce *our* acting on already existing desires" (ibid.). Thus, although Nozick avoids the claim that everyone can, or even if they can, will, realize their highest capacities via the market, he does hold that without the market they will not, for without it they cannot act in equilibrium. This assumes that the market is a necessary condition for acting in equilibrium, which Nozick does not establish. As I argued via the bus-boy example, an action being a market transaction can in certain circumstances be a sufficient condition for its being coerced.

Nozick's account of the basis for rights thus rests on a combination of his subjunctive conditional for acting in equilibrium and his leap of faith that people will want to "track bestness." On the second of these he believes that philosophy has nothing to say;[35] the first is assumed, ultimately without argument, to be guaranteed exclusively by the market.

iv. The purposes of rights

Apparently rejecting the doctrine of the priority of right propounded in *Anarchy State and Utopia*, in *Philosophical Explanations* Nozick presents an account of objective goods for all entities (plants, animals, humans, even solar systems) in terms of maximizing the "degree of organic unity" of the relevant entity. For humans this consists of a process of self-improvement or "harmonious hierarchical development," variously likened to stages in the Platonic hierarchy of the soul, to the Aristotelian notion of potential, and to the experiences of (usually unidentified) mystics. It is difficult to discuss this view without caricaturing it, especially since *Philosophical Explanations* begins with a homily on the vices of "coercive philosophy," the traditional (argumentative) mode that tries to "force" conclusions on people with "powerful" "knockdown" arguments (1981:4–11). Rather, Nozick argues, philosophy should illuminate with ex-

35 See Nozick (1981:410–11). This issue is taken up in Section II(iv) of this chapter.

planations, it should be motivated by "puzzlement, curiosity, [and] a desire to understand." Philosophers should not be "thought-police" (ibid.:13). This may sound disingenuous coming from the author of one of the most explicitly argumentative and ideological books of philosophy to achieve prominence in many years, but it would be churlish not to recognize that *Philosophical Explanations* is written in a quite different and much more speculative mood.

Apart from the doubtful plausibility of his distinction between coercive and noncoercive philosophy, the question arises whether Nozick practices what he preaches. The ethics presented in *Philosophical Explanations* is clearly intended, inter alia, to provide a moral foundation for the argument of *Anarchy State and Utopia*. When he mentions the earlier book, he makes no attempt to qualify its "coercive" doctrine. In this book Nozick clearly attempts to establish an argument about the existence of free will and a particular conception of the good, both being best realized in practice in unregulated capitalist markets. He outlines and argues for a position with substantive philosophical and political implications. His arguments therefore invite critical scrutiny.

Nozick's theory of objective good in terms of "degree of organic unity" is spelled out as follows: organic unity is "the common strand of value across different realms" of existence. Although there may be other things with particular values for entities, "degree of organic unity" accounts for at least "90 percent of the variance in intrinsic value." It is the "basic dimension of intrinsic value, accounting for almost all differences in intrinsic value" (ibid.:418–9). What is valuable for an entity is that which maximizes its degree of organic unity; what is disvaluable is that which tends to destroy this unity. Nozick takes a broad evolutionary view of entities striving always to act by this principle of unifying diversity. Thus he relates, from the *Book of Genesis*, "everything was formless and void and God then structured it and saw it was very good, whereas the parts were only said to be good." And, "[a]ccording to *Meshech Chachmah*, there was new goodness in the whole, greater than the sum of the parts" (ibid.:424–5n). More technically, for Nozick:

The value of X is the sum of its degree of organic unity plus the values of each of its parts. Since by hypothesis each of these parts has zero value, the second term will be zero. However, since X does have some degree of organic unity greater than zero, its value will be greater than zero, and equal to $O(X)$. Thus, the view that organic unity gives rise to new value allows value creation *ex nihilo:* the creation of intrinsic value out of nothing of intrinsic value. There need not be atoms of value, since there can be valuable molecules composed of valueless atoms. (Ibid.:423–4)

Although he reduces this statement to a formal equation, he supplies no dimension for measuring this degree of organic unity: the idea is the intuitive claim that values arise out of the objective structuring of the world, and goods are those things either conducive to the viability of existing structures, or leading to the creation of new unified structures.

The sense in which these structures are held to exist in the world is difficult to get at, but they appear to be something like noumenal entities.[36] Nozick is aware that any given entity (or action) admits of many true descriptions and that an explanation is always an explanation under some description. Because concepts without percepts are blind, however,[37] he must postulate objective structures "out there" that nonetheless form the basis of knowledge and value. Hence the following metaphor:

It is not impossible that there be beings who experience phonograph records differently, whose vision registers the microscopic contours of the grooves, the intricate relationships exhibited there; for them, the record itself is a visual art form. In this case, the spatial features (isomorphic to the relations among sounds and tones) would have important weight for them, and be crucial to (their view of) the identity of the object as the kind of thing it was. Here we would expect further relationships also to be salient to them, such as relations of adjacency between grooves (for instance, lying on the same radius from the center); these would make further unities possible, whereas the "corresponding" uniformly changing temporal relations among the musical sounds would not be a unifying mode for the

36 Nozick does not himself draw this comparison.
37 Again, this is not Nozick's phrase in this context.

music. Similarly one could imagine the record as a tactile art form, with its own salient organizing relationships. (Ibid.:426)

His claim seems to be that underlying all these different possible valuable experiences of the record is its basic "brute" structure which is, or stands in isomorphic correspondence to, its intrinsic value. Leaving aside the well known difficulties with such noumenal theories (such as how we can say anything about them at all, even identify them, if they are genuinely noumenal, and what the causal relationship between them and phenomenal entities is), note Nozick's claims not only that organic unity is desirable, but the greater the diversity that is unified the better. Thus he gives his pluralism its transcendental gloss. The more diversity an "ontologically unified structure" encompasses the more valuable it is. The degree of organic unity is a function of both the diversity and the degree of unifiedness. Even accepting all the rest, this is by no means intuitively obvious from Nozick's premises. For instance, the old AJS 500cc single-cylinder motorcycle was tremendously simple by contemporary standards. Do we say that a 1985 four-cylinder Honda 1000cc has more intrinsic value because it has three more pistons, extra wing-mirrors, electric starter . . . more diversity? Degree of organic unity does not necessarily entail greater value for more rather than less united diversity.

There also seem to be serious difficulties about the entities to which these value-predicates attach. Although degree of organic unity is the basic dimension of intrinsic value across different realms, this "does not mean that we can make value rankings across realms as well as within them" (ibid.:419). The nature of the structured diversity will be different in different cases, but Nozick does want to generalize to the extent of saying that whatever is conducive to the preservation of an organic unity is valuable. This obviously becomes problematical if unities are conceived so generally, because unities in nature and social life destroy one another, as he notes:

Some destroyers of organic unity are themselves highly organized unities, for example, concentration camps. Someone might say that therefore these are intrinsically valuable, though instrumentally disvaluable. The latter they certainly are, but I am reluctant to see them

190

as at all instrinsically valuable. For their purpose, their *telos,* is an important component of their unity; indeed, it is their central unifying factor. Since this purpose is destructive of organic unity, it itself is disvaluable and infects with disvalue the unity that it animates. (Ibid.:419)

This solution, however, is fraught with difficulties, some of which Nozick half acknowledges in a footnote.[38] By this logic a cancer-killing drug must be held to disvaluable, for instance. Nozick may not like concentration camps, but at this level of abstraction, they are no different than cancer-killing drugs.

To avoid these difficulties this argument would have to specify – at a much lower level of generality – the nature of the entity concerned, the conditions for its survival, the implications of those conditions for other entities, their imperatives for survival, and, above all, why some entities are valuable while others are disvaluable. Nozick's answers to these questions are at best implicit, as can be seen as soon as he applies this doctrine to political and economic life. Thus:

Is the most valuable society a tightly organized centrally controlled hierarchical society of fixed hereditary status, termed by some theorists an "organic society"? Although it would have a high degree of unity, it would not encompass the same vast diversity as a free and open society. A far-flung system of voluntary cooperation unifies diverse parts in an intricate structure of changing equilibria, and also unifies these parts in a way that takes account of their degree of organic unity. Enlisting a person's voluntary cooperation or participation takes account of his degree of organic unity to a greater extent than commanding him. (Ibid.:421)

Granting the unity/diversity thesis, the objective structure thesis, the value/disvalue thesis, this is an additional undefended empirical claim, not even intuitively plausible to boot. A cor-

38 "[W]e must take into account the alternative possibilities of what the organic unity can do, and whether destruction is a central aim of the entity. . . . Are people less valuable because they eat animals, which are organic unities? However if these animals eat plants, are they not destructive, so that it is better to eat them than to eat (innocent) plants? Yet to eat only animals who eat plants is to bask in the good fortune that there are such destructive entities, so that one does not have to eat (the less valuable because having a lesser degree of organic unity) plants oneself, and so one is a parasite on the disvalue of others. These animals themselves have no other alternatives, and so on" (Nozick, 1981:420). The implications of these observations for his more general argument are not considered by Nozick.

poratist society of the kind envisioned by Plato could conceiva-
bly be just as complex, have just as many interlocking but
independent constituent parts, as the most complex market
society imaginable; it might have more components than many
actual market societies. Alternatively, there are cases of markets destroying diversity through monopoly, or by promoting
mediocrity as Mill and Tocqueville feared. One might compare British and American television, for instance, where the
very much greater number of channels organized on a market
basis in America results in significantly inferior output. It is by
no means obvious that American television has greater intrinsic value, or even that it contains more genuine diversity,
though the market-based system may generate a greater number of channels.

It should by now be clear that Nozick's philosophical theory
of objective goods is quite irrelevant to his substantive claims
about objective value. These rest on little more than faith in the
utopian consequences held to flow from unregulated markets.
At no time does he explain why we should value the unification
of diversity which, he claims without evidential support, this
process generates. Thus he argues that "in my value ranking I
place people higher in instrinsic value than animals which are
higher than plants which are higher than rocks. There are
distinctions in value within these categories, as well as some
overlap; for example, I do not rank a mouse higher than an
800-year-old redwood" (1981:415). Two pages later, however,
he has attributed these idiosyncratic rankings to the rest of us:
"Thus the ranking of organisms in accordance with degree of
organic unity [complexity of unified diversity] matches *our*
value ranking of them, with people above other animals above
plants above rocks" (ibid.:417, emphasis added). In his list of
the valuable characteristics a self-choosing being would select in
order to be valuable, he feels "little doubt" that these include:
having free will, conscious, self-conscious, able to do something
because it is right, able to recognize value, able to guide behavior in accord with recognition of value, self-choosing. "You
would want your child to have these characteristics," he says
(ibid.:445). Perhaps one would, but perhaps one might think
other characteristics just as (or more) important, such as com-

passion for others, or a critical mind. One might even think too much self-consciousness a bad thing in some people, if it immobilizes them, for instance. We seek, not to debate general characteristics with Nozick, but to establish that he offers no reasons for the ones he prefers, nor does he remotely prove that they will effectively be realized via unregulated markets.

What of the big question confronting all who want to hold both a subjective theory of rights and an objective theory of goods: how are they to be mutually reconciled? Either they must be shown to entail one another (or at least not to generate mutually incompatible injunctions), or one must ultimately be held to be prior.[39] Hobbes and Locke believed they reconciled them in a view of science and an ontology not available to Nozick. What is his solution? He tries to side-step this question by arguing that if there is objective value its "allure" will be such that people will in fact strive for it.

Is it humanocentric to think that value must inspire us? Couldn't we be so sunk in sloth and darkness (original sin?) that we would not choose the good even under good conditions? Isn't it possible for some selves to be in that unfortunate state? Perhaps it is us. However, we are not sunk absolutely low, since we quest for value, and we are attracted to some things *qua* valuable. Since questing for value is itself valuable, it is a sign that we are not thoroughly bad; moreover, if questing for value also falls under the same dimension that allures us, that is a sign that the dimension itself is valuable. (Ibid.:439)

If we accept Nozick's claim that people strive for what they take to be valuable for them, this need not entail that they will strive for the particular things Nozick enumerates, nor exemplify his theory of individual "harmonious hierarchical development," as he is aware:

[D]o we believe that all selves who are attracted by anything in the peaceful contest will be attracted by the same thing? Leaving aside other beings described in science fiction novels, there is some evidence that every person will be attracted most by the same thing, once they encounter it. . . . Mystics report their experiences as over-

---

39 Leaving aside the nature of this priority: absolute, conditional, lexical, or some other.

whelmingly valuable and powerful in impact; certain types of these experiences not only transform the person's view of what the world contains, they also transform the person. If all those who experience it agree in their response and in the nature of their transformation, and no additional experience of anything else damps down this response, isn't this a sign that it is an objective response to value? (Ibid.:439–40)

It must be the apotheosis of implausibility to maintain there is objective value because there is consensus among mystics. This aside, it is still unclear why people should strive for the objectively valuable. "Is the thought," Nozick wonders "overly optimistic that underlies all this, namely, that value will inspire (under good conditions) more strongly than disvalue or non-value?" (ibid.). This is the crux of the question as far as rights are concerned. The closest Nozick comes to confronting it is the following:

If there is objective value, we should expect it sometimes to be divorced from a person's actual motivations, while being none the less valuable for that. Surely, some adverse biographical conditions, or even moods, can lead a person not to care about value. . . . "But if under some conditions value is divorced from a person's motivation, that person may lack (sufficient) motivation to behave morally; what then can we do?" There is much we can do in society, ranging from attempts at persuasion to punishment of the person who does not behave morally, by connecting sanctions to motivations he does have. There is no guarantee he will not be able to avoid our institutional network. However, it is not the task of philosophy to plug this gap and provide motivation for people. At any rate, that is not our task here. I want to understand how a person is worse off being immoral, not to convince the immoral person that he is worse off. "But he might just dig in his heels and refuse to be convinced without a knock down argument." When he digs in his heels and lives accordingly, his choice has the effect of determining the value of his life, whether or not he realizes this. What he needs is not a philosopher but inspiration. (Ibid.:410–11)

Thus it seems that ultimately the rights must be prior to the objectively valuable since the latter is critically dependent on the agent *choosing* to act in accordance with value. If he does not, so much the worse for him; but since a necessary condition for acting valuably is acting in equilibrium, individual choice must be prior. The rest of the theory of objective goods is irrelevant to the argument. The purpose of rights is for people to treat one another as self-choosing beings. This is Nozick's philosophical defense of the market, although we saw that it is riddled with arbitrary assertions and unsubstantiated empirical claims.

III. IDEOLOGICAL CONSEQUENCES OF NOZICK'S ARGUMENT

The force of Nozick's argument clearly derives from the neo-classical view of the world that it both invokes and seeks to justify. The neo-Kantian foundations supplied for this theory of rights are neither Kantian nor generative of his conclusions. Locke adumbrated a modified natural-law theory to give his rights their transhistorical force, but Nozick appeals to a modified version of the categorical imperative to give his rights their objective and transcendental gloss. Nozick's main appeal is to the liberal language of individual rights discussed in the last two chapters, although this language had, since its early formulations, been strongly influenced by the rise of equilibrium theory, the shedding of labor theories of value, and the impact of modern utilitarianism on its evolution. It remains to consider the ideological consequences of this appeal in detail.

Nozick believes, with Locke, that the isolated individual is the subject of asymmetrical rights of exclusive dominion, but now in a much more radical form. He takes over Locke's doctrine of the individual as proprietor of his capacities and possessions with two important modifications. First, God is removed from the picture, destroying the possibility of exogenous binding moral constraints on individual behavior. In *Anarchy State and Utopia* he claims that people in the state of nature "generally act as they ought," but we saw that this was (implicitly) circularly defined to mean respecting one another's rights. In *Philosophical Explanations* Nozick holds that people will "track bestness" to avoid what he sees as the nihilistic moral implications of not holding this. His strong attachment to the priority of right over good, however, and his claim that if there is an objective good the priority of right – necessary for acting "in equilibrium" – must be a necessary condition for its attainment, both preclude sanction of any exogenous constraints on individuals at all. There is Lockean liberty but no Lockean license for Nozick. For ideological reasons, he needs the conclusion that no redistribution by the state can ever be justified. He is thus forced to embrace a radical version of Pareto's noncomparable ordinal utilities, ruling out all "moral balancing acts" and "paternalistic judgments" that might limit the realm of individual autonomy. The workmanship model of intentional action as the source of all moral imperatives, together with the Cartesian privileged-access thesis, are thus neatly adapted to the neo-classical view of rights, stripped of their theological baggage.

Not merely is Locke's argument from scripture unavailable to Nozick; the arguments from reason and nature were embedded in a view of science to which he does not subscribe. His individuals are thus subject to no exogenous constraints at all. In making these moves Nozick is neither original nor alone: he falls squarely into the neo-classical tradition as adapted to politics by the modern discipline of public choice.[40] Second, although for Nozick the individual is proprietor of his actions, this entails no labor theory of value as it did for Locke, again in keeping with the neo-classical revolution against classical political economy. Neo-classical theory takes all property rights as given and explains value in terms of returns on the factors of production – land, labor and capital. A standard criticism of this has always been that to assume this is to assume much that is controversial. The standard reply, that questions about the original endowment of property rights are the proper concern of historians, not economists, is not especially convincing. Perhaps out of

40 For similar views that noncomparable utility functions are necessary for respecting individual rights, see Buchanan and Tullock (1962) and Arrow (1973). It might be argued that a comparable thesis is embedded in Mill's claim that "the sole end for which mankind are warranted, individually or collectively, in interfering with the liberty of action of any of their number is . . . to prevent harm to others. His own good, either physical or moral, is not a sufficient warrant. He cannot rightfully be compelled to do or to forbear because it will be better for him to do so, because it will make him happier, because, in the opinion of others, to do so would be wise, or even right" (Mill, 1975:15).

awareness of this Nozick acknowledges the need to have an account of justice in acquisition, although once he has jettisoned Locke's labor theory of value it is unclear why his particular (Grotian) theory, with a modified version of Locke's second proviso tacked on, should necessarily be chosen. Nozick avoids the issue of justice in acqusition by holding that even his more demanding version of the proviso will never be violated under capitalist market conditions, because of the productivity and other congenial effects of capitalist production and exchange. These factual claims are never defended and might easily be challenged, both as claims about long-term efficiency and productivity and as claims that the proviso will not be violated for any given individual. Thus, despite many internal difficulties with his formulations of it, Nozick uses the asymmetrical model of individual proprietorship to justify capitalist markets.

Nozick remains firmly in the tradition of Locke and Hobbes in separating right from law, and making individual private rights prior to civil law from which this latter is derived. For Nozick the issue is not to explain the relationship between public and private law in terms of private-law contracts; it is to deny that there can be *any* public law other than simple unanimity. There is no sense of a public sphere operating for different purposes and by different rules than the private. This logical outgrowth of the arguments of Hobbes and Locke is vastly more extreme than theirs. Hobbes's sovereign, once created, had very great (autonomous) powers. Locke's state, too, could act autonomously in the public interest, though this power was conditioned and dependent on its fiduciary trust. For Nozick, there is no public sphere; the market rules that Hobbes and Locke restricted to the private sphere are directly applied to politics. Thus can the state in all seriousness be conceived of as a business run by entrepreneurs, an insurance company from which clients buy a service for a fee. If this sounds implausible, note that Nozick is firmly anchored to the public-choice tradition that has made use of similar assumptions since the 1950s. In one of its formative works, for instance, Downs (1957) treats political parties as firms trying to maximize votes (the analogue of profits); and at least since

Buchanan and Tullock (1962) this entire school has treated
voting preferences as utility functions, and the search for "equilibrium" in the political "market" as an exact parallel of the
neo-classical conception of the economic market, based on voluntary transactions, Pareto-superior trades, and "stable" efficient outcomes. The Nobel Prize-winning Arrow theorem
could not even be stated without embracing this whole view of
the political world.[41]

The ideological implications of this are doubly ironic. First,
there is the simple fact of this "ecomorphism" of the political,
this view of politics as a simple extension of the market, and
therefore governed by the same assumptions, rules, and
procedures as the market. Ideology is never entirely at odds
with reality, and, particularly in the United States (where public choice has had its greatest impact), these developments to a
considerable extent reflect the expansion of the market system
into all walks of life—most notably politics. Politicians do, to a
greater extent than ever before, sell a commodity as entrepreneurs, employ agencies to "package" their products for advertising, and gear those products to what they believe the market demands.[42] Even in England, where two decades ago such
practices would have been inconceivable, professional political
managers, consulting firms, and advertising agencies have
made substantial inroads into the political process. However
much this ecomorphism clashes with more traditional conceptions of politics and the public sphere, it would be a mistake to
think it has no grounding in contemporary political practices.
To the extent that the ideology strikes us as quaintly extreme
this is a reflection of the degree to which political concerns
have actually come to be dominated by, and mimic, those of
the market.

41 For good recent summaries of the public choice literature with many illustrations
of these assumptions, see Mueller (1979) and Ordeshook and Shepsle (1982).
42 For a discussion of one significant illustration of this, see Mayhew (1974:1–77),
where it is shown that the most important factor affecting the behavior of U.S.
Congressmen in office is their set of beliefs about what will get them reelected,
and how other considerations are tailored to this end. I skirt the issue of whether
they actually do what they believe their potential electorate wants done, or
whether they try to describe what they do in terms that make it seem they are
doing what their potential electorate wants done; not always, needless to say, the
same thing.

The second ironic aspect of these developments concerns this wholesale importation of neo-classical equilibrium theory into political theory, which added much fuel to pretentions toward scienticity and value neutrality,[43] taking hold just as it was dawning on economists that traditional neo-classical (competitive) models bore scant relationship to the actual structure of contemporary capitalist markets. The much vaunted predictive prowess of neo-classical price theory was reduced to impotence as these economies entered sustained periods of combined low growth, high unemployment, and continuous inflation (even during periods of recession), from which they have yet successfully to emerge. The neo-classical price mechanism bore no readily discernible relationship to contemporary price behavior and many economists began to cast about for alternative models.[44] That in this situation the neo-classical model, seen as scientifically sound, as tried and tested by generations of economists since Marshall, should be adapted to political theory is thus deeply ironic. The myth of the political market was now built atop the myth of the economic market. Neo-classical price theory still retains tremendous prestige and influence among dominant intellectual elites, but it masks a quite different reality in the highly concentrated economies of the advanced capitalist world. Without these prevailing beliefs Nozick's modeling of the state on the firm, his presumption of the validity and adaptability of the axioms of (macro and micro) neo-classical theory to politics, could never get off the ground, let alone win him pride of place as a champion of contemporary libertarianism.

Closely related to this is his negative libertarianism, which falls into the classical mold discussed in the last chapter, but takes on much more extreme dimensions in its neo-classical form. Nozick's side-constraint view of rights, which literally

43 For one of many possible illustrations: "Since this theory [of Pareto-optimal equilibrium] admits prediction of an equilibrium and since the actual occurrences of numerous predicted equilibria [in economics] have been verified, the prestige of this theory is higher, I believe, than that of any other theory in the social sciences. Indeed, it seems to me that this success alone (i.e., predictions from the theory of price) elevates the science of economics above all other social sciences" (Riker, 1982:6).
44 See Shapiro and Kane (1983:6–28).

invokes the metaphor of a line or "hyperplane" in moral space surrounding an individual, wholly ignores the social and economic relationships that place people in the "moral spaces" they occupy, just as the Pareto system ignores the (determinants of) the initial conditions of the distributions to which it is applied. The neo-classical tradition denies the possibility of interpersonal comparisons of utility for fear of the distributive consequences that may result. The effect of this postulate on Nozick's formulation is to make the isolation of individuals from one another absolute. Small wonder that the view of the "meaning of life" at the end of *Philosophical Explanations* is so romantically individualistic, concerned with the "harmonious hierarchical development" of the individual soul, lapsing into appeals to mystical experiences, and at times almost autistic in tone. This is the logical outcome of taking deadly seriously a view of social life as constituted by a scatter of unrelated entities (or entities whose relatedness extends no further than acknowledging their mutual separateness), each spending its time running up and down its utility function, impervious to the activities of others except insofar as those activities might enhance or impede its own advancement.

Nozick is in the mainstream of classical and neo-classical tradition, too, in viewing the class of objects and actions to which there are private rights as potentially infinite. There is not the hint of a distinction between wants and needs in any of his writings. He openly embraces the empirical belief that unfettered capitalist production will lead to continuous productive growth. It is worth saying a word here about Nozick's utilitarian assumptions, because the claim that the productivity effects of capitalist production will be such that the proviso will not be violated smacks of traditional utilitarian consequentialism. Nozick explicitly rejects utilitariansim as an "end-state" principle. He also rejects the weaker "utilitarianism of rights" where the "total (weighted) amount of violations of rights is built into the desirable end-state to be achieved" (1974:28)—a kind of rule-utilitariansim. Nozick employs precisely this procedure, however, when he argues that in certain cases it is not worth getting an individual's consent to a rights violation because the transactions costs are too great. The logic of this claim is that of a rule-utilitarian maxim to minimize some weighted measure of rights violations. In addition, Nozick imports the whole (neo-classical) theory of value into his account of the substance of rights. He is content to refer to individual utilities, indifference curves, and utility maximization; the whole discussion of compensation obviously presumes the neo-classical utilitarian theory of value. In what sense is his account antiutilitarian? It is an attempt at the kind of synthesis of rights and utility undertaken by Mill in *On Liberty*, which has always resolved into either a restatement of rights in rule-utilitarian terms or a (consequentialist) claim that utilitarian efficiency will be best served by respecting individual rights. Nozick attempts both these strategies of argument at different times. His argument would not have the surface plausibility it does if it did not implicitly attempt this synthesis.

Nozick's account of the nature and functions of the state falls squarely into the classical tradition as modified by the rise of equilibrium theory. His reading of the minimal state into Locke involved an anachronistic misreading of Locke and a misleading conflation of minimalism with regulation. Nozick exemplifies the libertarian tendency to look back at what is taken to be a classical liberal past, when the state really was minimal, and the market was permitted to function unimpeded. The era of this supposed Golden Age is never clearly specified by Nozick or others who ritually invoke it, but we know from Polanyi, Supple, and others that classical laissez-faire capitalism lasted briefly in nineteenth-century England and was never fully adopted elsewhere, and that the creation of capitalist markets required a massively interventionist state. My analysis of the views on the state held by Hobbes and Locke confirmed that, although both thought the state should regulate a negative libertarian society, this in no way entailed minimalism. These writers, I argued, had no notion of equilibrium. When Nozick appeals to the neo-classical system he is appealing to the belief that capitalist economies can be efficiently self-regulating, an empirical claim for which little evidence has ever been supplied.

Nozick's belief that such self-regulating systems would emerge naturally has no basis in fact. A state would be (and in fact was) required to create the particular systems of property rights, contracts, torts, and other legal arrangements necessary to their preservation and reproduction. Once these are established the power of the state becomes latent and its inactivity will be sought by those desirous of preserving the broad socioeconomic status quo. The idea of the minimal state has always been a myth, not least today when it is invoked by the New Right on both sides of the Atlantic as a means for restoring the "traditional" competitive structure of these economies. In fact, deregulation has resulted in greater concentration of capital and less competition than ever before.[45] That Nozick invokes it is a primary reason for the ideological appeal of his work. It is the institutional manifestation of the conservatism inherent in a liberal tradition in which to be free is to be free above all from politics: the government that governs least governs best.

IV. CONCLUSION

A recent attempt by Jeffrey Paul to explain the impact of *Anarchy State and Utopia* sees it as a paradox:

In contrast to the moderate and conventional ideological stance of John Rawls's *A Theory of Justice*, its distinguished predecessor in political philosophy, Nozick's work announced a thesis so out of joint with its times that the critical acclaim accorded it by many of its reviewers must have astounded its author as much as it baffled its critics. That a treatise extolling the virtues of eighteenth-century individualism and nineteenth-century laissez-faire capitalism should not have elicited either hostility or silence, is both a puzzling and gratifying phenomenon; puzzling because its themes run counter to the *Zeitgeist* and gratifying because it is a work of considerable philosophical acuity. (Paul, 1978:1)

Paul's solution to this is to invoke the Kuhnian notion of a paradigm shift with Nozick at its center, which explains "why *Anarchy State and Utopia* was able to replicate the enthusiastic welcome accorded to Rawls's work only three years earlier." Rawls's work was written partly to restore the "impaired foun-

45 See OECD (1979) and Shapiro and Kane (1983:13–19).

dations of the current ideological paradigm," but Nozick's book "struck at the conceptual underpinnings of both contemporary Western society and its totalitarian adversaries in the East" (ibid.:2–3).

If the analysis offered in this chapter is broadly correct, Paul's assessment could not be further from the truth. Nozick's argument falls squarely into the well established traditions of neo-classical economics and conservative liberalism which are both rooted in classical liberalism and have always comprised a powerful strand of modern liberal thought. From Pareto to Friedman in economics, from Hayek to the modern discipline of public choice, these ideas have substantial twentieth-century intellectual pedigrees, apart from the earlier influences I have sought to establish. They are also deeply embedded in contemporary liberal culture, constituting a substantial part of the prevailing *Zeitgeist*. The metaphor of a paradigm shift could not be more misleading.

5

The Keynesian moment

I. INTRODUCTION

Rawls employs a hypothetical contract, like Nozick, but its structure and explanatory status are very different.[1] Nozick's appeal was to a modified version of Locke's state of nature, but Rawls sees himself as building on the work of Rousseau and especially Kant, who "sought to give a philosophical foundation to Rousseau's idea of the general will" (Rawls, 1971:264). His principal concern is comparable to Nozick's in that he is seeking to establish unanimity for the fundamental social contract. His aim is to argue for a theory of justice by convincing the reader that the principles he advocates would be chosen by imaginary persons in a hypothetical state of nature (or "original position"), ignorant of all "particular facts" about themselves and their actual lives in society that might impair their impartiality. From behind this veil of ignorance, Rawls argues, it would be rational for all persons to choose his two principles of justice over several other common candidates, notably intuitionism, two types of utilitarianism, perfectionism, and various combinations of these. The two principles chosen would constitute the basic social structure, as well as shape constitutional, legal,

---

1 It is in the nature of a book as long as *A Theory of Justice*, written over an extensive period and circulated in manuscript form for many years, that its central doctrines have been subtly qualified and modified at many points, to the degree that it is sometimes difficult to discover what the argument is, as Barry (1973:1–3), among others, has noted. This is complicated by the fact that, since its publication, Rawls has published several articles in response to critics, further clarifying and in some cases modifying his position. In this chapter I will take *A Theory of Justice* as the definitive statement of Rawls's view, referring to subsequent writings only where they decisively affect my argument. This seems defensible to me, first, because none of the central doctrines has been given up, and, second, because I am primarily concerned with the influence of Rawls's argument—and this undoubtedly derives from the central doctrines of the book, not the subsequent qualifications.

economic, and political practices. He sums up the essential impartiality of the conditions under which the principles are chosen in the phrase "justice as fairness." The principles are also held to be procedural expressions of the categorical imperative – to acknowledge and preserve our sense of justice and our essential nature *qua* autonomous beings capable of free choice. They are public in that everyone understands, acknowledges, and agrees to them, and permanent in that all subsequent decisions will be made in accordance with them and they are understood as applying to future generations as well as present.

II. RAWLS'S THEORY OF RIGHTS

Rawls often uses the words "right" and "just" interchangeably, but his considered view is that an account of right must be embedded in a theory of justice, that it is consequently on the question of justice that individuals in the original position must agree first and foremost. He argues that these individuals will first agree on a general conception of justice which rules out inequalities that are not to the benefit of all. More specifically, they will agree that "All social values – liberty and opportunity, income and wealth, and the bases of self-respect – are to be distributed equally unless an unequal distribution of any, or all, of these values is to everyone's advantage" (Rawls, 1971:62).

As a "special case" of this general view of justice Rawls formulates his two principles which, in their final form, read as follows:

First Principle
Each person is to have an equal right to the most extensive total system of equal basic liberties compatible with a similar system of liberty for all.
Second Principle
Social and economic inequalities are to be arranged so that they are both:
   (a) to the greatest benefit of the least advantaged, . . . and
   (b) attached to offices and positions open to all under conditions of fair equality of opportunity (ibid.:302).

These principles are "lexically" ordered, with the first prior to the second, and, within the second, (b) prior to (a).[2] Thus for Rawls a liberty protected by the first principle can never be sacrificed for improvements in economic well-being, no matter how extensive they may be or how minor the infraction of the relevant liberty. The only justifiable basis for sacrificing a liberty in whole or in part would be to "strengthen the total system of liberty shared by all" (ibid.).

Once the principles have been chosen under the relevant conditions of ignorance, the veil of ignorance is gradually lifted in a four-stage process. Individuals are given the information necessary to agree on more specific economic, political, and legal institutions, always in conformity with the two "constitutional" principles which, once established, constitute the permanent basis of social organization. Although this four-stage sequence is "suggested by the United States Constitution and its history" (ibid.:196n), the choice problem is conceived of as hypothetical, on the level of so-called "ideal theory." Once the principles have been justified in this way, however, they are held to be applicable to the real world, as a goal for which to strive and a yardstick for establishing the relative justice of extant institutions. They are conceived of quite generally[3] as applicable wherever the "circumstances of justice" (the most important of which is conflicting claims for scarce resources) obtain, and are discussed in relation to historical and contemporary societies. They are held to be applicable in both capitalist and socialist societies, although the only case Rawls considers in any detail is that of a "property-owning democracy" (ibid.: 274).

i. The subject of rights

Who are these persons in the original position, and what is the nature of their agreement? Although Rawls's individuals are hypothetical, they are intended to correspond to actual per-

2 A principle higher in a lexical ranking must always be given priority over a lower one, and can never be sacrificed for a lower one should conflicts arise.
3 There is a proviso that their strict application requires a certain level of economic development, but even in the case where this condition is not met, they are held to become increasingly relevant as economic development advances.

sons in all essentials relevant to questions of justice. The denial of particular information in the original position is justified by reasons that clearly presuppose a theory of human nature. The problems of partiality to one's particular goals, free ridership, and intolerance are all seen as features of the human condition needing to be controlled for in setting up the original position. In this respect, Rawls's purpose can be likened to that of Rousseau, who states in the opening sentence of *The Social Contract* that he proposes "taking men as they are and laws as they might be" to "consider if, in political society, there can be any legitimate and sure principle of government" (Rousseau, 1968:49).[4]

Rawls offers little by way of justification for the particular view of human nature to which he subscribes, except to say that it rests on weak assumptions that are widely shared. (He never attempts to establish the truth of this claim, for which he has been heavily criticized.)[5] Most of his energy is devoted to showing that if his assumptions *are* granted the persons in the original position must rationally choose his two principles. This contention has often been challenged[6] but for now we will concentrate on the assumptions themselves, and the view of human nature they presuppose.

For Rawls, mutually disinterested apolitical individuals behind a veil of ignorance are the subjects not only of all rights and principles of justice, but also of all "requirements" and "permissions" of social behavior – indeed of all moral predicates with the possible exception of those relating to the law of nations (which he mentions but does not discuss) (1971:108). They have no natural rights in the traditional sense. Their rights are restricted to those that would be chosen unanimously in the original position. The principles are those "that free and rational persons concerned to further their own interests would accept in an initial position of equality as defining the fundamental terms of their association" (ibid.:11). Their equality is forced on them by their universal ignorance,

---

4 Rawls does not compare his enterprise to Rousseau's in this respect.
5 See, for instance, Wolff (1977:208ff).
6 See, for instance, Barry (1973:116ff); Fishkin (1975:615–29); Lyons (1975:141–67); Wolff (1977:119–91); and Mueller (1979:227–46).

which also forces them to reason in general terms. Rawls distances himself from the view that human nature is not shaped in important ways by social institutions, by asserting that in fact it is. He even supplies knowledge of this fact to the contractors in the original position, but this is not fully convincing. He clearly believes that he can strip his individuals of natural and social "contingencies" that are "arbitrary" from "the moral point of view," and retain what is essential—his modified view of Kant's noumenal self. This noumenal self is conceived of as making the original agreement in order to "express" and preserve itself. The original position is "the point of view from which noumenal selves see the world" (ibid.:255ff).

What are the natures of these contracting agents? We are told they have no knowledge of "particular facts" about themselves, of their place in society, class position, social status, natural assets and abilities, or "special psychological propensities" (ibid.:12). Rawls does allow them, however, knowledge of the "general facts" of social life, they "understand political affairs and the principles of economic theory; they know the basis of social organization and the laws of human psychology" (ibid.:137). In fact they know a good deal more, and we know a good deal more about their motivation, but before getting onto these issues it will be useful to examine this account of the contracting agents with particular attention to the distinction between general and particular facts, and to the criteria by which Rawls imparts to, and excludes information from, individuals in the original position.

The principles chosen in the original position, Rawls tells us, must be general. That is, "it must be possible to formulate them without the use of what would be intuitively recognized as proper names, or rigged definite descriptions" (ibid.:131). Rawls does not define the term "rigged definite description." He acknowledges that it might be potentially problematical, but contends that in "presenting a theory of justice one is entitled to avoid the problem of defining general properties and relations and to be guided by what seems reasonable" (ibid.). This begs the question, for Rawls employs many definite descriptions in his characterization of the original position and they are "rigged" to produce precisely the conclusions he requires. Indeed, it is difficult to imagine a different interpretation, given the repeated claims he makes to the effect that "[w]e want to define the original position so that we get the desired solution" (ibid.:141).[7] There seems to be an ambiguity in Rawls's account between the requirement that the principles themselves embody no definite descriptions and the requirement that the information available to the parties in the original position contain no definite descriptions. The first of these might be plausible although it in no way requires the device of the veil of ignorance. Many principles (utilitarianism, for instance) are general and require no definite descriptions in (what seems to be) the relevant sense.[8] The second is clearly false. The fact that an empirical description makes no reference to an individual has no bearing on its definiteness or lack of it. Rawls's aim in ruling out reference to individuals is to achieve *impartiality* among the various parties in the original position. Justice-as-fairness is held to be impartial because the ignorance of the parties rules out their acting from motives of personal gain. The extent to which this procedure achieves impartiality is dubious, however, as we will see.

Rawls claims in many places that a substantive theory of justice need not concern itself with questions of ontology and epistemology. He also rejects out of hand any attempt at a purely a priori ethics, holding that some factual assumptions are essential for the conduct of moral theory (ibid.:51). He must be aware, however, that particular events, entities, and actions admit of multiple true descriptions, that explanations and justifications always presume one of several descriptions of an event, entity, or action, and that the process of description is itself inevitably loaded as a result. Yet Rawls asserts that relying on commonly accepted assumptions "implies no particular metaphysical doctrine or theory of knowledge. For this criterion appeals to what everyone can accept." This is blatantly false, as Hare (1975:86ff) and others have argued. Even

---

7 For similar assertions, see Rawls (1971:19, 26ff). For extended criticism of Rawls on this score, see Hare (1975:81–107).

8 I will argue in section II(ii) of this chapter, however, that what surface plausibility Rawls's difference principle has assumes a number of definite descriptions of reality that are certainly not uncontroversial.

if Rawls did show (which he never attempts to do) that any or all of the factual assumptions he builds into the original position were widely accepted, this would not demonstrate their truth or their impartiality without the added assumptions of a consensus theory of truth and the possibility of neutral principles of social organization.[9]

Rawls's individuals behind the veil of ignorance have a good deal of quite specific information presumably derived from their knowledge of the "laws" of economics and psychology and the "general facts" about society.[10] They understand and accept Rawls's theory of so-called primary social goods. These are "the things that every rational man is presumed to want" whatever else he or she wants. These include "rights and liberties, powers and opportunities, [and] income and wealth."[11] Rawls supplies the contractors yet more specific "general information." He argues that it would be irrational, given their ignorance, to make probabilistic calculations about their position once the veil is lifted. He claims their conceptions of the good are such that they care greatly about being the worst-off member of society, but care little about the increasing payoffs of being above this lower limit:

[T]he person choosing has a conception of the good such that he cares very little, if anything, for what he might gain above the minimum stipend that he can, in fact, be sure of by following the maximin rule [i.e. inequalities must maximize the position of the worst-off]. It is not worthwhile for him to take a chance for the sake of a

9 The alleged neutrality of Rawls's argument is taken up in section II(iii) of this chapter. The implications of his and Nozick's characteristically liberal failure to come to terms with the problems for political theory raised by multiple and competing true descriptions are taken up in Chapter 6.

10 For further discussion of Rawls's arbitrary uses of information in the original position, see Wolff (1977:119–32) and Mueller (1979:239ff).

11 In this discussion of his general conception of justice Rawls includes "the bases of self-respect" as a primary good. He also acknowledges there are other primary goods, including "health and vigor, [and] intelligence and imagination." These, however, are "natural goods" because "although their possession is influenced by the basic structure, they are not so directly under its control" (Rawls, 1971:62). The three main "social" primary goods are clearly intended to correspond to the principles and to be similarly lexically ordered. It is not entirely clear where the "social bases of self-respect" are to be ranked (with respect to the other goods), how they are to be measured, and by what specific principle(s) they are to be distributed, although Rawls clearly intends them to be very prominent. For discussion of some of the difficulties associated with the relationship between self-respect and the other primary goods, see Michelman (1975:340ff).

further advantage, especially when it may turn out that he loses much that is important to him. . . . The situation involves grave risks. (ibid.:154)

Their preferences thus constitute identical step-functions, which is why they will be partial to the difference principle. By the principle of insufficient reason all are equally likely to be the worst-off, and, given the nature of their preferences, they must devote prime concern to this eventuality. Rawls rejects the notion that individuals under conditions of ignorance would choose the principle of average utility, as Edgeworth argued, because it involves risks, and "[t]he essential thing is not to allow the principles chosen to depend on special attitudes toward risk" (ibid.:172).[12]

Neglecting the question of what makes an attitude toward risk "special," Rawls's description of the preferences (as step-functions at the position of the worst-off stratum) seems arbitrary. The various positions have no necessary material correlates (as they do, for instance, in Shue's (1981:13–87) account of "basic rights" or Barrington Moore's (1978:3–48ff) account of universal human needs). The worst-off position is defined relationally, purely by reference to the other positions to which it is compared. It is worth considering why this claim can seem plausible to Rawls.

There seems to be a general (Pigouvian) assumption in his argument that an efficiently functioning economic system may not function optimally for all, particularly the worst-off. It is therefore rational for the contractors to ensure that inequalities work to the benefit of the least-advantaged and to charge the state with responsibility for this. The strict neo-classical view would be that all inequalities that arise in a market system are efficient (else they would not arise), and necessary for investment incentives, and that the benefits will eventually trickle down to the worst off. Rawls is fearful of this assumption, arguing instead for a "trickle up" theory, discussed in detail in section II(ii) of this chapter. For the present, note only that Rawls must consider the position of the worst-off

12 For a critical discussion of Rawls's assumptions about risk-aversion, see Barber (1975:296ff).

because he acknowledges that market systems can generate very serious inequities, no matter how fast they grow, how much wealth they contain, or how well functioning they are in terms of technical efficiency. Apart from this problem of the worst-off (as well as some reservations relating to externalities and monopolies) Rawls is in general well disposed toward un-regulated markets. Thus:

[O]nce a suitable minimum is provided by transfers, it may be perfectly fair that the rest of total income be settled by the price system, assuming that it is moderately efficient and free from monopolistic restrictions, and unreasonable externalities have been eliminated. Moreover, this way of dealing with the claims of need would appear to be more effective then trying to regulate income by minimum wage standards, and the like. (Rawls, 1971:277)

Rawls does not reveal who will decide, and on what basis, which externalities are unreasonable, but his view that the market requires state management to prevent its worst in-equities is clearly at the root of his desire to build the "grave risks" assumption into the original position, thereby generating a predisposition toward the difference principle on the part of the contracting agents. This is close to explicit in the following:

Suppose that law and government act effectively to keep markets competitive, resources fully employed, property and wealth (especially if private ownership of the means of production is allowed) widely distributed by the appropriate forms of taxation, or whatever, and *to guarantee a reasonable social minimum.* Assume also that there is fair equality of opportunity underwritten by education for all; and that the other equal liberties are secured. *Then it would appear that the resulting distribution of income and the pattern of expectations will tend to satisfy the difference principle.* In this complex of institutions, *which we think of as establishing social justice in the modern state,* the advantages of the better situated improve the condition of the least favored. Or when they do not, they can be adjusted to do so, for example, by setting the social minimum at the appropriate level. (Ibid.:87, emphases added)

Rawls evidently assumes that the most important economic factor in making market systems just is providing a "reasonable social minimum," and to predispose his contracting agents to a state which ensures this, the "grave-risks" assumption is built into the original position.

Rawls's account of his "thin theory of the good," those minimal assumptions about rational life plans on which individuals would allegedly agree behind the veil of ignorance, is also empirically and ontologically loaded, as has been observed by several critics.[13] One of Rawls's primary concerns is to show that his principles would be chosen over various types of utilitarianism. His main objection to utilitarianism is that it is a teleological theory; it specifies the good independently of and prior to the right, the latter being "defined as that which maximizes the good" (ibid.:24). In classical utilitarianism the good is regarded as the sum of satisfactions across all individuals; in aggregate utilitarianism it is the average social satisfaction that has to be maximized. In both these cases "there is no reason in principle why the greater gains of some should not compensate for the lesser losses of others; or more importantly, why the violation of the liberty of a few might not be made right by the greater good shared by many" (ibid.:26). Rawls repeats this standard objection to classical utilitarianism many times. It parallels Nozick's objection that utilitarianism involves "moral balancing" of the interests of some against the interests of others. Like Nozick, Rawls wants to argue for the priority of right over good to avoid this, but the kind of solution Nozick adopts is not available to him, for two reasons. First, he is aware that the market may not preserve the interests of all, and that it cannot be appealed to, a priori, as the preserver of individual rights. Second, Rawls does want to make some comparisons among persons. He wants to do this, however, without violating the priority of right and so collapsing into the kind of teleology that, for him, makes utilitarianism objectionable. "A competitive price system," he writes, "gives no consideration to needs and therefore it cannot be the sole device of distribution" (ibid.:276). Statements of this kind presume a theory of needs. It is to the solution of this problem that his "thin theory" and "primary goods" are directed.

13 For one recent discussion, see Galston (1983:625ff). See also Hare (1975:81–107).

Rawls argues that there is a plurality of conceptions of the good, but that they all require certain things, namely his primary goods. Thus he can have his cake and eat it, too, for he can have a theory of objective needs without falling into teleology. What is the nature and extent of this theory of needs? Rawls attempts to downplay the interpersonal comparisons involved in it, holding that an attraction of his difference principle is that it requires only that we identify the worst-off member in any distribution. He claims that the difference principle "meets some of the difficulties in making interpersonal comparisons" because, "as long as we can identify the least advantaged representative man, only ordinal judgments of well-being are required from then on." The "further difficulties of cardinal measurement" allegedly do not arise because no further interpersonal comparisons are necessary. If we can determine whether a change in the basic structure makes the worst-off individual better or worse off, according to Rawls, we can determine his best situation.

We do not have to know how much he prefers one situation to another. The difference principle, then, asks less of our judgments of welfare. We never have to calculate a sum of advantages involving a cardinal measure. While qualitative interpersonal comparisons are made in finding the bottom position, for the rest the ordinal judgments of one representative man suffice. . . . The only index problem that concerns us is that for the least advantaged group. The primary goods enjoyed by other representative individuals are adjusted to raise this index, subject of course to the usual constraints. It is unnecessary to define weights for the more favored position in any detail, as long as we are sure that they are more favored. (Ibid.:91–4)

This is very murky. All interpersonal comparisons require at the very least a definition of the dimension along which individuals are to be compared and the criteria for ranking all relevant individuals along that dimension. To identify the worst-off individual we must compare every individual with every other individual along the relevant dimension. If we had a bag of marbles and wanted to know which was the most scratched, we should have to compare every marble with every other marble in this respect.[14] In regard to Rawls's primary goods, too, we need to have them sufficiently well defined to compare all individuals along the relevant dimension. (The one application of his principle on pages 153–4 assumes that primary goods can be given dollar values, although it is by no means obvious that this is feasible given their very broad definition and the range of situations to which this principle is meant to be applicable, but I will pass over this issue here.)[15]

Once the worst-off individual has been identified, what of Rawls's claim that we can proceed to ordinal meaures? How will we know that the individual's situation *has* been improved on an ordinal scale? Ask her? What if we give her a million dollars and she replies in the negative? Give her another million and see what she says then? Surely not.[16] How can we know, without reverting to cardinal scales, whether she still *is* the worst-off individual? After any distributional change we should again have to compare every individual with every other along the relevant cardinal dimension to know who was now the worst-off. Thus Rawls's weak cardinality turns out on closer inspection not to be so weak. If it is a full-blown cardinal system, however, as it seems that it must be, Rawls is

14 We could take some shortcuts in this process by assuming various transitivity rules, but it would be a mistake to think that this in any way (in this context) reduces the comparisons involved. A transitivity rule is only a form of short-hand – it entails comparisons of all the entities covered by it.

15 Arrow (1973:254) has noted that so long as there is more than one primary good there is an index-number problem in commensurating the different goods, in principle just as difficult as the interpersonal comparisons problem. Little (1950) and others have argued with some force that as soon as ordinal utilities are given a dollar value they implicitly become cardinal.

16 Rawls (1982:164) avoids some of these difficulties by retreating to the claim that "the least advantaged are defined as those who have the lowest index of primary goods, when their prospects are viewed over a complete life. . . . The two principles of justice allow for social mobility through the principle of fair equality of opportunity: it is not a primary good to be weighted in the index." This move creates new difficulties of its own. It certainly weakens the already weak egalitarian component of the difference principle (discussed later in this section), since this now requires only actions that improve the situation of the worst-off but do not alter their situation *as* worst-off. Given Rawls's assumptions about grave risks and risk-aversion this would seem to make the difference principle even less attractive to the parties in the original position. These issues aside, this move does nothing to mitigate the difficulties involved in identifying the worst-off and deciding what would benefit them sufficiently to satisfy the difference principle, without interpersonal comparability.

clearly in danger of collapsing into precisely the kind of teleology he finds so objectionable in utilitarianism.[17]

His only real bastion against this is his additional claim that primary goods "are things which it is supposed a rational man wants whatever else he wants. Regardless of what an individual's rational plans are in detail, it is assumed that there are various things which he would prefer more of rather than less" (ibid.:92). This must be true if the principles are to be neutral between different conceptions of the good as Rawls claims:

Justice as fairness . . . does not look behind the use which persons make of the rights and opportunities available to them in order to measure, much less to maximize, the satisfactions they achieve. Nor does it try to evaluate the relative merits of different conceptions of the good. Instead, it is assumed that the members of society are rational persons able to adjust their conceptions of the good to their situation. There is no necessity to compare the worth of the conceptions of different persons *once it is supposed they are compatible with the principles of justice.* (Ibid.:94, emphasis added)

This is a big supposition and by no means intuitively self-evident. It is clearly an empirical claim, yet Rawls seems to regard it as a logical requirement. That all persons would agree that it would be rational always to want more rather than less of his primary goods is not self-evident, particularly when the

17 More recently, in response to Arrow's criticisms, Rawls has acknowledged that his theory requires explicit interpersonal comparisons. He has retreated to the view that I termed Pigouvian in the last chapter: that interpersonal comparisons are unavoidable in a theory of just distribution. Thus to "an economist concerned with social justice and public policy an index of primary goods may seem merely *ad hoc* patchwork." For a moral theory, however, the "use of primary goods is not a makeshift which a better theory can replace, but a reasonable social practice which we try to design so as to achieve the workable agreement required for effective and willing social cooperation" (1982:184–5). Plausible as this might be as a point about the inevitability of interpersonal comparisons, it leaves Rawls with the problem of defining an index for comparison not teleological in what he takes to be the relevant objectionable sense. In this paper he does not define such an index, and primary goods are again "estimated in terms of income and wealth." This is problematical, as he acknowledges, since it is not at all clear, for instance, that such primary goods as the social bases of self-respect can be so estimated, and if so, how it will be done (ibid.:162–3). If the bases of self-respect are taken seriously as primary goods, this is likely to involve many things that cannot be measured in this way (cf. Walzer, 1983). Problems of index-definition aside, Rawls offers here no new concrete reasons why his particular primary goods, in their particular lexical order, are to be preferred.

primary goods are so loosely defined. Kane (1982:249–52) has mentioned the case of religious sects that may eschew worldly wealth as well as religious toleration for other groups. Without going to such extremes we might well imagine, for example, someone holding with good reason that the desire for income and wealth beyond a certain limit becomes self-destructive and/or socially destructive. It has thus been a standard objection to Rawls's argument that the values he claims everyone can accept are in fact those of a relatively small group of liberal intellectuals. Rawls nonetheless takes his theory of motivation as axiomatic.[18] In his discussion of toleration, for instance, he holds that it is legitimate to be intolerant of conceptions of the good incompatible with the two principles (Rawls, 1971:216–7ff), if circumstances arise in which they become threatening to social stability.[19] If the two principles are held to be nonteleological, however, as neutral among different conceptions of the good, they cannot be used as a basis for rejecting a particular conception of the good on the grounds that it violates the two principles, unless it is held a priori that only conceptions of the good consistent with the two principles are rational. If *this* is the claim, Rawls's argument is irreducibly teleological.

The criteria employed by Rawls to characterize the original position and the motivation of, and information available to, the contracting agents seem thus quite arbitrary. They are clearly geared to producing the conclusions he desires, yet he feels no compunction to argue for many of the factual claims he makes or presupposes along the way. The closest he comes to a justification of his procedures is the following:

[I]t is obviously impossible to develop a substantive theory of justice founded solely on truths of logic and definition. The analysis of moral concepts and the a priori, however traditionally understood, is too slender a basis. Moral philosophy must be free to use contingent

---

18 For further discussion of the arbitrariness of Rawls's theory of primary goods see Fishkin (1979:105–20).

19 Rawls makes the empirical claim that this is unlikely to be a problem in practice because initial toleration of the intolerant "may persuade them to a belief in freedom" so that an intolerant sect will "tend to lose its intolerance and accept liberty of conscience" (Rawls, 1971:219). This is wishful thinking, however, based on his (undemonstrated) claim that just institutions will tend to be stable.

assumptions and general facts as it pleases. . . . This is the conception of the subject adopted by most classical British writers down through Sidgwick. I see no reason to depart from it. (Ibid.:51)

It is one thing to claim that a substantive theory of justice must make factual assumptions, and quite another to say that it is licensed to do so "as it pleases." We saw in earlier chapters that seventeenth-century writers in the tradition to which Rawls refers felt it incumbent upon themselves to demonstrate their empirical claims, insofar as they were able, and to argue for their assumptions about knowledge and reality. This was also true in varying degrees of writers such as Bentham, Hume, and Mill. Only under the extreme division of labor prevailing in the academy today can a writer like Rawls simply ignore issues clearly relevant to his enterprise, and make factual claims about the world that suit his theory, leaving the validation of those claims to others whose job it is held to be within the academic division of labor.

ii. The substance of rights

Rawls's first principle grants everyone the most extensive system of basic liberties "compatible with a like liberty for all," and his second principle requires, first, that all offices be open to everyone under "conditions of fair equality of opportunity," and, second, that inequalities be arranged for the benefit of the least advantaged. These requirements must be satisfied in the order stated, an injunction lower on the list always giving way to a higher one.

Notice first that these principles presuppose that it is possible to consider issues of liberty independently of issues of equality. As Rawls puts it:

As their formulation suggests, these principles presuppose that the social structure can be divided into two more or less distinct parts, the first principle applying to the one, the second to the other. They distinguish between those aspects of the social system that define and secure the equal liberties of citizenship and those that specify and establish social and economic inequalities. (Ibid.:61)

It is an exceedingly large assumption to hold that parties in the original position would make a division of this kind, particularly knowing that in the society in which they will be living, being the poorest individual would involve "grave risks." It might be argued with some force that from the point of view of the worst-off individual (which the principle of insufficient reason, according to Rawls, requires us to take),[20] eligibility for public office, voting, and so on should be seen as secondary to ensuring that some basic economic guarantees are fulfilled. What good is the right to run for President to someone who is dying of starvation? The response to this – that the parties to the agreement know conditions of "moderate scarcity" and a certain "level" of economic development obtain – does not suffice to meet this objection. Rawls's objections to utilitarian efficiency and his "grave risks" argument require the contracting agents to assume that, even if the level of economic development is considerable and the wealth in a society extensive, this does not ensure the situation of the worst-off will not be precarious. Whatever the average per capita income there may be bag ladies living out of railway station lockers, and we might be them.

It is more than a little naive to suppose that the political and economic spheres of society are distinct in the way Rawls suggests, governed by different principles of organization. Not only does Rawls regard the first principle as morally prior, in the sense that it should take precedence should conflicts arise; he seems to think that it can be specified independently of, and somehow temporally prior to, the principles governing the economic organization of society:

The first principle of equal liberty is the primary standard for the constitutional convention. Its main requirements are that the fundamental liberties of the person and liberty of conscience and freedom of thought be protected and that the political process as a whole be a just procedure. . . . The second principle comes into play at the stage of the legislature. It dictates that social and economic policies be aimed at maximizing the long-term expectations of the least advantaged under conditions of fair equality of opportunity, subject to the equal liberties being maintained. *At this point* the full range of general economic and social facts is brought to bear. (Ibid.:199, emphasis added)

20 See Rawls (1971:167–73)

It is surely possible, without buying into any very rigid determinism, to wonder whether this makes much sense; whether the forms of political organization in medieval Europe had not something to do with feudal methods of production and exchange; whether the forms of political organization in the contemporary capitalist world have not something to do with market-based industrialization; whether the forms of political organization in the communist countries have not something to do with late planned industrialization in a capitalist world economy; whether the forms of political authoritarianism that prevail in such third world countries as Brazil have not something to do with the economic conditions under which industrial modernization is taking place there. Yet Rawls seems blithely unaware of such considerations; so, too, are the parties in the original position – for all their knowledge of the "general facts" of social life and the "laws" of economic and psychological theory.

What is this "most extensive system of basic liberties compatible with a like liberty for all" required by the first principle? What is a liberty for Rawls? This is not entirely clear. Despite the fact that he endorses MacCallum's analysis of freedom as a triadic relation[21] (Rawls, 1971:201–3; MacCallum, 1972:174–93), he takes little or no account of it in his subsequent discussion of freedom, which is littered with phrases like "the standpoint of liberty itself," "the priority of liberty," and "the principle of equal liberty" (Rawls, 1971: 207; 211). The point of MacCallum's analysis, however, was to show it is meaningless to speak of freedom or liberty in these ways. If Rawls were to take that analysis seriously as a basis for talking about freedom, he would always need to describe his freedoms relationally, specifying which agents were to be free from which constraints to perform which actions. It seems highly unlikely, on this view, that one could formulate a general principle guaranteeing freedom that "holds unconditionally, that is, whatever the circumstances or state of society" (ibid.:125). Further, it could certainly not be specified independently of the principles governing social

---

21 For discussion of MacCallum's view, see notes 11 and 14 to Chapter 1.

and economic organization. Once the term "freedom" is held to entail reference to constraints, enabling conditions, and actions, we cannot talk sensibly about freedom without reference to substantive questions concerning economy and society, which so obviously determine the nature of many constraints on, and enabling conditions for, actions, and indeed the class of actions available to a given individual.

Rawls sometimes seems aware of these complications, making one attempt to sidestep them via a distinction between "liberty" and "the worth" of liberty:

The inability to take advantage of one's rights and opportunities as a result of poverty and ignorance, and a lack of means generally, is sometimes counted among the constraints definitive of liberty. I shall not, however, say this, but rather I shall think of these things as affecting the worth of liberty, the value to individuals of the rights that the first principle defines. . . . Thus liberty and the worth of liberty are distinguished as follows: liberty is represented by the complete system of the liberties of equal citizenship, while the worth of liberty to persons and groups is proportional to their capacity to advance their ends within the framework the system defines. Freedom as equal liberty is the same for all; the question of compensating for a lesser than equal liberty does not arise. But the worth of liberty is not the same for everyone. Some have greater authority and wealth, and therefore greater means to achieve their aims. (Ibid.:204)

Inequalities in the *worth* of liberty are to be governed by the difference principle. They are secondary to, and can never dictate any changes in, the definition of the liberties themselves. No affirmative action could be justified, for Rawls, if it involved the mildest infraction of the equal liberty of the most advantaged.[22]

22 I will not discuss in detail Rawls's argument for fair equality of opportunity – the weaknesses of which have been well explored by Fishkin (1975:623ff). Suffice it to note that the issues discussed in the last two paragraphs and the next arise in that connection also: the priority of very generally defined liberties seriously limits the possibility for achieving meaningful equality of opportunity. As Williams (1962: 110–131) has shown, and as Rawls seems at times to be aware (e.g., 1971: 74ff), the notion of equality of opportunity, if taken seriously, is potentially highly radical. I would argue that in the cases where it began to make significant differences to the social structure, it would be rendered inactive by the general provisions of the first principle.

Rawls defines "freedom" here quite independently of the uses to which it is put, a definition clearly at odds with MacCallum's formula which analytically requires reference to the action performed and the means for performing it as part of the meaning of statements about freedom. If we grant Rawls his distinction between "liberty" and its "worth," it seems implausible that the individuals in the original position would only be concerned with unconditional guarantees concerning the former. Knowing that having a liberty entailed nothing about having the capacity to exercise it – as in the old saying that the poor are equally free to dine at the Ritz – is an insufficient guarantee to our risk-averse contractors who view the situation from the point of view of the worst-off.[23]

Rawls's definition of freedom is the standard negative libertarian one that we have encountered, in one form or another, in each of the last three chapters. It is no accident that the first kind of liberty he discusses in any detail is religious toleration, or that he takes this as his basic model of substantive freedom. Thus the "reasoning in this case [of religious toleration] can be generalized to apply to other freedoms" (ibid.:206). He begins by arguing that "equal liberty of conscience is the only principle that the persons in the original position can acknowledge." They cannot "take chances with their liberty by permitting the dominant religious or moral doctrine to persecute or suppress others if it wishes." To do so "would show that one did not take one's religious or moral convictions seriously, or highly value the liberty to examine one's beliefs" (ibid.:207). Rawls acknowledges (ibid.:208) that these remarks may not be consistent with all views of religion. He nonetheless maintains it is the only rational view to adopt. This surely begs the question, since it is often in the nature of religious conviction precisely to deny the kind of ethical pluralism that these remarks presuppose. On reading them one cannot help but think of the English statesman whose solution to the Middle East conflict was that Jews and Arabs should settle their differences in a

---

23 For a more elaborate discussion of this issue, see Daniels (1975:253–81), who avers that if Rawls's argument for equal liberty is to be accepted it must entail an argument for equal worth of liberty, and that Rawls implicitly makes such an appeal in his arguments for equal liberty of conscience.

Christian fashion. Rawls's view of toleration derives from the standard Protestant view of the importance of individual conscience, and the centrality of the personal relationship between man and God. It is inconsistent with crusading religions such as Islam (or Medieval Catholicism), and with the doctrines of the present-day Catholic Church – which still include Papal infallibility and the acceptance of doctrine as interpreted by the church hierarchy whatever one's individual convictions happen to be. Rawls holds that the contracting agents must regard religious obligations as "self-imposed" (ibid.:206); to ensure this the parties must acknowledge pluralism and require toleration.

We confront here the same type of circularity we encountered in relation to the thin theory of the good. Religious toleration is held to be a good because it is the only means of ensuring that one can be free to practice one's religion. Religions incompatible with the doctrine of toleration are ruled out since they are inconsistent with this principle. It may be that religious toleration is a social good, but if Rawls is to be convincing on this score he must supply some independent reasons why this is so. The claim that the doctrine of toleration is neutral among different religions is false – it is neutral only among the (historically and geographically) few religions that embrace it. The tactic of defining acceptable religions as those which acknowledge (or at least do not threaten) the principle of toleration is as unconvincing as that of defining acceptable conceptions of the good as those which conform to the thin theory.

Rawls nonetheless takes this doctrine of toleration as paradigmatic for the freedoms guaranteed by the first principle.

Justice as fairness provides, as we have now seen, strong arguments for an equal liberty of conscience. *I shall assume that these arguments can be generalized in suitable ways to support the principle of equal liberty.* Therefore the parties have good grounds for adopting this principle. *It is obvious that these considerations are also important in making the case for the priority of liberty.* (Ibid.:211, emphases added)

The "basic liberties" of citizens are thus defended by Rawls through an appeal to the conventional negative libertarian arguments of Locke, and oft repeated by Mill, Berlin, Nozick, Dworkin, and many others.[24]

Leaving aside, for now, questions that have been raised by Hart (1975: 230–52) and others concerning the coherence of Rawls's idea of "the most extensive system of basic liberties" and his apparently arbitrary translation of this into the standard liberal freedoms of the right to vote and be eligible for public office, freedom of speech, assembly, conscience, and thought, and the right to hold personal property and to be free from arbitrary arrest, notice that these freedoms are purely formal and procedural. Questions about their substantive content, or "worth," are treated as of secondary import, and protected from serious discussion by the a priori commitment to pluralist conceptions of the good. It might be argued that Rawls's attachment to the negative libertarian notion of rights as spheres surrounding individuals is even stronger than Nozick's. In outlining why his account of rights is not vulnerable to Sen's paradox of the Paretian liberal,[25] Rawls likens his position to Nozick's, asserting that the "basic liberties are, in effect, unalienable and therefore can neither be waived nor limited by any agreements made by citizens, nor overridden by shared collective preferences" (1982:171n). These liberties are conceived of as on a higher plane than preferences, and can therefore not be part of the pairwise comparisons that generate Sen's paradox. Rawls notes that this is actually a stronger claim for inviolability than Nozick's (for whom rights can be traded by agreement or compensation, as we saw). In justice as fairness, by contrast:

. . . any undertakings to waive or to infringe them [basic liberties] are *void ab initio*; citizens' desires in this respect have no legal force and

24 If we forget for a moment Locke's arguments for the suppression of atheists and Papists (though, as we saw in Chapter 3, his reasoning for this is very Rawlsish) his defense of toleration could be straight out of *A Letter Concerning Toleration*. All the main ingredients are present: the view of religious and other freedoms as rights to privacy, the view of religious groups as voluntary associations whose internal activities should never be interfered with unless they violate an individual's freedom, and the view of the state as reserving the right to regulate these associations in the interests of "public order and security," but remaining otherwise neutral with respect to different religions (Rawls, 1971:211–2).

25 Which purports to demonstrate that the Pareto principle is incompatible with the most minimal assignment of individual rights, given some very weak conditions (Sen, 1970:82ff).

should not affect these rights. Nor should the desires of however many others to deny or limit a person's equal basic liberties have any weight. Preferences which would have this effect never, so to speak, enter into the social calculus. . . . Both the agreements and preferences of citizens in society are counted as hierarchically subordinate to these [highest-order] interests, and this is the ground of the priority of liberty.

The metaphor of a sphere in moral space is almost too weak to capture this: Rawls's view of man *qua* moral being seems almost monadic. If this is a more internally consistent statement of the negative libertarian view than Nozick's, it still remains to be shown why this highest-order interest in absolute inviolability would rationally be agreed on in the original position, something by no means self-evident.

Rawls is a liberal who has read Keynes and welfare economics seriously. He therefore feels compelled to enter the thickets of substantive conceptions of the good, although he tries to downplay this, and of the active regulation of economy and society by the state. His assumptions on these counts are even more clearly apparent in his second principle, as I will now argue.

In its final formulation the difference principle postulates that inequalities can only be justified if they work to the advantage of the worst-off. It is important to note, however, that Rawls has changed his formulation (in both the general and special conceptions). In its first (and much less contentious) form the difference principle held that inequalities are justified only if they can reasonably be expected to work to *everyone's* advantage (ibid.:60–2). He often writes as though these two injunctions are synonymous. They clearly are not, without the addition of extremely powerful empirical assumptions concerning the multiplier effects on the welfare of every stratum above the worst-off, and on the economy as a whole, of increasing welfare at the bottom. Not only must such increases improve the welfare of every stratum, but they must somehow generate the expansion necessary to make this possible (otherwise at least one stratum must be less well off by definition). The only attempt Rawls makes at justifying this assumption is his very brief discussion of "chain connection" and "close-knitness" (Rawls, 1971:80–3).

Rawls makes two distinct empirical claims in this regard: first that the application of the difference principle generates a tendency toward equality; second, that it can be expected to increase the welfare of all social strata. Taking the second of these first, he claims that inequalities in expectations are chain connected: "if an advantage has the effect of raising the expectations of the lowest position, it raises the expectations of all positions in between." Thus, for Rawls, "if the greater expectations for entrepreneurs benefit the unskilled worker, they also benefit the semiskilled." Furthermore, he argues, "expectations are close-knit: that is, it is impossible to raise or lower the expectation of any representative man without raising or lowering the expectation of every other representative man, especially that of the least advantaged." Under these empirical assumptions, Rawls concludes, "there is a sense in which everyone benefits when the difference principle is satisfied. For the representative man who is better off in any two-way comparison gains by the advantages offered him, and the man who is worse off gains from the contributions which these inequalities make" (ibid.:80–2). These are powerful empirical assumptions, not obviously warranted. In this connection Rawls remarks:

I shall not examine how likely it is that chain connection and close-knitness hold. The difference principle is not contingent on these relations being satisfied. However, one may note that when the contributions of the more favored positions spread generally throughout society and are not confined to particular sectors, it seems plausible that if the least advantaged benefit so do others in between. (Ibid.)

What is the force of this claim? Rawls's position appears to be that, although he does not know to what extent chain connection holds in the actual world, in a just society it would hold most of the time, and it therefore rests on "natural assumptions" (ibid.:80). He is aware, however, that in cases where this is so there will be no difference between the practical results of his principle and of classical utilitarianism. If this is taken to be the typical case it surely undercuts the effectiveness of his objection to utilitarianism, as has been

Table 1 *The difference principle without chain connection for distributional changes where the sum of advantages remains constant, with three representative individuals*

Individuals ranked by possession of primary goods	Distributions				
		Departures from status quo			
	Status quo	D_1	D_2	D_3	D_4
A	90	90	89	91	6
B	7	6	8	5	90
C	3	4	3	4	4

observed by several commentators.[26] Rawls offers no evidence that chain connection occurs in the world to any significant extent, and as Barry (1973:111ff), Rae (1975b:641), and others have noted, it is a highly unwarranted assumption. Rawls sidesteps this issue by claiming his principle does not *require* that chain connection holds, but if the intuitive force of the principle is not contingent on chain connection, why talk about it at all? The truth is that it *is* so contingent, as can be seen when we consider the distributive possibilities without chain connection. There are three main types of cases: where the sum of advantags remains constant, where it is increasing, and where it is decreasing.[27]

Where the sum of advantages remains constant, some examples of which are given in Table 1, it can *never* be true that the difference principle works to everyone's advantage (therefore, strictly, chain connection cannot hold), since improving the position of C requires worsening the position of someone else, either A (as in the move from the status quo to D_4) or B (as in the move from the status quo to D_1). Rawls's argument does not prevent improvement in the position of the worst-off

26 See especially Rae (1975b:635–41); see also Fishkin (1975:625–6).
27 Some of the examples presented in the following paragraphs are logically analogous to those discussed by Rae (1975b). They are all special cases of a more general rule demonstrated by Rae et al. (1981) in Chapter 6, "Relative equalities," especially pp. 110–23. Some implications of Rae's discussion are taken up in the next chapter.

Table 2 *The difference principle without chain connection for*
distributional changes where the sum of advantages decreases,
with three representative individuals

Individuals ranked by possession of primary goods	status quo	Distributions			
		Departures from status quo			
		D_1	D_2	D_3	D_4
A	90	10	7	4	4
B	7	7	4	4	5
C	3	4	4	4	4

member at the expense of the middle strata, while either leaving the most well-off as they were before (as in the move from
the status quo to D_1) or improving their situation (as in moving from the status quo to D_3). The difference principle sanctions both these moves from the status quo.[28] These anomal-
ous results, and others, can also be produced if the difference
principle is applied when the sum of advantages is decreasing,
as can be seen from Table 2.

Rawls never discusses the implications of his principle for a
contracting economy, but it is a case he must confront if only
because of the standard conservative argument that planned
downward distribution has precisely this contracting result,
due to its long-run effects on investment incentives. In this
case it is obvious that improving the situation of the least advantaged does not improve that of all. By definition the sum
of advantages is decreasing, thus again chain connection cannot strictly hold.[29] Notice that by the difference principle we
would prefer all four departures from the status quo in Table
2, though they are radically different distributions, ranging
from perfect equality in D_3, to D_1 where the best-off individ-

28 For further discussion of why the difference principle would be unacceptable to
the middle classes, see Rae (1975b:635ff).
29 If we enter the realm of counterfactuals, more complexities arise concerning what
would have occurred had the distributional change not taken place, and the
extent to which the change is responsible for overall expansion and contraction.
Rawls never considers these issues, but surely any general principle of distribution
that claims such broad application as Rawls's would have to deal with them.

Table 3 *The difference principle with and without chain connection for distributional changes where the sum of advantages is increasing, with three representative individuals*

Individuals ranked by possession of primary goods	Distributions				
	Status quo	Departures from status quo			
		D_1	D_2	D_3	D_4
A	90	90	90	6,000	6,000
B	7	7	6	10	6
C	3	7	5	4	4

ual has two and a half times as many primary goods as the worst-off, to D_4 where the middle stratum actually replaces the top stratum. All these moves constitute chronic reductions in overall wealth for the sake of very minor increases for the worst-off.[30] From these considerations it can be seen that the difference principle is highly undetermined, that many of its possible injunctions violate many intuitive notions of rational distribution, and that it will in all likelihood remain silent on many, if not most, controversial questions about distribution.

Where the sum of advantages is increasing, both with and without chain connection, many of these anomalies remain and others arise. In Table 3, again, all four departures are preferred to the status quo; D_1 is preferred to D_2, which is preferred to D_3, which is preferred to D_4. It is by no means intuitively obvious, however, that we should prefer D_1 to D_3, for instance, or D_3 to the status quo. The move from the status quo to D_3 (where chain connection holds) is highly inegalitarian and could be shown to embody the logic of the distributive consequences of across-the-board percentage-based tax cuts of the type implemented by the Reagan administration during the early 1980s. The even more inegalitarian move from the status quo to D_4 (where there is no chain connection) would be sanctioned by the difference principle.

30 More generally, Rae (1979) has shown that the difference principle can militate against both equality and efficiency at the same time.

From these examples it is clear that if the chain connection assumption is relaxed many additional absurd distributive consequences can result. The difference principle can work to the benefit of all only if we assume a continuously expanding economy, and even in this case (with or without chain connection) it can produce highly inegalitarian results. In short, there are few rational grounds for embracing the difference principle as a general principle for distributing income and wealth. It takes so little information into account, either about the impacts of its application on other social strata or about the circumstances in which it is applied, that it would be unwise to embrace it under conditions of ignorance as the only and permanent principle of social distribution. Whether the sum of advantages is constant, decreasing, or increasing, there are circumstances in which there are at least prima facie reasons for rejecting it. Finally, it is simply false that there is any necessary egalitarian tendency in the principle as Rawls and many of his conservative critics have claimed.[31] The principle is based on such sparse information that, although it can sanction some distributional changes that increase equality (somehow defined), it can sanction many which obviously either have no significant distributional impact or have an inegalitarian impact.

Only if it is packed with Keynesian assumptions about the multiplier effects of increasing the position of the worst-off can this argument make intuitive sense. This would further require the postulate that the effects on aggregate demand of applying the difference principle will be such as to increase investment, production, output, and wealth for all. Such logic is compatible with the one concrete illustration Rawls gives of his principle (1971:153–4) wherein the sum of advantages is greatest in the distribution favored by the difference principle.[32] There are no

---

31 For further discussion of the weakness of Rawls's claims about equality in relation to the difference principle, see Fishkin (1975:624–5). For a conservative attack on Rawls's supposed egalitarianism, see Bloom (1975).

32 It is not clear, however, whether or not chain connection holds in this example. It does not hold in his three "decisions" as compared with one another, but since Rawls fails to describe the status quo from which the decisions are considered, it is unclear whether moving from the status quo to D_3 improves the situation of each stratum above the worst-off.

special reasons for thinking this is the typical case, however, and Rawls never supplies us with any. He does make the empirical claim that in a society governed by his principles very substantial inequalities will not arise. The difference principle "relies on the idea that in a competitive economy (with or without private ownership) with an open class system excessive inequalities will not be the rule. Given the distribution of natural assets and the laws of motivation, great disparities will not long persist" (ibid.:158). By way of justification for these assumptions Rawls continues:

Now the point to stress here is that there is no objection to resting the choice of first principles upon the general facts of economics and psychology. As we have seen, the parties in the original position are assumed to know the general facts about human society. Since this knowledge enters into the premises of their deliberations, their choice of principles is relative to these facts. What is essential, of course, is that these premises be true and sufficiently general. (Ibid.)

Rawls, however, supplies no reasons for us to suppose that his premises are true or sufficiently general. He is here not appealing to the "general facts" of any society: one thing we know with little doubt is that competitive market systems generate massive inequalities, always have done, and perhaps even require them – or so many (defenders and critics) would claim.[33] Rawls is appealing here not to any generally accepted facts or laws, but to his own highly speculative account of economic systems in Chapter 5 of *A Theory of Justice,* wherein he claims that his principles can apply equally to capitalist and socialist economies, and that "there is no essential tie between the use of free markets and private ownership of the instruments of production" (ibid.:271ff). Contentious empirical claims, at the least, yet Rawls feels no compulsion to descend to the realms of evidence to establish either of them. He makes one reference to the fact that markets predate capitalism (although what he should show is that they predate private ownership of the means of production). He pays no attention to the immense differences between medieval markets and national and international markets today, or to the huge

33 See, for example, Parkin (1971:163ff).

difficulties encountered by socialist countries such as Poland and Hungary that have attempted to conjoin socialist institutions with competitive market practices in some areas.[34]

For two reasons it is difficult to make much sense of his claim that his principles can apply to both capitalist and socialist societies. First, he offers no account of what the socialist institutional manifestations of his principles would be. Many of our intuitive notions of socialism are in tension, to say the least, with his account of the priority of liberty and his insistence on plural conceptions of the good. Second, his assumptions about market systems are so lacking in evidential support it is difficult to imagine *any* system conforming to the one he describes. The assumptions about chain connection and the absence of substantial inequality are two cases in point. Questions could also be raised concerning the efficiency and viability of a distributive system based solely on the difference principle, assuming it could be implemented, and about the lack of any thoroughgoing account of how, in the absence of substantial inequalities, investment incentives will be maintained.

Rawls's application of his principles in a "property owning democracy" presumes a highly benign view of how competitive markets operate. He claims that a market-based system, if fully competitive, just happens to be consistent with the first two of his three lexically ordered principles:

A . . . significant advantage of a market system is that, given the requisite background institutions, it is consistent with equal liberties and fair equality of opportunity. Citizens have a free choice of careers and occupations. There is no reason at all for the forced and central direction of labor. Indeed, in the absence of some differences in earnings as these arise in a competitive scheme, it is hard to see how, under ordinary circumstances anyway, certain aspects of a command society inconsistent with liberty can be avoided. Moreover, a system of markets decentralizes the exercise of economic power. (Ibid.:272)

On this basis Rawls feels justified in claiming that market arrangements constitute the only way "that the problem of dis-

---

34 I have argued elsewhere that, at least with respect to Poland, the attempt to introduce market-price systems where there is no private ownership seems to run into intractable difficulties (Shapiro, 1981:469–502).

tribution can be handled as a case of pure procedural justice" and that this has the additional advantage of "efficiency" and leaves us able to "protect the important liberty of free choice of occupation" (ibid.:274). Leaving aside the claim that the market system is held to be neutral between capitalist and socialist worlds, leaving aside the claims that market systems decentralize the exercise of economic power or that they give everyone the freedom to work to begin with, let alone in the occupation of their choice (again, no evidence is offered for any of this), it is clear from his discussion of "exploitation" that Rawls has an essentially benign view of markets:

It may be objected . . . that a perfectly competitive economy can never be realized. Factors of production never in fact receive their marginal products, and under modern conditions anyway industries soon come to be dominated by a few large firms. Competition is at best imperfect and persons receive less than the value of their contribution, and in this sense they are exploited. The reply to this is first that in any case the conception of a suitably regulated competitive economy with the appropriate background institutions is an ideal scheme which shows how the two principles of justice might be realized. It serves to illustrate the content of these principles, and brings out one way in which either a private-property economy or a socialist regime can satisfy this conception of justice. Granting that existing conditions always fall short of the ideal assumptions, we have some notion of what is just. Moreover we are in a better position to assess how serious the existing imperfections are and to decide upon the best way to approximate the ideal. (Ibid.:309)

We have to patch up the market and approximate the ideal as best we can. This whole argument assumes that "exploitation" only arises under "imperfect" market conditions, a view that Rawls takes from Pigou (ibid.:309).

This benign notion of exploitation is not, strictly, available to Rawls. Pigou's notion of exploitation turned on his concept of external diseconomy which, as we saw in Chapter 4 and as Pigou never thought of denying, in turn requires a full-blown cardinal utilitarian system and interpersonal judgments of social utility. This was anything but a minimal commitment for Pigou. As even the most cursory reading of his chapter on unfair wages (Pigou, 1960:549–71) will reveal, he thought substantive judgments about unfairnesses worked by the market due to the low mobility of labor, ignorance of workers, power of employers, and the weak bargaining position of certain sectors – notably women – could and should be made. This is a far cry from Marx's notion of exploitation, which turned on the claim that under an advanced division of labor human labor-power produces more fresh exchange-value than is required to produce it (and more, therefore, than the worker can command in wages). Pigou's is, however, unquestionably a teleological theory in Rawls's sense, requiring independent judgments concerning the "most advantageous" distribution of resources. Rawls explicitly rejects it in his discussion of classical utilitarianism (Rawls, 1971:32ff). It is difficult to see how part of it can be invoked without implicitly accepting the system in its entirety, with all its uncomfortable teleological implications. As with his account of the identification of the most disadvantaged for the difference principle, and with the discussion of the thin theory of the good, Rawls here equivocates concerning the interpersonal comparisons he is prepared to sanction, understating the extent to which they are required by the arguments he endorses. The overarching commitment is to the notion that the market system can be made fair and efficient when "suitably regulated," although criteria for suitability are nowhere expressly laid out.

iii. The basis for rights

What is the force of Rawls's argument that his principles would be chosen unanimously in the original position? Strictly speaking, it is not the hypothetical unanimity that is decisive, but our agreement that unanimity for his principles would occur under the relevant conditions. To understand fully this claim, we must examine Rawls's views on the nature of moral theory.

Rawls holds that we "should strive for a kind of moral geometry with all the rigor which this name connotes" and says that his eventual aim is to produce a theory of justice that is "strictly deductive" (ibid.:121). He rejects out of hand, however, all attempts at a priori ethical systems, arguing that empirical considerations must inevitably be part of the subject matter of moral philosophy. Rawls's method is difficult to characterize. He rejects "Cartesian" views of moral justification which presume "that first principles can be seen to be true, even necessarily so; [and] deductive reasoning then transfers this conviction from premises to conclusion," as well as so-called naturalist attempts to derive moral conclusions from alleged facts about the human condition. These two methods of justification, he holds, are the two main ways philosophers have sought to justify moral arguments, and both are unsuccessful (ibid.:577–8). "[W]e do better," he argues, "to regard a moral theory just as any other theory" (ibid.:578) and model it on scientific explanation. Rawls has long been concerned with giving an account of ethical justification analogous to (his understanding of) scientific justification. In his "Outline of a Decision Procedure for Ethics" (1951:177–97) he argued that just as the objectivity of the sciences turns on the reliability of their methods, so an objectively justifiable ethics must be founded on a reliable method. At a minimum this must include a procedure for isolating the relevant set of facts, a procedure for formulating a set of principles that would satisfactorily "explicate" the relevant facts, and an account of the reasons why the principles formulated are held to be rationally justifiable (ibid.:177–97).

Applying these notions to *A Theory of Justice,* we may say that the procedure for isolating the relevant set of moral facts is the veil of ignorance. The relevant moral facts to be "explicated" are the principles of justice that hypothetical individuals in the original position would choose as the permanent basis for the organization of their society. The procedure by which the choice of these principles is validated is a "thought experiment" the reader is asked to conduct, by imagining the persons in the original position, and considering whether the principles for which Rawls argues are not in closer agreement with our "considered judgments" in "reflective equilibrium" (the moral convictions we hold after careful consideration of the choice problem Rawls constructs) than a limited class of alternatives.[35] Hence:

35 For a discussion of the influence of Rawls's early methodological writings on *A Theory of Justice,* see Delaney (1977:153).

By going back and forth, sometimes altering the conditions of the contractual circumstances, at others withdrawing our judgments and conforming them to principle, I assume that eventually we shall find a description of the initial situation that both expresses reasonable conditions and yields principles which match our considered judgments duly pruned and adjusted. (Rawls, 1971:20)

Before examining these arguments in detail, it is worth pointing out that the claim that these procedures in any significant sense parallel the procedures of science is highly questionable. Kane (1982:232–40) has argued with some force that, although the practitioners of science must strive for impartiality, this is not typically achieved by enforcing ignorance on them in the manner Rawls advocates. In addition to this general difference between Rawls's procedures and those regarded as relevant to the pursuit of objectivity and impartiality, several questions arise concerning his more specific claims for his procedures.

First there is the sense in which he appeals to "our" considered judgments. Rawls intends the idea of reflective equilibrium to capture the "Socratic" element in moral philosophy, the sense in which we might "want to change our present considered judgments once their regulative principles are brought to light" (1971:49). Whether or not this is accurate, it does not entail that the process or results of reflective equilibrium will be the same for everyone, at least not without the addition of several other substantial premises. Rawls is aware of this complication, but his attempt to deal with it is not unproblematical:

I shall not even ask whether the principles that characterize one person's considered judgments are the same as those that characterize another's. *I shall take for granted that these principles are either approximately the same for persons whose judgments are in reflective equilibrium, or if not, that their judgments divide along a few main lines represented by the family of traditional doctrines that I shall discuss.* (Ibid.:50, emphasis added)

This procedure is held to be justified by analogy to Chomsky's theory of linguistics, in terms of which Rawls claims, "if we can describe one person's sense of grammar we shall surely know many things about the general structure of language. Similarly, if we should be able to characterize one (educated) person's sense of justice, we would have a good beginning toward a theory of justice." We can assume that everyone has "the whole form of a moral conception," so that "the views of the reader and the author are the only ones that count" (ibid.). This appeal to linguistic rules rests, however, on a misleading conflation of levels of abstraction. Earlier Rawls says more fully:

A useful comparison here is with the problem of describing the sense of grammaticalness that we have for the sentences of our native language. In this case the aim is to characterize the ability to recognize well-formed sentences by formulating clearly expressed principles which make the same discriminations as the native speaker. This is a difficult undertaking which, although still unfinished, is known to require theoretical constructions that far outrun the ad hoc precepts of our explicit grammatical knowledge. *A similar situation presumably holds in moral philosophy.* There is no reason to assume that our sense of justice can be adequately characterized by familiar common sense precepts, or derived from the more obvious learning principles. A correct account of moral capacities will certainly involve principles and theoretical constructions which go much beyond the norms and standards cited in everyday life; it may eventually require fairly sophisticated mathematics as well. (Ibid.:47, emphasis added)

It is one thing to claim that the use of moral terms, like other terms, involves the invocation of (often highly complex and implicit) rules of grammar and reference, and that such rules might (perhaps even necessarily) be the same for all users of a particular language. It is quite another thing to move to the view that peoples' substantive judgments will be in agreement, that a "moral grammar" will thus yield universal substantive moral judgments. The fact that a group of persons knows and agrees on the correct usages of the terms "good" and "conduct" in no way entails that they will agree on which conduct is good. They could not debate the issue without agreement on the meanings of the terms, and the correct use of those terms may well presuppose highly complex grammatical rules speakers could not typically articulate. No amount of analysis of the logic of those meanings and rules, however, would be sufficient to produce agreement in their substantive judgments. There is no reason to suppose that the views of a particular reader in Rawlsian reflective equilibrium might constitute generalizable substantive judgments, certainly not for the reasons Rawls offers.

Second, it might plausibly be wondered what the particular significance of "educated" persons is for views generalizing about substantive questions of justice. Perhaps only intellectuals with nothing better to do will be properly equipped and have time to engage in Rawls's thought experiments. It is difficult to see why this gives them any special claim to make substantive moral judgments for others. In this respect Rawls's appeal to the assent of the reader is arbitrary.

Perhaps this is to miss the force of Rawls's claim. His appeal is not strictly (at least at first sight) to the reader's assent to his substantive propositions, but to his assent that those proposals would be chosen unanimously in the original position. The difficulty with this formulation is that it throws us back on Rawls's highly speculative descriptivism, on what he takes to be the "general facts of society," the "laws" of economics and psychology, and the "facts of everyday life." We are invited to agree with these and to suppose that the individuals in the original position agree with them as well, and to conclude that these persons would unanimously choose his two principles of justice. Since he has devoted so much attention to defining the so-called laws and facts in such a way that they generate (he believes) his conclusions, and since he openly admits he would change them if they did not, this argument can have little force for anyone who does not agree with Rawls's conclusions in advance. There is a basic appeal to a consensus theory of truth implicit in Rawls's argument: even if it could be shown that some of Rawls's assumptions were widely believed, this would demonstrate nothing about their truth or the rational basis for thinking about justice. Should Rawls, as he claims, "avoid introducing" any "controversial ethical elements" into his account (ibid.:14) this would in itself be no justification. At different times there has been wide consensus on the flatness of the earth, the divine right of kings, and the rationality of slavery.[36] Rawls does not even begin to establish that there is (or would be in the original position) consensus on many of his critical propositions. The assumptions behind his appeal to consensus thus need not concern us here, although this question will inevitably arise in Section III of this chapter.[37]

The whole battery of theoretical devices relating to the thought experiment Rawls proposes has one end: to achieve impartiality or fairness in the original position. The least convincing and most criticized aspects of this are Rawls's tactical uses of "knowledge" and "ignorance" in pursuit of this goal. Note, however, that Rawls's paradigm case of a fair decision in no way necessarily involves the use of ignorance. The example he uses to illustrate his "pure procedural justice" is that of the fair division of a cake; the aim is to devise a procedure that makes it rational for the cake-cutter to divide it equally. The obvious solution is to have the cutter get the last piece, since, by hypothesis, he "wants as large a piece as he can get" (ibid.:85). Yet what is the nature of the impartiality generated here? There is certainly no ignorance involved. Given Rawls's maximizing notion of rationality ("standard in economic theory"), the potential cutter can presumably predict exactly who will take which pieces for all possible ways of dividing the cake as soon as he knows the order in which they will choose, and indeed the logic of the example requires this knowledge. The "impartiality" or "fairness" seems to lie in devising a set of procedures that will produce an outcome we intuitively regard as fair *on wholly independent*

36 For further discussion of Rawls's appeal to consensus, see Hare (1975:81–107).
37 In the Dewey lectures Rawls retreats slightly from this consensus theory to the rather Millian claim that the principles must rest on "common knowledge and on shared practices of inquiry" and that the "parties must reason only from general beliefs that are suitably common," not on the grounds that these are necessarily true, but because there is no justifiable alternative. Indeed, he notes, in a democratic society "there is no settled and enduring agreement on these matters;" they are part of the "subjective circumstances of justice" that at best rest on "part of the truth" (1980:540ff). Despite this, neither in *A Theory of Justice* nor in his subsequent clarifications, does Rawls ever try to establish that the particular factual assumptions and "laws" of economics and psychology *are* widely shared. Even if a particular belief were shown to be widely held, this would not be a sufficient reason for basing an argument for political principles on it, without first investigating why it is widely held, with a sharp eye out for any ideological uses to which it might likely be put. This issue is taken up in detail in the next chapter.

grounds, assuming only self-interested behavior on the part of the relevant agents.[38]

To the extent that this is the logic of Rawls's enterprise, two (related) questions arise. First, can the argument for the two principles be made without appeal to the problem-ridden device of the original position, and, second, what independent justification can be given for the notion of fairness embodied in the two principles? As in the cake-cutting example, the desired distributive result must be desirable on grounds independent of the procedures that produce it, if the procedures are to be defended because they produce the desired result.[39] Rawls must tell us why the fair way to divide a cake *is* to divide it equally before we can evaluate his proffered account of pure procedural justice. He must also tell us why his two principles are a desirable basis for institutions of social justice before we can evaluate his claims that mutually disinterested persons, acting in accordance with some exogenously determined rules (in this case the relevant conditions of ignorance), would choose these principles.

What are the grounds on which the two principles and the priority of right *are* held to be desirable? Rawls has two basic types of response. First he claims that his principles are desirable because they are neutral among different conceptions of the good. His primary goods supply people with the wherewithal to achieve their goals and the priority of liberty gives them the freedom to do this. We have seen, however, that these claims are fallacious, partly because his principles are not neutral among different conceptions of the good (rather they arbitrarily *define* one class of conceptions as acceptable), and partly because his principles need not generate either the freedom or the wherewithal as Rawls claims. The distinction between freedom and its "worth" places Rawls in the standard negative-

---

38 The fact that Rawls's account of the original position presupposes an independent criterion of fairness has been noted by several commentators, including Sen (1970:135) and Mueller (1979:229ff).

39 In this connection notice Gewirth's (1982:44) observation that Rawls's doctrine "that if persons were to choose the constitutional structure of their society from behind a veil of ignorance . . . they would provide that each person must have certain basic rights" becomes a circular argument if viewed as an answer to the question "whether human beings have equal moral rights."

libertarian mold, and entails that in most significant essentials peoples' lives will be governed by the difference principle. This principle is so ill-specified, however, and compatible with so many different distributive arrangements, that it cannot be evaluated as a principle of social distribution. Once Rawls comes to discuss the application of his principles he takes great pains to show they are compatible with competitive markets, duly regulated to get rid of problems of monopoly, externality, and free-ridership. He further claims that his principles, as now expressed via "the price system," have the additional advantage of promoting "efficiency." He grows increasingly ambiguous, however, between this claim and the claim that the market system is desirable because it embodies his principles, as in the claim that market arrangements are efficient and preserve the important liberties required by the first principle (ibid.: 274ff). Indeed, although Rawls often claims to eschew arguments from efficiency (1971:276; 1980:562), at times he moves teeteringly close to precisely these. In one more recent formulation of the reasons for departing from equality in the original position, for instance, this is quite explicit:

Now since we are regarding citizens as free and equal moral persons . . . the obvious starting point is to suppose that all other social primary goods [beyond those covered by the first principle], and in particular income and wealth, should be equal: everyone should have an equal share. *But society must take organizational requirements and economic efficiency into account. So it is unreasonable to stop at an equal division.* The basic structure should allow inequalities so long as they improve everyone's situation. (1979:15, emphasis added)

This sounds suspiciously like another attempt at the good old rights-utility synthesis via the market, since the difference principle is being justified by a direct appeal to efficiency.

Thus Rawls explicitly rejects, in general, appeals to efficiency or utility as justifications for principles, but he avers that his principles (which are just for other reasons) happen to be compatible with a distributive system designed to maximize efficiency. If these are not grounds for holding that the principles are justifiable, why mention them? Why get involved in contentious and controversial arguments about the compatibility or otherwise of competitive markets and market-based price systems with socialist economic and political institutions, if these considerations are irrelevant to the justification of his principles? The truth is that they are not irrelevant at all. He assumes, for instance, that although market institutions are "riddled with grave injustices," there "presumably are ways of running them compatible with their basic design and intention so that the difference principle is satisfied consistent with the demands of liberty and fair equality of opportunity" (1971:87). *This* assumption, I submit, is intended to give his argument its intuitive appeal. It "underlies our assurance that these [market] arrangements can be made just" (ibid.).

If this is so, Rawls's appeal is ultimately an intuitionist one to the complex of liberal moral commitments behind the rights-utility synthesis. Despite his oft repeated antipathy to intuitionism, this conclusion seems inescapable. By Rawls's own account the force of his argument depends not on the claim that the individuals in the original position would choose his principles under the specified conditions, but on the claim that the principles themselves are fair, just as in the cake-cutting example the primary question must be: is an equal division fair? The appeal is to "our considered judgments" about the justice of the principles themselves and the institutions they entail. Once the question is cast in this light we are left only with Rawls's many assertions about what "seems reasonable," what is "desirable" and what is "plausible."[40]

The only other attempt at an independent justification for the principles is Rawls's much commented upon, but nonetheless very brief, "Kantian interpretation" of his two principles (1971:251–7), which he has since (1980:515–72) elaborated on as a form of "Kantian constructivism." If we consider the problem of justice, Rawls argues, from the point of view of Kant's noumenal self, the two principles are what this autonomous being would rationally choose. They are thus a procedural "interpretation" of the categorical imperative and the Kant-

---

40 It has been argued at some length by Hare (1975:83ff) that Rawls provides very little argument on these points and that the appeal is almost invariably to intuition, something which Rawls himself in several places grudgingly acknowledges.

ian conception of autonomy, since they express and preserve our nature as "free and equal rational beings with a liberty to choose" (1971:256).

The central difficulty that Rawls confronts in relation to his Kantian interpretation parallels that confronted by Nozick. Rawls wants a principle with the force of the categorical imperative, but he wants to alter its content to suit his own purposes. He wants to say that the only justifiable principles of justice are those which are freely chosen, but he then wants to constrain the class of principles and load the choice problem so that it "must" be rational to choose his principles. As Sidgwick objected to Kant (in Rawls's view decisively), however, if one takes seriously the notion of free will as Kantian autonomy, the possibility has to be accepted that people may choose evil over good, or irrational over rational. Either the right is derived from the good or it is not. To try to escape this via the "thin theory" is a red herring, for this amounts to no more than saying the priority of right is (a part of) the good. The question remains as to whether this is held to be the case because it is chosen or because it conforms to some exogenously determined conception of the good (whether this is based on natural law, intuition, "reflective equilibrium," or anything else).

Like Nozick, Rawls wants to attach Archimedean significance to individual choice in legitimating the principles which regulate human behavior, but also, like Nozick, he cannot live with the subjectivist consequences of holding this. Therefore he attempts to rig the choice that "autonomous" individuals would make, to ensure that the principles chosen conform to what he intuitively takes to be "reasonable" values. The discussions of his "Kantian conception of equality" in "A Well Ordered Society" (1979:6–20) and of "Kantian constructivism" in the Dewey lectures (1980:515–72) do not begin to meet this difficulty, because in both these discussions Rawls's primary concern is to elaborate the claim that his Kantian conception of equality is embodied in the theoretical device of the original position. He advances no new substantive arguments for his particular theory of primary goods or for the particular assumptions he makes about "general facts" and "laws" of society, all of which are needed to generate the claim that, in the original position, his principles would "freely" be chosen over the various alternatives. Thus even if his neo-Kantian conceptions of equality and autonomy are accepted, this does not generate a justification for the specific principles constituting his theory of justice. Such a justification requires additional assumptions about economics, psychology, and society that are problematical quite independently of the view we take on the desirability or usefulness of Kant's theory of moral autonomy. The concept of the original position, therefore, does not resolve Sidgwick's objection to Kant, as Rawls claims it does, because by itself it does not show "which principles, if any, free and equal rational persons would choose," or that these principles are "applicable in practice" (1971:255).

Rawls's departures from Kant's ethics in both method and content are so extensive it is difficult to see how anything resembling a genuine Kantian foundation could be given his theory of justice. First, as Rawls (ibid.:256–7) acknowledges, it is one thing to require individuals to act as though the principles guiding their actions are to become universal laws, or always to treat others as ends as well as means to your own ends, and quite another to say that such injunctions can be turned into principles of collective choice and as such will yield the same substantive principles for all. We have no better reasons for saying this than for saying if it is rational for each individual to maximize his total utility then it is rational for society to maximize *its* total utility, a view that can quickly be shown to generate paradoxes and absurdities. Kant's argument, it bears repeating, does not generate any substantive principles for collective welfare decisions. Kant was unequivocal about this, although at times he ignored some of its implications. In *The Contest of the Faculties,* for instance, in a discussion of the role of government in providing for the welfare of the citizenry, he squarely asserts that:

[W]elfare does not have any ruling principle, either for the recipient or for the one who provides it, for each individual will define it differently. It depends, in fact, upon the will's *material* aspect, *which is empirical and thus incapable of becoming a universal rule.* (Kant, 1970:183–4n, second emphasis added)

If Rawls wanted to claim that his principles, if implemented, would never violate the categorical imperative, this would be something different, but he would have to show this – something he never attempts to do. Many would take issue with such a claim. It might be argued, for instance, that the distinction between liberty and its "worth," and the massive inequalities that can be sanctioned by the difference principle, might well generate situations where given individuals are not in any convincing sense respected as ends.

A second major departure from Kant, which Rawls also acknowledges but attempts to downplay (ibid.:257), is his free use of empirical considerations, so-called empirically established laws of human behavior, facts of society, and so on – huge quantities of material Kant would have regarded as "anthropological" and irrelevant therefore to questions of moral philosophy. Rawls's eventual goal is for a "strictly deductive" ethics. It is unclear, however, what this is supposed to rest on, given his hostility to what he calls "Cartesian" views of ethics purporting to rest on self-evident premises – unless he seriously believes the empirical claims he makes or presupposes in describing the original position have been established with sufficient certainty to generate a deductive ethics. If this was his view it is difficult to see how it avoids being a kind of naturalism, since it would rest ultimately on the claims that since all men naturally reason alike, and since all men naturally require certain things, they must rationally choose his principles. It is clear that Rawls's views on the nature of moral philosophy differ markedly from Kant's. Kant must represent one of the most extreme cases in the history of philosophy of what Rawls refers to as a "Cartesian" theory, based on supposedly self-evident premises, perceivable by introspection and transcendental reasoning, in no way dependent for their truth or plausibility on considerations "borrowed from" experience.

Finally, Rawls differs from Kant in that much of his mode of thought and argument is heavily consequentialist. The specific sense in which Rawls endorses consequentialism is not entirely clear.[41] In his appeals to the market as embodying his principles, he makes many consequentialist claims about efficiency and the priority of right being preserved by the market. His objections to utilitarianism, too, are generally consequentialist in nature: he imagines specific situations in which application of the utility principle might have deleterious consequences for a given individual. He explicitly defends a kind of limited consequentialism, saying that although it is the virtue of institutions that determines their justness, "other things equal, one conception of justice is preferable to another when its broader consequences are more desirable" (ibid.:6). This view may well have much to commend it and it may be unavoidable given the empirical premises in Rawls's argument. It is, however, unquestionably anything but Kantian: Kant notoriously held that the only relevant factor in evaluating the moral worth of an action is the motive with which it is performed.

Given these difficulties, Kant's ethics obviously cannot provide a moral foundation for Rawls's principles of justice. They rest, in fact, on no more than an intuitive appeal to what "seems reasonable" to the reader, and much of that appeal is to a reader already predisposed to the empirical beliefs and substantive moral judgments Rawls is interested in establishing.

iv. The purposes of rights

The underlying purpose of the rights embodied in Rawls's principles is that mutually disinterested individuals may most effectively realize their individual conceptions of the good. He also claims, however, that a society organized to achieve this is desirable in the broader sense that it conforms to "our" considered judgment about what is socially optimal. Prudential and moral rationality are intended to coincide at this point. Thus a just society is a "social union of social unions" ranging from individuals through families, friendships, and larger associations (1971:563); it is an objectively fair and rational arrangement in which individual conceptions of the good can "endure and flourish" (1975:554). These individual concep-

41 This matter is taken up more fully in Chapter 6.

tions of the good are conceived of as essentially private, embodied in the "rational life plans" of persons. In describing these purposes in detail in *A Theory of Justice* and subsequently, Rawls invokes the metaphor of religious toleration:

[T]he notion of a well-ordered society is an extension of the idea of religious toleration. Consider a pluralistic society, divided along religious, ethnic, or cultural lines in which the various groups have reached a firm understanding on the scheme of principles to regulate their fundamental institutions. While they have deep differences about other things, there is public agreement on this framework of principles and citizens are attached to it. (Rawls, 1979:8)

A well ordered society is thus one in which people institutionalize agreement on what is possible and sensibly regulate conflict over what is not, in the interests of a flourishing plurality of individual achievement. The pursuit of this latter provides the overriding purpose of their cooperation.

For Rawls, where social cooperation is possible, its basic purpose remains individual private gain – it is geared to each "disinterested" individual's realization of his rational life plan. Like Hobbes, Rawls defines "good" relationally and argues that it is determined, for a given individual, by his rational life plan. The definition of the term "good," in his descriptivist account, is presented as morally neutral (ibid.:401–7ff). Thus, for instance, he takes over the standard neo-classical definition of public goods (from Buchanan) as being essentially public only in the sense of being indivisible (such as national defense). Public goods are thus implicitly defined as things individuals want which, for one of several contingent reasons, cannot be individually attained, and which therefore necessitate state action to provide them. "Many of the traditional activities of government, insofar as they can be justified, can be accounted for in this way" (1971:267–8ff). This is a negative definition of public goods in the sense that the need for them only arises with the breakdown (or potential for breakdown) of private market arrangements.

Rawls, then, has the standard negative libertarian view of mutual cooperation for individual advancement. Even the groupings that constitute social unions are no more than

247

Lockean voluntary associations. We might, therefore, conceive of Rawls's view of human association in terms of Oakeshott's notion of *societas*. The purpose of social organization, for Rawls, consists primarily in the preservation of individual freedom which consists in turn of two things. First, it consists in mutual acknowledgment of each individual as the "self-originating source of [moral] claims," which translates in practice into "not requiring the parties to justify the claims they wish to make." Second, it consists in acknowledging in all persons the "moral power to have a conception of the good" which generates "the right to view their persons as independent and not identified with any particular system of ends" (1980:544ff).[42] This freedom is held to be compatible with, and required by, our moral equality, inhering in our capacity to act in compliance with the public conception of justice (1980:546ff).

Despite Rawls's use of the term "social union of social unions," and his various assertions that mutual cooperation is inevitable, desirable, and even that "the self is realized in the activities of many selves" (1971:565), as well as more recent attempts to deemphasize his individualistic assumptions (1975: 539–47), it is difficult, as Sandel (1982:151ff) has persuasively argued, to discover much content behind these phrases. I will suggest later that there is some ideological significance to these quasi-liberal corporatist assertions, but in terms of substantive intellectual content they appear to be entirely lacking. Whatever the surface attraction of Rawls's account of the mutual reinforcement of freedom and equality in a well ordered society, he does not begin to establish that this will occur in the actual world as organized in accordance with his principles of justice. I have argued that there is no necessary sense in which these are egalitarian, and that they might well function – particularly when instantiated via "the price system" – to the serious detriment of the autonomy of some, as Rawls understands this term.

42 A third "aspect" of freedom is that citizens are responsible for their ends in the sense of being authoritative in adjusting and revising their conceptions of the good (Rawls, 1980:544).

Rawls's blithe political optimism[43] is compounded here by his failure to consider seriously the likely obstacles to his social union of social unions. It might be argued, for instance, that although economic growth is a good which serves everyone's interest, there may be no system of achieving this neutrally, and different systems will distribute the benefits and burdens in different ways. Rawls misses this because he makes an implicit distinction between the *type of economic system* and the *level of economic development,* disallowing knowledge of the former, but not of the latter, to individuals in the original position. Implicit in the idea of the consensus at the contractual stage is the view that once a certain level of economic development has been reached there *is* a just or fair distributive principle to which all might agree (once sufficient account has been taken of their basic liberties): namely maximize the position of the worst-off. It may be argued that there are causal links between the type of economic system and the level of economic development such that the achievement and maintenance of "moderate scarcity" requires the systematic impoverishment of certain groups. History has surely not disconfirmed this view. The distributional status quo is at least in part a function of the type of economic system prevailing in a society. Whether or not a single distributive principle can be found "rationally" and equally dictated by the interests of all will depend on whether or not the constant reproduction of the level of economic development (moderate scarcity plus) effectively divides society into different groups whose needs and interests conflict with one another.[44]

Rawls seems to assume that the economic system can work in some kind of neutral way, if not to the benefit of all at least to the detriment of none. No historical society has worked in this way. It is precisely this assumption, however, which, for Rawls, generates consensus on one distributive rule for all. Rawls fails to understand that, although there may be social goals universal in the sense that everyone needs them, this in

---

43 On which Barber (1975:310ff) has commented in some detail.
44 On this subject, see Miller (1975:206–30).

no way entails that there are neutral means of distributing the costs necessary to produce them. Aspects of social life may be inherently cooperative, but they nonetheless involve activities which are inherently conflictual.[45]

Rawls never addresses these questions because he conceives of economic problems as problems of distribution, without giving serious attention to the production of what is to be distributed. Thus in the original position we assume a certain level of development, the availability of certain quantities of primary goods, and the instrumental rationality of the parties; the problem then becomes how to distribute these goods most rationally in accordance with the relevant constraints. The question of how these goods are produced in the first place is never considered and presumably held to be irrelevant to the initial decision. Yet the implicit distinction between type and level of development is deeply artificial. One wonders, given the different possible ways of producing wealth to the required level of "moderate scarcity," whether our initial contractors might not want some assurances about the mode of production to be employed.[46] It is a measure of his lack of attention to questions about production that Rawls can believe once a certain level of economic development has been achieved his principles can be neutral between capitalism and socialism, and applicable equally to both.

The social union of social unions, in which "everyone's conception of the good as given by his rational plan is a subplan of the larger comprehensive plan that regulates the community" (ibid.:563) requires a highly benign view of the world. It

45 When Rawls (1979:6ff) notes that some aspects of life are conflictual and others amenable to cooperation he does not answer this point, because this truism does not address the issue of the unequally distributed *costs* of cooperative, mutually beneficial, activities.

46 The few remarks Rawls does make relating to production seem to presuppose a conventional view of investment incentives in competitive markets. Thus inequalities are adjudged rational when "as we raise the expectations of the more advantaged the situation of the worst off is continuously improved. Each such increase is in the latter's interest ... For the greater expectations of the more favored presumably cover the costs of training and encourage better performance thereby contributing to the general advantage" (Rawls, 1971:158). Although he asserts that his principles are applicable under socialism as well as a "property owning democracy," he never explains how production there would occur; presumably his notion of incentives in competitive markets could not be applied.

is almost as if Rawls perceives a well functioning ecosystem, with the difference that no organism ever gets eaten. He does not begin to show, however, that this would be generated by his principles, or that it could ever be exemplified in the actual world.

III. IDEOLOGICAL CONSEQUENCES OF RAWLS'S ARGUMENT

The ideological force of Rawls's argument derives mainly from his appeal to and legitimation of the Keynesian values and assumptions outlined in Chapter 4. Rawls presents his argument as a deontological alternative to what he takes to be the dominant teleological mode of political theory. He sees his contractarian account of justice as an alternative to utilitarianism in all its unsatisfactory forms. Nevertheless, these claims obscure as much as they reveal; like other canonized writers in the liberal tradition, Rawls offers an account of the rights-utility synthesis via the market. His views of what market practices entail, what their limitations are, and how they are best managed and regulated, all powerfully shape the particular account of the synthesis he offers, as we will see by examining the ideological consequences of his argument in more detail.

For Rawls, as for Nozick, the isolated individual is the subject of all political rights and his voluntary actions are decisive in legitimating all political practices. The principles are what mutually disinterested individuals would rationally choose unanimously. Although Rawls argues that his principles are desirable on other grounds – most important that they are held to conform to "our considered judgments" and to preserve a Kantian notion of individual freedom – what makes them legitimate, he claims, is that they would be freely chosen in the original position.

The whole idea of the original position assumes that moral and political questions can be considered independently of man's social relationships. In this respect there is an important affinity between Rawls's procedures and Hobbes's resolutive-compositive method, specifically in the assumption that the most profound way to understand the nature of social relationships is to reduce them to their individual component parts. Claims to the contrary notwithstanding, this generates a powerful atomistic bias in Rawls's argument. The closest he ever comes to defending it is the following:

The essential idea [of justice as fairness] is that we want to account for the social values, for the intrinsic good of institutional, community, and associative activities, by a conception of justice that in its theoretical basis is individualistic. For reasons of clarity among others, we do not want to rely on an undefined concept of community, or to suppose that society is an organic whole with a life of its own distinct from and superior to that of all its members in their relations with one another. Thus the contractual conception of the original position is worked out first. It is reasonably simple and the problem of rational choice that it poses is relatively precise. From this conception, however individualistic it might seem, we must eventually explain the value of community. (Ibid.:264–5)

There is no reason why beginning with assumptions about individuals, and a denial that societies are in any significant sense more than the sum of their (individual) constituent parts, is in any way conducive to greater "clarity" than beginning with (arguably more accurate) assumptions about man's natural sociality and about societies as irreducibly complex structures. The extent to which such assumptions are clear will depend on how well defined they are, and the extent to which they are useful in understanding questions of justice will depend on their accuracy and their relevance to the problem at hand. Rawls pays scant attention to these issues. It is a measure of the powerful hold atomistic assumptions about man and society have over the mainstream of contemporary political theory that he is able to rely on such vacuous off-the-cuff assertions, in lieu of serious argument, for the position he holds. The whole cluster of ideas relating to the original position and the veil of ignorance can be thought of as generating rigor and clarity only against a particular view of moral philosophy, one that sees moral imperatives as timeless universals predicated of isolated individuals, whatever their social and political circumstances. It is precisely because this view cannot be applied to substantive political and moral issues that Rawls is forced, as we have seen, to smuggle in panoplies of unsub-

stantiated empirical and consequentialist assumptions about
the actual structure of the political and economic world.

Rawls's appeal to simplicity is ideologically loaded in a similar way. He frequently appeals to the notion of simplicity,
either in a direct claim that simpler principles are preferred
to complex ones, or merely to make his problem workable at
all. Thus he refuses to consider the notion that different
substantive principles of justice might be justifiable in different cultural and historical circumstances, on the grounds
(among others) that if views of this kind were added to the
list of principles to be chosen from in the original position,
"our problem would become very complicated if not unman-
ageable." He therefore considers only universal principles "to
keep things simple" (ibid.:125). An appeal to theoretical simplicity, holding that we should always seek out ways to cut
out redundant theoretical entities, would be one thing but
Rawls's claim is quite different. He constructs a highly artificial procedure (not notable for its theoretical economy) for
choosing among alternative principles of justice. He then
rules out of consideration principles many would regard as
plausible on the grounds that it is too complicated to apply
them under the procedure as he has defined it (presumably
because different substantive principles of justice that might
be required in different historical circumstances could only
be considered in light of factual knowledge not available
behind the veil of ignorance). One might, at this point,
reasonably anticipate some reconsideration of the adequacy
of his procedure for evaluating alternative principles of justice. On the contrary, Rawls regards this as *grounds* for ignor-
ing complex principles of various types. There is no more
reason to expect the best justifiable substantive principles of
justice in one society to be theoretically simple than there is
to assume that all societies beyond a certain level of economic
development are governed by the same principles. That
Rawls assumes there *must be* a solution to the choice problem
he has constructed is equally clear in the Dewey lectures,
where "Kantian constructivism" is conceived of as follows:
"[I]t starts by allowing the parties no information and then
adds just enough so that they can make a rational agree-

ment." The contracting agents are endowed with "sufficiently specific desires that their rational deliberations reach a definite result" (1980:549; 525). It seems more likely, however, given the difficulties we and others have encountered in his internal reasoning, that this artificial device will yield no "definite result." Certainly there is no noncircular sense in which the agreement reached can be termed "rational."

These various simplifying assumptions seem plausible to Rawls, I think, because, despite the very broad claims he makes for his theory, the only alternative that he takes at all seriously is utilitarianism. He considers and rejects versions of intuitionism, perfectionism, egoism, and various "mixed" conceptions, but his discussion of these is quite cursory. A close reading of *A Theory of Justice* reveals that most of Rawls's critical argument is devoted to attacking utilitarianism in what he takes to be its most influential forms, and to showing his own argument avoids its most serious weaknesses. Rawls clearly regards utilitarianism as the most serious alternative to contract theory.[47] This may explain why the limitations of his procedures seem acceptable to him. If one's view of the class of serious substantive moral positions is restricted to rights-based contract theories and utilitarianism, so long as one's procedures allow consideration of these they will seem reasonably all-encompassing (particularly if they can be shown to allow consideration for one or two other positions as well). It is a measure of the extent to which contemporary political theory is dominated by the so-called choice between rights and utility that such arbitrary limitations can seem intuitively plausible.

Hare (1975:83ff), among others, has argued that Rawls's argument rests on a disguised subjectivism rooted in his appeal to consensus in validating moral claims. Rawls very much wants to avoid this position, but he does make the basic subjectivist move, as Kane (1982:249–52ff) has pointed out, of identifying the good with what is desired (so that primary goods

---

47 This should not be taken to imply that Rawls is not influenced by the various other doctrines mentioned, particularly intuitionism. As I follow Hare (1975:83ff) in arguing, his appeal to "our considered judgments" is essentially intuitionist, proclamations to the contrary notwithstanding.

are held to be such on the contingent grounds that all persons *want* them, whatever else they *want*). Rawls (1971:406–7) acknowledges that his argument may be consistent with emotivism. He also defends something of a rationalist theory of interests, but what does this amount to? He defends a notion of "goodness as rationality," according to which a person's plan of life is held to be rational if and only if:

(1) it is one of the plans that is consistent with the principles of rational choice when these are applied to all the relevant features of his situation, and (2) it is that plan among those meeting this condition which would be chosen by him with full deliberative rationality, that is, with full awareness of the relevant facts and after a careful consideration of the consequences. (Ibid.:408)

The first part of this definition hearkens back to his earlier one (ibid.:142–50ff) of rationality in purely instrumental terms as the most effective means to a given end ("standard in economic theory"). The second part, referring to "full deliberative rationality," is notable for its similarity to Nozick's account of acting in equilibrium discussed in the last chapter. Leaving aside the various difficulties raised there in connection with this notion (how full awareness of the relevant facts is established in practice, and how choices can be designated free in some "open" sense – without reference to the determinants of the options among which choices are made), this move does seem to confirm the case for a kind of moral subjectivism at the heart of Rawls's account. The ultimate appeal, in validating his claims that certain courses of action are rational and others not, is to what individuals would want to *choose* under some (not very well specified) optimal conditions. There is no room here for a notion that what is good for an individual may (in a nontrivial sense) conflict with what he desires, since the good is derived from an idealized notion of desire. Therefore, Rawls, like Nozick must devote much attention to proving that voluntary unanimity is theoretically possible at the constitutional stage: voluntary individual assent is necessary and sufficient for validating moral claims.

A second (connected) consequence of Rawls's argument concerns his account of the relationship between the right and

the good, which in an important respect parallels the traditional liberal distinction between right and law. Rawls's central
reason for attacking utilitarianism, it will be remembered, is its
teleological character. Specifically, what Rawls objects to is that
"the good is defined independently from the right, and then
the right is defined as that which maximizes the good"
(ibid.:24). This is a misleading formulation. It suggests that he
objects to the independence thesis itself, whereas in fact he
objects to the priority of the good. This is obvious as soon as
we reflect that Rawls's argument for the priority of right must
rest on the converse of the independence thesis he identifies
in "teleological" theories: he defines the right independently
of the good and the good as that which maximizes the right. It
might be objected that Rawls's account of the priority of right
is derived from his "thin" theory of the good, but we saw that
if *this* is his position it is teleological in exactly the sense that he
regards as objectionable.

Rawls descends into incoherence on this point, on the one
hand because his powerful attachment to the notion of individual choice impels him to reject teleology and argue for the
priority of right, on the other because his fear of the consequences of subjectivism makes him want somehow to constrain
this priority. He needs something like a theory of Lockean
license, but in the absence of a philosophy adjuring us to obey
the injunctions of our creator because he created us, or a
naturalist or rationalist theory of the imperatives for human
survival, this is not readily forthcoming. Rawls's way out of
this conundrum is to assert that the priority of right *is* the
good and that his particular definition and ranking of primary
goods, and his particular account of pluralism, are neutral
among all possible rational conceptions of the good.[48] These

48 In "Fairness to Goodness" he appears to retreat somewhat on this position, saying
he is not holding that the original position is neutral "in the sense that its description uses no moral concepts." He even acknowledges that it might favor some
conceptions of the good (Rawls, 1975:539ff). He retains his "thin theory" unmodi-
fied, however, and still argues that questions of right can be "bracketed" and
considered separately from issues about substantive conceptions of the good. The
negative libertarian model remains: "[W]e want to work out principles of accommodation between different moralities much as a constitution insuring liberty of
conscience and freedom of thought contains principles of accommodation between different religions" (ibid.:539).

claims do not withstand much scrutiny, but it is of greater significance for us that Rawls feels constrained to make them. Like Nozick, Rawls evaluates actions partly in terms of their consequences. Unlike Nozick, he does not pretend not to be doing this. He addresses gross injustice and inequity as he perceives it. He will not rely on an a priori appeal to the market *qua* preserver of the priority of right (although he does hold that market relationships can be made just). Rawls lacks a theory of needs on which to base his alternative claims, largely because his strong commitment to a subjectivist conception of persons requires identification of the good with what is desired. This makes it impossible to distinguish clearly between wants and needs, or to have any basis for moving away from a theory of revealed preference. A theory of needs would have to be argued for on the basis of evidence and claims about interests, all of which would be objectionable to Rawls as forms of naturalism and teleology.

The limitations on, and limited character of, his attempts to avoid the weaknesses of traditional accounts of the priority of right are even more clearly evident in the negative libertarian account of freedom. The freedoms guaranteed by the first principle are, we saw, wholly formal and dealt with independently of (and prior to) questions concerning their substantive worth. In addition, the fact that Rawls models his discussion of liberty on religious toleration generates an exceedingly limited view of political participation. He is mainly concerned, in his brief discussion of this latter subject (ibid.:228–34), with the traditional liberal problem of defining constitutional checks to limit problems of tyrannous majorities. His exclusive concern, however, is with the formal liberties enumerated under his first principle; questions about their "worth," or about peoples' capacities to exercise those liberties, receive no attention in the procedural guarantees of political participation.[49] Again we find broad endorsement of the standard liberal view of procedural democracy as sufficient to guarantee democratic participation in its important forms. Rawls's claim (ibid.:230) that

---

49 "[P]rocedural constraints are said to mitigate the defects of the majority principle. The justification appeals to a greater equal liberty. At no point is there a reference to compensating economic and social benefits" (Rawls, 1971:229).

those "who place a higher worth on the principle of participation will be prepared to take greater risks with the freedoms of the person, say, in order to give political liberty a larger place" hardly meets this point. First, political liberty as he defines it is purely procedural. Second, even if it were not, this argument would have the force of a claim that if workers valued owning the factories in which they worked, they would go out and buy them. The point is that the disadvantaged may not have the capacity to participate.

Regarding the difference principle, the only coherent account of it is in terms of a Keynesian view of capitalist markets that can make sense of the assumptions of "chain connection" and "close-knitness," and consequently the move from what benefits the worst-off to what benefits everyone. Even with these strong assumptions, not borne out by the experience of the capitalist democracies over the past fifteen years at least,[50] the difference principle is not without its difficulties, largely because it supplies so little of the information one would want to consider in judging the justness of particular distributions.

A further consequence of Rawls's discussion of distributive justice concerns his assumption that such questions can be considered in isolation from questions about production. This is a weakness for which Nozick takes him to task, arguing with some force that an adequate account of distributive justice must include an account of justice in acquisition. Having raised this question, Nozick proceeds to avoid it via the simple assertion that market-based acquisitions are just by definition. Rawls never even considers it. In this he is in the mainstream of the reaction against classical economics which rested primarily on the rejection of labor theories of value and the relegation of questions about the genesis of property rights to disciplines outside economics. This development was of considerable ideological importance in the evolution of liberalism: it placed limits on the extent to which the workmanship metaphor could be invoked to criticize relations of private property. The last remaining vestiges of radicalism in Locke's argument were cast off with this reaction, since issues of the origin of rights of

50 See Shapiro and Kane (1983:5–39).

private property were removed from the agenda of serious political debate.

Once the labor theory of value had been jettisoned, all questions of history could be seen as quite irrelevant to moral and political philosophy. This, in turn, is in significant part responsible for the speculative rationalism, "ideal theory," and moral philosophy based on hypothetical examples and counterexamples dominating so much of the discipline today, and exemplified in the work of Nozick and Rawls. I will have more to say about so-called ideal theory in Chapter 6. Note for now that Rawls's exclusive focus on distributive outcomes is one of the main sources of the deep conservatism in his argument. His evident indifference to so many questions relevant to issues of distributive justice places serious limits on the extent to which his arguments might be used critically to evaluate existing economic institutions. This is hardly surprising since, as we have seen, Rawls has little desire to do this. He clearly believes that, provided the worst problems of externality, free ridership, and monopoly are dealt with and the weak requirements of the difference principle are satisfied, capitalist markets are just distributive mechanisms that function simultaneously to preserve the priority of right and economic efficiency.

Rawls's account of rights falls into the traditional liberal mold, as well, in that the class of objects to which there are entitlements is potentially infinite, so long as the difference principle is satisfied. The difference principle functions like Locke's second proviso and can generate monumental inequalities for the same reasons as can the proviso. There is some lack of clarity in Rawls's conception of the worst-off. He begins by defining them purely relationally (in terms of the difference principle), but in discussing the functions of the "transfers" department of government, he clearly intends physical subsistence to be guaranteed. Neither of these views, however, entails anything about the relative equality in the systems as a whole. Rawls argues (not very coherently as we saw) that once the worst-off have been identified we can work with ordinal utilities for all other purposes. Thus, beyond identification of the worst-off, statements about relative inequality cannot, strictly, even be made.

It should not be thought that my claim that the difference principle can justify serious inequality rests on theoretically possible but empirically unlikely eventualities. I pointed out in section II(ii) that the benefits of the Reagan administration's tax cuts in the early 1980s, highly regressive in their overall effect, were in perfect conformity with the difference principle.[51] It could be argued, with reference to the postwar experience in the United States, that welfare policies improving the position of the worst-off have coexisted with virtually no change in the relative inequalities in the system as a whole on several measures, even with increased inequality on some measures.[52] Similar claims could be made about many of the so-called socialist economies in the post-Stalinist era. I have argued elsewhere that in Poland, for instance, the economic position of industrial workers has improved since the 1950s but inequality in the system as a whole has increased (Shapiro 1981:469–502). Rae et al. (1981:104–29) have shown more generally that the difference principle is one of a whole class of distributive mechanisms that can be more and less egalitarian depending on the circumstances, most particularly on whether the economy expands, contracts, or remains constant. The view that welfare policies geared to providing sustenance for the worst-off are in any necessary sense egalitarian is a highly influential myth, of which Rawls is both a victim and a perpetrator.

Rawls's use of utility functions in identifying the worst-off raises the broader question of the extent to which his argument is at odds with utilitarianism in all its forms as he so often claims. There is a strawmanish quality to Rawls's discussions of utilitarianism, deriving from the fact that he takes Sidgwick's classical statement of it as paradigmatic. Although he considers several variants of this, as well as the so-called doctrine of "average" utility, he never considers the strict neoclassical version based on noncomparable ordinal utilities. Whatever the difficulties with this doctrine (and they are

51 I refer here only to the actual reductions in income tax rate schedules. No doubt if we took into account the additional losses in services and welfare benefits suffered by those at the bottom of the income scale, and calculated the overall changes in the position of the worst-off social stratum, we might find its position had in fact declined.

52 For an illuminating discussion of evidence on this question, see Cameron (1978).

many), it is not, strictly speaking, vulnerable to Rawls's stock objection to utilitarianism. By denying the legitimacy of inter-personal comparisons of utility, it does not permit the sacrifice of some for the benefit of others.

To the extent that Rawls invokes ordinal utilities he might be said to be appealing to a version of this argument. Like Mill, however, he wants to add some ground-floor guarantees. Rawls's attack on Mill's utilitarianism (ibid.:562ff) focuses pri-marily on the notorious "proof," but it is in *On Liberty* that Mill argues that a single system can be created that both preserves individual rights and maximizes utilitarian efficiency. Rawls's claim is strikingly similar. It is frustratingly difficult to pin him down to a precise view on this question because he constantly shifts his ground depending on the particular claim he is try-ing to establish. Thus, when trying to minimize his "paternal-ism," he makes his claims for weak cardinality and ordinality once the worst-off is identified, but when discussing primary goods and needs he makes vastly more extensive interpersonal claims. In making his argument for the priority of right his thin theory is held to be confined to characteristics contin-gently shared by different conceptions of the good, but when he comes to argue against particular conceptions of the good to which he objects, the thin theory begins to thicken.

Whatever Rawls's final position on these questions, his argu-ment clearly imports much of the method and substance of neo-classical utilitarianism. His instrumental definition of ra-tionality, the psychology of his persons as mutually disinter-ested and always wanting more means to the good than less, the very idea of the radical separation of means and ends embodied in the theory of primary goods, the unquestioning use of the theoretical paraphernalia of utilitarianism (includ-ing utility functions), individuals engaged in acting out indi-vidually conceived "rational life plans," the identification of the good with what is desired, and the claim that his system is in general conducive to utilitarian efficiency, all these are indi-cations that the utilitarianism he rejects has left its indelible stamp on his argument. The main difference between Rawls and Nozick on this count is that Rawls recognizes that need for some limited state action if his version of the rights-utility synthesis is to be achieved, whereas Nozick does not. Rawls's view of the role of the state is remarkably similar to what students of comparative politics refer to as a liberal corporatist one.

The image of a corporate state is associated primarily with the fascist and Nazi states of the 1920s and 1930s. The idea of liberal corporatism is linked to these, stripped, however, of its violently coercive and statist implications.[53] Instead of being seen as an arena of class conflict, or as a plurality of groups striving on behalf of their own interests with the state providing a passive "aggregating" function, society is construed as an organic unity in which each group has its essential function to perform, the true interest of each being found within the general interest of the whole organism. The state actively negotiates a consensus between different social groups, most important business, labor, and its own representatives via liberal-democratic forms. It takes ultimate responsibility for the efficient functioning of the system, and can require sacrifices from particular groups, via taxation and prices and incomes policies, for instance, in what is held to be the interest of the system as a whole. The state is decisively reliant on the private economy for its existence, and its actions are geared toward this latter's efficient functioning. There is no presumption, however, that left to its own devices the private economy will be naturally efficient or that it can deal with all questions of social justice. The liberal corporatist state derives its legitimacy from taking responsibility for those matters. It works actively for agreement between business and labor, ensures mass support by guaranteeing the basic social and economic mechanisms of the welfare state, and by making government publicly responsible for full employment, price stability, and growth. It seeks support from business by promising a workable investment climate, beneficial currency and tariff arrangements, and, above all, the orderly integration of labor. The liberal corporatist state is held to be nonpartisan with respect to internal constituent members, enforcing rules essential to the survi-

---

53 For a useful discussion of liberal corporatism, see Panitch (1977:66ff).

val of the system as a whole and consequently to the individual interests of all members.

Rawls's account of social justice in a well ordered society appeals to all the main elements of this view. This is particularly clear in his account of the activities to be performed by the state. In the only case he considers in detail he assumes a "properly organized democratic state that allows private ownership of capital and natural resources" (ibid.:275), and then ascribes to the state four main functions.[54] First, the "allocation" branch "is to keep the price system workably competitive and to prevent the formation of unreasonable market power . . . [which] does not exist as long as markets cannot be made more competitive consistent with the requirements of efficiency and the facts of geography and the preferences of households" (ibid.: 275–6). This branch also strives (via taxes and subsidies) to ensure that the price system reflects actual social costs and benefits (although the criteria by which such decisions will be made are not described). Next there is a "stabilization" branch which "strives to bring about reasonably full employment in the sense that those who want work can find it and the free choice of occupation and the deployment of finance are supported by strong effective demand" (ibid.:276). These first two branches are thus concerned with the efficiency of the system. The other two, the "transfer" and "distributive" branches, deal with questions of distributive justice, ensure the preservation of basic liberties and equality of opportunity, the social minimum, tax and savings structures, and regulate inheritance of wealth (which "is no more inherently unjust than the unequal inheritance of intelligence"), all in accordance with the difference principle (ibid.:276–8).

These institutions are sufficient to ensure that capitalist markets will be both just and efficient. By enforcing a view of justice aiming to "reduce disagreements and to bring divergent convictions more in line" (ibid.:53), the state maintains a negotiated consensus and a social system that is relatively

54 There is a fifth function discussed separately (Rawls, 1971:282ff), dealing with the expansion of expenditure on public goods when unanimously agreed on. This is taken up in section IV of this chapter.

stable over time. Since exploitation is held to derive from inefficiencies and malfunctions of the market, there is no sense that the two goals of promoting efficiency and distributive justice might systematically conflict; indeed the presumption clearly is that they will be mutually reinforcing. By "policing the conduct of firms and private associations and by preventing the establishment of monopolistic restrictions" (ibid.:275), the state ensures that free equality of opportunity is maintained. Demand management is implied to generate employment (ibid.:276). Welfare payments to the worst-off are presumed to benefit all because of the multiplier effects of chain connection. In short, something very like a liberal corporatist state, in pursuit of social justice in a market society via something very like Keynesian economic policies, appears to constitute Rawls's view of the legitimate role of the state in a well ordered society. The intuitive appeal of Rawls's "social union of social unions" inheres in the fact that it invokes this view of the nature and purposes of the state. The appeal to liberal corporatism, however, as Panitch (1977: 61–90) and others have argued, is essentially an ideological one under conditions of capitalist markets, since it invokes a picture of an internally complex but intrinsically harmonious social structure to describe relationships in reality that are profoundly opposed.

IV. CONCLUSION

Enough has been said to establish the case outlined at the outset of the last chapter. As with Nozick, for Rawls the appeal to a Kantian ethics as the basis for his political theory is seriously misleading. In both structure and content Rawls's argument differs so markedly from Kant's it is difficult to know in what precise sense it is supposed to be Kantian. Rawls does not begin to establish his case that his principles constitute procedural expressions of the categorical imperative and Kant's notion for autonomy. Like Nozick, Rawls is especially attracted to this latter notion because it seems to embody what he intuitively understands as the priority of liberty; it seems to attach prime importance, in the formulation of a moral position, to the decisive validating function of free individual choice. It has the further attraction of seeming to offer a way of attaching primary importance to these notions without falling victim to the bugbear of modern liberalism, subjectivism, since it purports to have some objective basis and universalist tendencies. Thus pluralism need not be based on indifference to alternative moral positions, or on a claim that all moral positions are equally (in)valid. It can appear to have some more robust philosophical status.

Wherein this robustness lies is deeply problematical for Rawls, because of his antipathy for what he takes to be teleological modes of philosophical argument. This prevents his arguing for a pluralist society on the grounds that it is a good idea, reducing him instead to the claim that his particular brand of pluralism is neutral among all rational substantive conceptions of the good. This claim is either false or tautologically true from Rawls's definition of rationality, in which case it is teleological in precisely the sense that he takes to be objectionable.

Rawls does not even try to establish that his principles would, in practice, preserve the categorical imperative or Kant's notion of autonomy. This claim could easily be challenged with reference to the difference principle alone, not to mention the considerations about the "worth" of liberty mentioned earlier. This principle ensures that the worst-off individual is not used exclusively to others' advantage; it says nothing, however, about the use of other strata for the benefit of the worst-off, or of one another. The only case in which observing the difference principle would ensure conformity to the categorical imperative would be the case where benefiting the worst-off really did benefit all, which requires both an expanding economy and strict chain connection throughout the system. Rawls does not even try to establish that these empirical circumstances typically prevail. Were he to do so, this would show only that, several very benign empirical conditions happening to hold in the world, Kant's categorical imperative would not be violated if we acted by Rawls's principles. This would be true of many principles in these circumstances, including utilitarianism, as Rae (1975b: 630–647) has shown. Something has clearly gone awry here, however, since the categorical imperative supposedly holds quite independently of empirical considerations. If the two principles are held to be "procedural expressions" of it, so, too, should they.

If Rawls replied that all distributive principles make empirical assumptions, one could agree but this must inevitably raise two further questions: first, to what extent is Rawls's argument really based on Kant's ethics, and, second, what grounds does Rawls offer for thinking that the particular empirical assumptions embodied in his principles in fact hold (or might hold) in the actual world to a significant extent? The decisive answers to these questions are, we have seen, not much and not many. His appeal is principally an intuitionist one to a hodgepodge of normative and empirical beliefs I have broadly designated as Keynesian. The three most important of these beliefs are, first, that stimulating income at the bottom will have beneficial multiplier effects throughout the economy – which presumes a particular thesis about the causes and consequences of weak demand; second, that market systems are only exploitative when they malfunction – which presumes a Pigouvian analysis of exploitation; and, third, that actions necessary to make the system more just will tend to make it more efficient – which is not strictly held to be a justification but is clearly held out as bait to ensnare the reader on his or her prejudices.

A somewhat different assessment of Rawls's argument has recently been offered by DiQuattro (1983:53–78) and it will be useful to conclude by considering his claims in light of the analysis offered here. DiQuattro's main aim is to demonstrate that Rawls's "left critics" (by which he means principally Brian Barry, C. B. Macpherson and Kai Nielson) have misunderstood both the spirit and the letter of *A Theory of Justice*, which not only can accommodate all the serious criticisms they make of it, but actually rules out a capitalist organization of production and exchange; although it does not require socialism, it would be consistent with it. This is a strong claim. It requires that Rawls be mistaken about the political implications of his argument (not in principle impossible), since, in his discussion of just political institutions, Rawls presumes a "state that allows private ownership of capital and natural resources" (1971:275).

DiQuattro's thesis rests on two arguments. First, he claims that since Rawls does not have a Marxist concept of class he does not have a Marxist concept of exploitation:

> If Rawls meant by "class" what Marxists mean, who wouldn't share Macpherson's befuddlement over Rawls's presumed attempt to reconcile an egalitarian theory of justice with class divisions and their inherent exploitative mechanisms? . . . [H]e could not consistently claim that the existence of social classes is compatible with a theory of justice if he believed that class division entailed exploitation of one class by another. (DiQuattro, 1983:54–55)

Leaving aside the extent to which Rawls's theory of justice is genuinely egalitarian (which there are serious grounds for questioning), what is the force of this? DiQuattro's point is that since Rawls uses the term "class" much as contemporary social scientists use the term "stratum," and defines classes in terms of their relative shares of primary goods, he is not sanctioning exploitative relationships. If class relationships under capitalism are inherently exploitative (which DiQuattro implies is his own view), they cannot be sanctioned by Rawls's argument. This is more than a little like Tully's claim (discussed in Chapter 3) that since Locke does not have Marx's concept of wage labor, he cannot be considered as legitimating capitalist wage–labor relationships. DiQuattro's claim is fallacious as Tully's is and for a parallel reason. Tully misses the point when he says that for Locke employment relationships are not coercive because they are voluntary. DiQuattro misses the point when he says that since Rawls is opposed to exploitation, his argument cannot sanction exploitative relationships. Tully attacks a strawman in countering Macpherson's proposition that Locke had Marx's concept of wage labor (when, in actuality he had something like Smith's). DiQuattro seems to think this question turns on whether Rawls has Marx's concept of exploitation (when *the point is* he has something like Pigou's).

When DiQuattro says the "principles of justice (and the entire argument backing them) *plus* the truth of the Marxian

267

account [of exploitation] rule out capitalism as just" (DiQuattro, 1983:69) he is saying no more than if Rawls had a different (arguably more accurate) theory of how capitalist markets operate, and if Rawls took a different (arguably more plausible) view of what constitutes exploitation, he would have made a different argument, one which specifically denied the justness of capitalism. Hence Rawls's argument rules out capitalism. This is plainly absurd. It misses the fact that the ideological force of Rawls's argument derives precisely from his belief that capitalist markets can be "made just" since exploitation only arises when they malfunction. Largely because his theory is thought to provide a moral basis for this view has it been as influential as it has. If the first page of *A Theory of Justice* had stated that one of the implications of the argument would be that capitalism can never be justified, this book would not have had the impact it has had. Much of the ideological force of Rawls's argument derives precisely from the fact that it can legitimate the managed capitalism of the Keynesian state.

DiQuattro's second strategy of argument (not obviously consistent with his first) is to follow Rawls through his tortuous claims about the compatibility of markets with socialist political institutions (as Rawls understands these terms). DiQuattro notes that Rawls distinguishes allocative from distributive functions of markets and argues that under socialism the market might be employed for the former but not the latter. Whether or not this is true, it is clearly not Rawls's view since he regards the distributive functions of markets as their raison d'être, as DiQuattro is well aware (ibid.:69–70). Rawls's discussion at the level of "ideal theory" makes "considerable use of market arrangements. It is only in this way . . . that the problem of *distribution* can be handled as a case of pure procedural justice" (Rawls, 1971:274, emphasis added). It is, however, DiQuattro's view that "how capitalism fares under the difference principle depends [in part] on Rawls's distinction between ideal and nonideal normative theory" (DiQuattro, 1983:67). With this in mind he proceeds to Rawls's discussion of economic systems, noting that Rawls employs a conventional definition of public goods as those things which are uniquely public, essentially indivisible, and goods and services that are particularly vulnerable to problems of externality and free ridership. He argues, too, that for Rawls the notion of a public good must inherently be so limited (whether in the production or the consumption of goods) "because of the distributional consequences of its [the market's] allocative function" (ibid.:70–1). He follows Rawls in arguing that, although the class of goods that is *necessarily* public is limited, there is no reason why it cannot be expanded by the voluntary agreements of persons, should they unanimously agree to make their society more communitarian or socialistic.

In this sense socialism is an open question for Rawls's principles: it could justly be instituted in varying degrees without violating his theory of justice, provided this was done in accordance with Wicksell's "unanimity criterion" which requires near-unanimous approval on the public financing of collective goods. Beyond this, Rawls's position is that (provided the market-based distributive status quo is just, a large and pregnant assumption) "[t]here is no more justification for using the state apparatus to compel some citizens to pay for unwanted benefits that others desire than there is to force them to reimburse others for their private expenses" (ibid.:72; Rawls, 1971:283ff). This Nozickian language betrays the limited extent to which Rawls takes the concept of public goods seriously. It seems difficult to reconcile it with the proposition that Rawls's argument is compatible with, let alone requires, socialist political institutions.

Much of what Rawls has said militates against this conclusion. Most significant is that his open embrace of the view that individuals have rights of exclusive dominion over all objects of value except neo-classically defined public goods misses the social character of production on which arguments for the public control of means to "the good" are usually based. When socialists argue that the fruits of the division of labor should be publicly controlled, they appeal to the fact that our capacity to own the things we do own is critically dependent on the actions of others. Thus they are maintaining (perhaps, often, implicitly) that all goods beyond what an isolated individual could produce absolutely unassisted *are* public goods; it is therefore illegitimate to suppose that individuals can have rights of exclusive dominion over them.

The claim that an expanded (perhaps even comprehensive) public sector might legitimately emerge from bilateral agreements among all members of a society based on private ownership is a quite different *moral* claim (not to mention its being palpably unlikely). It presumes the existence of legitimate individual rights of exclusive dominion over parts of the social product, which any intelligent defender of socialism would not grant to begin with. The claim that Rawls's principles are neutral between "property owning democracies" and "socialism" on the grounds that they do not rule out individuals choosing to finance as extensive a public sector as they can unanimously agree to presumes that the market-based status quo can be made just (something Rawls never establishes since he never explains the origins of individual rights of private property). It also presumes that justifications of social institutions must appeal to the voluntary consent of every individual, a key liberal assumption which, I will suggest in the next chapter, we have grounds for questioning. For the present I conclude that by allowing these theoretical possibilities (empirically so unlikely that no one need worry about them) Rawls, DiQuattro, and others can pretend (possibly even to themselves) that they are agnostic about socialist political institutions. We have seen that the only socialist institutions Rawls could accept are those that maintain the integrity of well functioning capitalist markets.

Part IV
Conclusion

6

The liberal ideology of individual rights

I. HISTORICAL SUMMARY

The case I have sought to establish is that there is a distinctive way of conceiving of individual rights that has been central to the Anglo-American liberal tradition of political theory since the mid-seventeenth century, and that is very much alive in it today. Elements of this view have important roots in Renaissance and medieval European political thought, and in Roman law, but the seventeenth-century contract theorists combined these elements in new ways, thereby constructing a view of rights that formed the armature of modern liberal ideology. This view is so deeply embedded that it infects not only explicit rights theories, but is presupposed in the most influential traditional liberal alternative to these, utilitarianism in its major historical forms. Although my focus has been on rights-based theories, enough has been said to indicate that, just as these have always co-existed with powerful utilitarian commitments, a history of utilitarianism could be written that would bring out its reciprocal dependence on the evolving language of individual rights. The whole idea that liberals somehow face a choice between rights and utility[1] assumes misleading accounts of the concept of a right and of the goals of liberal writers, historical and contemporary. The nature of the term "right" is such that reference to the substance and purposes of

1 See, for instance, H.L.A. Hart's (1979:77) assertion that the philosophy of government in England and America has, for much of this century, been based on a "widely accepted old faith that some form of utilitarianism, if only we could discover the right form, *must* capture the essence of political morality." According to Hart, however, this old faith is finally being replaced by a "new faith" which is "that the truth must lie not with a doctrine that takes the maximisation of aggregate or average general welfare for its goal, but with a doctrine of basic human rights, protecting specific basic liberties and interests of individuals, if only we could find some sufficiently firm foundation for such rights to meet some long familiar objections."

273

rights is inevitably entailed by its use. Defenders of rights *theories* have typically focused their attention on the subject of and basis for rights (sometimes exclusively on the first of these), but their treatments of the other terms in the relation reveal much of the utilitarian conceptions of value and ends, both individual and collective. A more accurate picture of their endeavor, both historically and conceptually, portrays it as the search for a synthesis of rights and utility.[2]

The liberal view of rights has not gone unchanged historically. Rather than argue that there is some family resemblance, or even weaker relationship, among the various views discussed, I have presented the liberal view of rights as an internally complex set of evolving doctrines, theories, beliefs, and assumptions. This has advantages over the view argued for by Macpherson, that a single unit idea, "possessive individualism," triumphed after the Reformation and has governed all our philosophical and political preconceptions ever since, or MacIntyre's arguably comparable account of "the emotivist self," and also over general categories of traditionalism and modernity for which Marxists and Straussians are often summarily derided by historians. I have tried to preserve, without overstating, the elements of truth in these views, recognizing a core structure to all assertions about rights, and tracing the doctrines that constitute the liberal view of rights through several incarnations: transitional, classical, neo-classical, and Keynesian. These categories are very broad and might usefully be further subdivided in a more comprehensive study, although they seem to me to capture at least some of the most significant "moments" in its evolution. In contrast to the writers just mentioned, I have emphasized the

2 It would take a different book to argue this case in detail from the point of view of the history of utilitarianism, but note that even Bentham, who rejected all doctrines of natural law and natural right out of hand, made central use of the language of individual rights and the negative libertarian view of freedom we have been examining. A poignant illustration of this can be found in his *Principles of the Civil Code*, where he argues that "[l]aw does not say to man, *Labour, and I will reward you*, but it says: *Labour, and I will assure to you the enjoyment of the fruits of your labour – that natural and sufficient recompense which without me you cannot preserve, I will insure it by arresting the hand which may seek to ravish it from you. If industry creates, it is law which preserves*" (reprinted in Macpherson, 1978:50, emphases added). On this subject, see Long (1977:3ff); see also Rosenblum (1978:58–9, 71, 152).

internally complex evolving nature of the liberal view of individual rights, the particular philosophical conception of the subject (to which they devote almost exclusive attention) being one (evolving) part of it. It remains to consider the liberal conception of the subject, as well as the other evolving parts of this ideology, in more detail.

i. The subject of rights

The view of the subject of rights embraced by the seventeenth-century contract theorists is usefully termed Cartesian. It assumes that the individual will is the cause of all actions, individual and collective; it ascribes decisive epistemic and hence moral authority to the individual over his actions, on the grounds that he has privileged access to the contents of his own mind. For this reason individual consent becomes vital to the whole idea of political activity. The doctrine of individual consent was not, however, synonymous with that of individual right for the seventeenth-century writers, because it was embedded in and limited by explicit theories of objective interests. For Hobbes this turned on his view of science, and in particular on his belief in the possibility of a deductive ethics, intersubjectively demonstrable with the certainty of Euclidean geometry. For Locke the creationist view of knowledge took a more explicitly religious form, but produced a moral theory similar in structure if not in content. Neither writer seriously doubted that there *were* rational rules of social organization that could be demonstrated so to be, and that must, as a result, be chosen freely by rational persons acting in their genuine interests, and neither doubted that true interests could be known – such was their faith in the possibility of an objective science of morality. Thus the importance they ascribed to the subject of rights and individual consent was not seen as threatening to their beliefs in objective standards of value and interest. Hobbes's relational theory of the good and Locke's account of toleration did generate doctrines of pluralism, but these were circumscribed by definite and explicit limits: in Hobbes's case by the rule of law as imposed by the sovereign in accordance with the laws of nature, and in Locke's by a

275

more limited view of the rule of law and more complex appeals to the distinction between liberty and license and the imperatives for social stability. Neither writer took seriously for a minute the possibility that liberal writers since Hume have been attempting to escape: that the centrality ascribed to the will and convictions of the isolated subject would undercut their natural-law constraints, so that their limited moral pluralism might collapse into the kind of ethical relativism that seems to many to be entailed by emotivism in its dominant contemporary forms. Hobbes and Locke were transforming the natural-law tradition from within. The extent of the transformation was obscured, I argued, by their attachment to a view of science not destined to survive the eighteenth century.

Contemporary liberals face the consequences of this longer-term transformation. Their primary concern has been to find a way to hold onto the ontological conception of the individual of the seventeenth-century writers, but simultaneously to find some alternative moral basis that both acknowledges the centrality of his freedom and limits his power to act in any way he pleases. This has been attempted principally by embracing a version of Kant's ethics that appears both to acknowledge the centrality of the autonomous individual and to generate universal moral injunctions. The great difficulty this faces, embodied in Sidgwick's objection to Kant, lies in showing that the autonomous Kantian agent must choose any particular substantive moral or political principles. Even the injunction that he must act rationally, however defined, or consistently, appears to undercut the freedom of the individual contemporary liberals feel compelled to defend in a radical form. The Cartesian agent is given a centrality in the modern theories it lacked in the earlier ones: it trumps all other considerations.

ii. The substance of rights

The negative libertarian view of the substance of rights has been an integral part of the liberal conception of individual rights since its inception. It, too, has been through several metamorphoses. In Hobbes's argument it is literally defined negatively, as a residual, by the silence of the law, and although it constitutes "the greatest liberty of subjects," it exists at the sovereign's pleasure and can be invaded by him at his will. The rights of subjects vis-à-vis one another, however, are inviolable. These rights constitute the modern notion of exclusive proprietorship that was eventually to be turned against the state, as the system of public law shed its independent foundation and came to rest on the evolving system of private law. The notion of private-law rights of exclusive dominion having force against the state first achieved currency with Locke and the Whigs during their radical phase in the early 1680s. Ashcraft (1980:429–34ff) points out that it was they who adapted the metaphor of invasion from the nation to the individual, in order to argue that the king had invaded the liberties of his subjects. This was an important move because it entailed a separation of the concept of the public interest from that of the ruler, and because it meant that the rights of "the people" were reducible to, and perhaps even derived from, rights of individuals.[3] These ideological changes paralleled changes in public law, private law, and the relations between the two that were then in process.

This view of man's negative freedom, of a private sphere surrounding him that cannot be entered (first by other individuals and eventually by the state) without his consent, became the standard view of freedom in the liberal tradition, interlocking neatly with the Cartesian view of the person. We saw that it takes on extreme proportions with Nozick, that he

---

3 Skinner (1978, II: 239–348; 1980:309–30), as part of his concern to overturn Walzer's thesis in *Revolution of the Saints* that the modern notions of resistance originated with the Calvinists, traces a number of key components of the secular theory of resistance articulated in Locke's later writings, and of the Calvinist and Huguenot theories of resistance, to the Lutheran Reformation and in particular the Conciliarist writers of the early sixteenth century, Almain and Mair. As he points out, however, Locke's account is distinctive in that, first, the right to resist is held to be inalienable; second, the possibility of resistance in cases of tyrannical government is treated as a straightforward right, and, third, "the right of resistance is treated as the possession of each individual citizen, and hence of the whole body of the people viewed as a legal entity." These features distinguish Locke's theory "from a number of earlier and less radical strands of revolutionary thought, and at the same time license us to describe it as having a wholly secular and populist character." Thus for Locke in the state of nature each individual "has a right to punish the transgressors of that Law [of Nature] to such a Degree, as may hinder its Violation" (Locke, 1963:312).

is even prepared to jeopardize the coherence of large parts of his argument to maintain it intact. It requires his tortuous compensation arguments, his arbitrary definition of acting in "equilibrium," and his whole "side-constraint" theory of rights. Although Rawls claims to take a different, relational, view of freedom, his need to maintain the content of the negative libertarian view leads him to model his definition of freedom on a version of Locke's account of religious toleration, to distinguish liberty from its "worth," and to argue for the priority of the former, all hallmarks of the standard negative libertarian view. Leaving aside the vagueness of the difference principle, its injunctions are secondary to, and can never override, the priority of liberty understood in this negative libertarian form. In these various formulations private individuals are thus conceived of as having exclusive proprietorship over their capacities and actions, the latter constituting, in Nozick's phrase, a sphere in "moral space" surrounding them. This sphere can never be entered by other individuals with (formally) equal rights, except by consent.

The only exceptions to this in Rawls's argument consist in limitations on liberty for the protection of "liberty itself," a view most famously associated with Mill's harm principle, but also present in all its essentials in *A Letter Concerning Toleration*. Since Locke wrote, this view has been conceived of as holding equally against the state and against other individuals, with the difference that the state ceases to have the rights of a legal person, descending eventually in status in modern doctrines of constitutionalism to the role of "servant of the people." In this context Nozick can argue that the state has no rights beyond those unanimously conferred on it by the citizens. Rawls can limit its activities to those necessary when the mechanism for conferring consent (the market) breaks down—as in the case of public goods where problems of free ridership arise—or when the market breaks down for other reasons of externality or monopoly. The essential idea of preserving spheres surrounding individuals remains, however. Individuals conceive of and execute their "plans of life" separately, are indifferent to one another, and, above all, Rawls feels it incumbent upon himself to show, would unanimously consent to his principles at the constitutional stage, the assumption being that anything less would illegitimately violate the rights of some. This is built into the so-called Kantian conception of equality that guarantees everyone a *"right* to view their persons as independent and not identified with any particular system of ends" (Rawls, 1980:544, emphasis added). Rawls's "social union of social unions" consists essentially of Lockean voluntary associations. To the extent that the state has a more active role than mere aggregator of the interests of these various groups, I argued that this is best understood in terms of the ideology of liberal corporatism.

iii. The basis for rights

The two main changes that ushered in the modern liberal view of the basis for rights were the collapse of history and precedent as modes of political justification and the radically diminished possibilities of religious justification of political principles. The first of these, I followed Pocock (1957) in arguing, was an indirect by-product of the discovery by Spelman and the common lawyers that English law was largely feudal in content and German in origin. This decisively laid to rest the myth that its legitimacy lay in an Ancient Constitution, lost in the mists of time. Pocock held that Locke was something of an exception to anti-Royalist writers of his time in not attempting to argue for a version of the Ancient Constitution. I suggested, however, that this was a decisive reason for his longer-term influence in the liberal tradition. Locke shifted the basis of antiabsolutist conceptions of political legitimacy away from history and toward a moral justification based on an appeal to reason. Despite the tremendous differences in their substantive arguments and their politics, Locke shares this mode of argument with Hobbes. Both sought to show that a political constitution could be justified when and only when it functioned in the rational individual interests of each citizen. Whatever other religious and anthropological force their laws of nature were intended to have, it is in this that their longer-term influence is to be found.

The decline in religious bases for political legitimacy and

the growth of secularism have been so often discussed it would be superfluous to rehearse the arguments here. Two points are worth noting, however. First, religious skepticism on the part of Hobbes or Locke was not critical to their contributions to the secularization of liberal conceptions of political legitimacy. (The nature and extent of both their religious views remain controversial.) Both succeeded in making religious considerations largely irrelevant to their arguments. Locke did rely at times on his arguments from scripture and it may be impossible to establish the distinction between liberty and license, one of the mechanisms by which he limits the scope of his individual rights, without some such appeal. Precisely this aspect of his argument, however, was destined to be ignored in the dominant strand of the liberal tradition, as we saw in Chapter 4. Had Locke not offered an alternative rationalist construction of his argument it is doubtful he could have achieved the sustained prominence he did in that tradition.

Second, whatever the particular religious views of Hobbes and Locke, their Cartesian views of genuine knowledge in the moral sciences as subjective certainty of essences, undercut the possibility of religious, and indeed all forms of, extrinsic moral justification. Hobbes's railings against arguments from authority (religious and secular) and his appeals to the individual convictions of his readers, Locke's heady rationalism and his Protestant view of the sanctity of the individual conscience all militated against forms of justification based on anything other than individual assent. Neither writer perceived the potential implications of this because of their intense convictions that people could be decisively convinced of the truth of their arguments. It is arguable that even within their own terms of reference these contentions were vulnerable, and that both writers played on the ambiguity in the workmanship metaphor between one's having essential knowledge of what one makes, and holding that all persons will and/or should make the same things. The latter claims involve very strong additional assumptions not only that all men reason alike, but that they have identical (but separate) interests that can be preserved by an act of common consent. Neither of these assumptions would have seemed implausible to seventeenth-century writers, who had no ideological stake in denying interpersonal comparability or in holding that a concept of human nature grounded in a theory of objective interests was unavoidable in a full account of legitimate rights. Nonetheless, these assumptions could be, and eventually were, challenged by appeal to the very Cartesian conception of the self these writers had articulated, and on which both had, in different ways, relied.

Hobbes and Locke abandoned historical and religious modes of justification and sought instead for universal principles of rational social organization. They did not, however, strive for *afactual* theories in the post-Kantian sense that pervades the writings of contemporary rights theorists. The whole idea of the contract was, for the earlier writers, intended to have a basis in (their understanding of) actual political events. This is entirely lacking in the hypothetical arguments of Nozick and Rawls, as well as those of other contemporary liberal theorists, most notably Ackerman (1980).[4] The whole notion of "ideal theory,"[5] according to which concrete principles of justice are worked out in purely abstract terms and then applied to the "second best" situations of the actual world, would never have occurred to the earlier writers. This is a further reason, perhaps, why they perceived no significant tension between their "subjective" account of the subject of rights and emphasis on free choice, on the one hand, and their objective theories of the good, on the other. Although they thought that people must choose freely in some significant sense if their rights are to be respected, they never really doubted what people should choose, or that substantive, partly empirical, conceptions of the good could be argued over in terms of evidence and reason. I have argued that this is unavoidable in fact, and that the contemporary writers also presume substantive, partly empirical, conceptions of the good. They do so, however, as Rawls puts it,

4 Aspects of Ackerman's account are taken up in section III of this chapter.
5 His particular account of ideal theory is arguably one of Rawls's most influential innovations. Thus, for instance, Galston (1980:13), who is critical of much of Rawls's argument asserts that: "[o]ne of the main virtues of Rawls' *Theory of Justice* is his reliance on the concept of 'ideal theory'." The mere fact that so much of the Rawls literature consists of derivations of similar principles, and arguments over whether his initial conditions generate different conclusions than he claims, testifies to the degree to which is mode of moral argument has been influential.

"as they please," with little attention to the truth or plausibility of the empirical assumptions they make. There is thus an air of unrealism to contemporary arguments which the earlier ones lacked. This partly explains the tendency of contemporary liberal political theory to feed off its own controversies, since it is largely unconstrained by anything else.

iv. The purposes of rights

At the heart of the liberal conception of the purposes of rights in all its formulations is a pluralist account of the good. The nature of, and limits to, this pluralism have varied, as have the practical injunctions believed necessary to sustain it. Taking the second of these first, we saw that a critical development in the liberal tradition was the emergence of classical equilibrium theory in the eighteenth century. Before this Hobbes, and to a lesser extent Locke, saw no conflict between a pluralist view of human goods and a highly interventionist state; the Mandevillian belief that radical egoism would work for the benefit of all would only arise in conjunction with the view that the market system could be self-equilibrating. Although Hobbes recognized, somewhat equivocally, the inevitability of market relationships in large areas of social life, and although Locke openly endorsed such relationships, both believed they would have to be actively regulated, and in some critical areas even created, by the state.

This view went into decline with the rise of classical equilibrium theory, in terms of which the state appeared to be unnecessary for market regulation. The inherently vulnerable position of the state created by the changes in public law previously mentioned was exacerbated by this development. The regulative state became identified with the minimal state in the neo-classical revival, although it has been anachronistically read back into the views of earlier liberals by writers such as Nozick. The principal departure in the Keynesian tradition articulated by Rawls derives from a questioning of the equilibrium assumptions of neo-classical economics, generating a liberal corporatist view of the state geared to a managed capitalist economy. The equation of regulation with minimalism is given up, but the primary role of the state – to regulate a negative libertarian society and a market-based private economy – remains. The nature and content of Rawls's primary goods, and the empirical assumptions behind the difference principle, reveal both to be geared toward this end. The writers examined all see the purpose of political organization generally, and the civil rights constituted by it in particular, as being to preserve a negative libertarian society in which individuals can pursue their different individual goals unimpeded. The institutional manifestations of this, however, have varied greatly with external circumstances, and with related assumptions about the driving causal mechanisms of market societies.

An important difference between the pluralism of Hobbes and Locke and that argued for by Rawls and Nozick is that the former did not argue that pluralism was in any sense a morally neutral doctrine. This is one of the most problematical claims in the contemporary arguments. It is worth considering why it is defended at all. The central reason is the fear of "paternalism" and "teleology" that permeates their writings; dictated by their Cartesian view of the self trumping all other considerations. Many elements of the modern doctrine of subjectivism were present in the seventeenth-century arguments, but not all were. Perhaps more important, although Hobbes and Locke subscribed to a Cartesian view of the self, their view of the nature of moral knowledge meant that this Cartesian self was not inevitably subjectivist, where this is understood to entail that moral imperatives are statements of "mere" appetites and aversions. They believed that objective moral knowledge was both possible and necessary, thus were not forced to make the claim that pluralism was desirable because of its putative neutrality among different individual conceptions of the good. They held that it was a necessary and desirable method of social organization, a view for which they adduced both arguments and evidence, however internally problematical these might be revealed to be. The modern writers, fearful of the broader implications of substantive assertions about the good, fall back on neutrality as a (not very convincing) way out of this dilemma. We saw this most clearly in our discussions of Nozick's claim that his argument presupposes no "end state" or "patterned" theory of distribution, and of Rawls's "thin theory" of the good.[6]

II. PROBLEMS OF COHERENCE

Many of the internal difficulties confronted in the arguments discussed derive from a tension between the negative libertarian view of freedom, to some formulation of which these writers all subscribe in their accounts of the subject and substance of rights, and other moral positions they feel impelled to hold. More precisely, the Cartesian self with decisive authority over its private sphere as the basis for political life, and to whom all political arrangements must be shown to be justifiable, and even causally reducible, militates against other sentiments to which these writers are powerfully attached. It is for this reason that the modern writers particularly try to disguise these sentiments, claiming that they are somehow entailed by the negative libertarian view. Thus what is actually a quite limited form of pluralism is presented by Rawls and Nozick as a much more extensive form of moral neutralism, a claim for which, ironically, liberals have sometimes been strongly criticized.[7] Although this tension is present in an embryonic form in the early arguments, it does not become manifest until after the time of Hume. In its contemporary form it leaves liberal writers running from subjectivism with nowhere to go. This fact is at the root of the search for a Kantian basis for their arguments, in the hope that the radical notion of free choice embodied in Kant's conception of autonomy can somehow itself constitute an Archimedean point. This amounts to a complex restatement of the problem, however, rather than a solution to it.

An important substantive consequence of this tension is that

6 It is true that Rawls (1975:536–54) has more recently added some qualifications to his neutrality claim, but they do not in any essentials alter his accounts of primary goods being necessary for all rational conceptions of the good, the "thin theory," or of the possibility of coherently "bracketing" questions of the right from questions of the good. The considerable attention Rawls devotes to attempting to make a (suitably qualified) version of his claim to neutrality plausible underscores the importance he attaches to this question.

7 See, for instance, Bloom (1975:648–62) on Rawls, and more generally Strauss's indictment of this aspect of modernism in *Natural Right and History* (1953:9–80).

the liberal state is presented as a neutral arbiter or aggregator of different individual interests. Even in Rawls's liberal corporatist account the state's raison d'être is to enable individuals to pursue their individual conceptions of the good. He differs from Nozick only in his account of how this is to be achieved and what it entails in practice. Both writers view the (legitimate) state as neutral among citizens, performing essentially regulative functions. The liberal state, however, is no more neutral than the conception of the good on which it rests. This is not a sufficient reason for rejecting it, but it is sufficient for claiming that, if it is to be advocated in the contemporary world, some reasons must be given other than the fallacious claim that it is neutral among different conceptions of the good, and hence enables everyone freely to achieve his or her individual goals. The modern rights theorists, however, are prevented from formulating independent justifications of this kind by their attachment to the negative libertarian conception of freedom, and their concomitant need to show that it is preserved by the liberal state.

This negative libertarian view of freedom is conceptually problematical, in that it rests on a misunderstanding of the relational character of the term "freedom." The whole idea that persons can in some general sense be free, either because they are surrounded by a "sphere" in "moral space" or because they have some formal guarantees that are specifiable independently of their "worth," misses the point that freedoms are of agents from constraints to perform actions. The notion that we may be free to perform actions we are unable to perform, that both writers must take seriously, rests on this politically pregnant confusion. If the claim were that formal guarantees are an insufficient necessary condition for most significant substantive freedoms, this would be one thing. But Nozick regards the formal guarantees as necessary and sufficient, and although Rawls acknowledges difficulties with the "worth" of liberty, these are conceived of as secondary to liberty "itself" (whatever that is) and governed by different principles.

A second major internal difficulty with the liberal conception of individual rights in its dominant contemporary forms is that its proclaimed opposition to utilitarianism is fundamentally bogus. From its first formulations it has embodied what were to become utilitarian assumptions concerning individual rationality, preference valuation, and the justification for mutually cooperative behavior. Liberal rights theorists underestimate the degree to which utilitarian assumptions are incorporated into their arguments largely because they fail to consider (or, in Rawls's case, take seriously) the relational character of assertions about freedom, right, and justice.[8] Many of their utilitarian assumptions about value and ends are therefore suppressed, and obscured by the false claim that they do not make "paternalistic" or "teleological" claims about these matters. These claims are, however, present implicitly, in many places appealed to as back-door intuitive justifications for their arguments.

The most obvious of these, we saw, concerned claims of Rawls and Nozick (supposedly irrelevant to their arguments) that their proposals would work to maintain utilitarian efficiency. In addition, both adopt much else of the theoretical paraphernalia of neo-classical utilitarianism including ordinal utility functions (again dictated by the negative libertarian definition of freedom), mutual disinterestedness, and instrumental rationality. Both obscure this fact by rejecting classical utilitarianism for its teleology, at the same time appealing to a version of the neo-classical brand of this doctrine, widely believed to be antiteleological because based on ordinal noncomparable utilities. Although both writers implicitly employ cardinal (and hence uncontroversially teleological) measures (Nozick in his compensation argument and Rawls in his "thin theory" and the application of the difference principle), both attempt to downplay this and present themselves as relying principally, if not exclusively, on ordinal noncomparable measures.[9] This is done, I argued, out of the (false) conviction

---

8 Although I did not argue for a relational account of the term "justice" in Chapter 1 this could be done, as Rawls (1979:6) makes clear when he says: "[w]hen fully articulated, any conception of justice expresses a conception of the person, of the relations between persons, and of the general structure and ends of social co-operation."

9 Although I noted that Rawls (1982) has more recently retreated from this position to something more like a Pigouvian account of the inevitability of interpersonal comparisons.

that if it can be consistently achieved, what is intuitively useful in utilitarianism can be incorporated without "moral balancing" to maximize some exogenously defined conception of the good. Both avoid admitting that they embrace substantive conceptions of the good of any kind, including utilitarian, because they perceive this to be at variance with their subjectivist assumptions about persons that invariably trump. Because, however, an account of rights is more than an account of persons they find themselves willy nilly with substantive accounts of value and ends that are largely utilitarian in content.

Closely related to the tensions between the account of a free person embraced by the neo-Kantian writers and others of their substantive moral commitments, is the importance they attach to abstract doctrines of individual consent. Some notion of the consent of the citizenry has played a part in arguments for political legitimacy in the West since the Renaissance at least,[10] but the doctrine of individual consent as it has evolved in the contractarian tradition since Hobbes is distinctive in that it has become steadily more abstract and individualist. Hobbes's emphasis on a political regime needing to appeal to the subjective assent of the people was grounded in a fear of the masses quite common and perfectly understandable among the English ruling classes in the early and mid-seventeenth century. Hobbes's analysis rested, at least in part, on the descriptive thesis that unless the sovereign could command the assent of the citizenry it would not long survive, a view quite understandable historically. Locke's critique of Hobbes rested in part on a disputation of Hobbes's empirical claim that the state of nature might not be worth returning to in certain circumstances, and that the principal impetus for leaving it was its "inconvenience." Locke's claim, obviously felicitous for the Whigs in the early 1680s, has since supplied the basis for vastly more abstract theories of consent in the post-Kantian liberal tradition, where the "normal" or "essential" human condition *in* civil society is conceived of as both asocial and apolitical.

The increasing abstractness of the anthropological claim for the necessity for individual consent to all political arrange-

10 See Skinner (1978:Vol I).

ments is closely bound up with the radical transformation of the moral claim that individual consent forms the basis of political legitimacy. Hobbes's materialism resulted in a fusion of the anthropological and moral arguments via a deterministic psychology. From Locke on, however, influential writers in the liberal tradition have avoided this view, or at least been deeply uncomfortable with its implications. It was natural that Locke should give the moral doctrine of consent greater critical bite than Hobbes, since he was concerned with a theory of legitimate resistance to a corrupted sovereign – an oxymoronic notion for Hobbes. The historical legacy of Locke's discussion of consent has been complex and many sided. One aspect of it is of particular interest. It supplied the conceptual foundation for modern negative libertarianism, since it made the activities of the state intrinsically vulnerable to the charge that they lacked the consent of all or some of the governed and were by definition illegitimate as a result.[11] Locke's aim had been to specify conditions under which it could be legitimate to resist the supremacy of the rule of law. His argument also supplied the conceptual tools for questioning the legitimacy of the law itself. Instead of asking in what circumstances resistance might be justified (assuming that in general it was not), the question would become: in what circumstances is government justified? Thus Nozick, at the logical extreme of this conceptual transformation, defines his task with the casual assertion that the "fundamental question" of political theory is whether there ought to be a state at all (1974:4). For Rawls, too, except in cases of indivisible public goods, or where the market breaks down, the only criterion for expanded state action is Wicksell's unanimity criterion.

So deeply embedded have negative libertarian conceptions of freedom become that the sheer absurdity of this view escapes many people. If someone said that the fundamental question of dental theory is whether people should have teeth at all, no one would take him seriously for a minute. Yet if the existence of politics and states are an inevitable part of social life – which the weight of the evidence surely

11 Hence the liberal preoccupation, also since Locke, with the deeply problematic notion of tacit consent.

suggests – Nozick's question and many of the assumptions behind the negative libertarian conception of freedom are no
less absurd. At the heart of the negative libertarian ideal is
the notion that the state *presence or action* needs to be justified, not state *absence or inaction.* This assumes, fallaciously,
some "normal" or "expected course of events," in Nozick's
terminology, morally benign or at worst morally neutral. It
takes as its model of "normal" human interaction a view of
simple voluntary transactions among isolated persons, unme-
diated by external authority structures and power relations,
that has never prevailed anywhere in human history, is un-
imaginable in practice, and even in theory.[12] Thus the negative libertarian conceptions of freedom defended by these
writers are inevitably loaded ideologically. They clearly presume many of the latent power structures and relationships
that in fact prevail in contemporary market societies in their
accounts of their "prepolitical" initial conditions. This is quite
blatant with Nozick but Rawls, too, holds that unless they
malfunction markets are essentially neutral mechanisms that
preserve individual freedom. He seems unaware that market
systems require particular legal and political institutions and
definitions of property and contract that do not prevail
everywhere, had to be created historically, and have to be
reproduced if they are to survive. His assertion that markets
predate capitalism is not remotely sufficient to deal with this
problem and is, in any case, irrelevant to the question of
their moral neutrality. The myth of the minimal state could
only arise once these market relations were established. Thus
the ideological force of negative libertarianism in the contemporary world derives from the fact that, to the extent that
new state action or initiatives are held to be illegitimate, the
power relations embedded in the existing market system can
function unimpeded.

Closely connected to the arbitrary distinction between action
and inaction is the view of all social relationships as nothing
more than relationships among individuals, to be evaluated by
the same sorts of criteria by which we typically evaluate indi-

12 See the discussion of the theoretical breakdown of unanimity rules in Chapter 4,
section II(i).

vidual actions. This view is fundamentally inappropriate to theorizing about questions of political right and social justice, that by their nature involve complex structures that condition and shape individual actions, and the options available to individuals, in ways often directly intended by no one, even when they are understood. Thus the enterprise of normative theorizing about questions of distributive justice must be a heavily descriptive and consequentialist endeavor. This makes the problems of political philosophy vastly more difficult, because it implies coming to terms with hotly contested and ideologically loaded competing descriptions of the actual social world and the causes of its problems, and this in turn often necessitates counterfactual empirical argument that may be impossible to settle definitively. I have sought to establish that even the deontological liberals engage in these activities – proclamations to the contrary notwithstanding. The descriptive choices they make, most often by assumption, predetermine their normative conclusions. They seem blithely unaware that there may be true alternative descriptions with competing claims to relevancy, or even that their own descriptions are controversial. In this connection Elizabeth Anscombe (1969:175–95) has argued with some force that one of the greatest weaknesses of English (and, we might certainly add, American) moral philosophy since Sidgwick is its inability to come to terms with the problems entailed by multiple descriptions that she, Davidson, and others have identified.[13] Anscombe's explanation of this is that it has been dominated by consequentialism, necessarily a "shallow philosophy" (ibid.:187). Without wishing to take issue with Anscombe's general assessment of modern moral philosophy, I should like to suggest that it is not consequentialism as a doctrine that is problem-ridden, but rather the particular naive version of it that dominates the tradition we have been examining.

Neither Nozick nor Rawls regards himself as a consequentialist in the classical sense. Nozick's "historical" entitlement theory is expressly opposed to "patterned" theories that focus on a particular outcome of an action in evaluating its moral

13 See Davidson (1968:79–94) and Anscombe (1969:175–95, 1958:69–72).

worth. Rawls explicitly embraces only a very limited form of consequentialism resting heavily on *ceteris paribus* clauses that invoke other (deontological) requirements. Both appeal to Kant's concept of autonomy in validating moral claims that would seem to be radically anticonsequentialist. There is an important sense, however, in which these appeals are only skin-deep; much of both their modes of argument is implicitly consequentialist in character; not only in their intuitive appeals to the consequences of enacting their principles, but in their back-door appeals to efficiency and in the logic of their objections to classical utilitarianism. In short, some assumptions about utilitarian efficiency seem to be quite close to the center of the modern liberal's metaphorical Quinean field, and to do some surreptitious trumping of their own.

I do not take issue with the fact of appealing to consequences. This is inevitable in substantive moral argument. My objection is that they do not look hard at or far enough into the consequences of actions, almost never beyond their intended consequences.[14] They tend to take the agent's conception of what he is doing at face value and commit what I once described as the *meaning-of-the-act* fallacy as a result. This is the fallacy of assuming that an agent's intentional description of an action he performs is the only, or the primary, relevant description of that action (Shapiro, 1982:546–7ff). Perhaps the paradigmatic instance of this occurs in a recent book by Bruce Ackerman in which he takes the "ideal theory" approach to political philosophy to its logical extreme, shifting the constitutional choice problem to an imaginary planet discovered by a spaceship. Ackerman argues for three principles that must govern all arguments over the distribution of power, which he takes to be the basic problem of politics. First, persons are constrained to argue rationally, that is "the power holder must respond not by suppressing the questioner but by giving a reason that explains why he is more entitled to the resource than the questioner is." Second, arguments must be

---

14 The exceptions are Nozick's use of "fundamental" explanations that he arbitrarily switches on and off to suit his purposes, and Rawls's acknowledgment that in certain cases individual actions will have unintended "externalities" needing to be rectified by the state. Such cases are seen as exceptional, however.

consistent in that the "reason advanced by a power wielder on one occasion must not be inconsistent with the reasons he advances to justify his other claims to power." Third, all dialogue is to be constrained by the principle of neutrality, requiring that no reason is a good reason if the power holder must assert either that his "conception of the good is better than that asserted by any of his fellow citizens" or that he is "intrinsically superior" to them. By conducting "constrained power talk" in accordance with these requirements, Ackerman argues, the inhabitants will govern themselves via a liberal state as he understands it (Ackerman, 1980:3–30).

It is beyond the scope of this discussion to consider Ackerman's spirited and often ingenious arguments for his particular version of social justice in the liberal state. The only point I wish to establish is that it never seems to occur to him in setting up his constraints on dialogue that some of the most important disagreements about politics and political power arise not out of assertions about intrinsic superiority or the refusal to supply reasoned arguments, but out of conflicting depictions of the relevant situation itself. He seems to think there will be no intractable questions about this. All three of Ackerman's constraints presume it is clear who in fact wields the relevant power, over whom it is wielded, and what the power consists in. The problem is conceived of as how to justify this neutrally, rationally, and consistently. He does not consider the case where *A* maintains that *B* has power over her and *B* denies this – that is, they have competing descriptions of the situation and both supply what they take to be reasonable answers. It is in this sense, I think, that Ackerman's assumptions about neutral discourse exemplify the liberal tendency to ignore the difficulties of competing descriptions; this is what constitutes shallowness in Anscombe's sense. Some of the most difficult and important questions of right and justice arise from such competing descriptions. The route to their resolution, if there is one, will lie in arguing over the nature of the situation itself, which will no doubt rapidly lead to complicated factual disputes about what is causally relevant to its characterization. To ignore these questions by assuming that there is an accurate consensus on the nature of the situation is palpably question-begging.

In addition to the difficulties that arise (for evaluating issues of social justice) out of the liberal predisposition toward the *meaning-of-the-act* fallacy, the fact that modern liberals view social relationships as essentially additive of individual intentional actions, to which social relationships are reducible, means they ignore the senses in which it might be justifiable and necessary to make moral judgments about social relationships quite independently of (and sometimes even in conflict with) moral judgments about individuals. A strong case can be made, for instance, for intentions being centrally relevant to the assessment of individual culpability, although I would follow Anscombe (1969:175–95) in placing some limits on this where a person acts in ignorance of consequences of which we might reasonably expect him to be cognizant. I would distinguish between the case where no harm is intended by an agent out of complete ignorance of the consequence of his actions, and the case where he does not intend the harm but is aware of the causal consequences.[15] There are exceedingly complex issues involved in evaluating these kinds of actions, and they depend on a great many factors. However we finally resolve these issues concerning the evaluation of individual moral actions, assuming that we can, they are separate from those relating to judgments concerning the justice or otherwise of social institutions and relationships, which must be evaluated in terms of different, and almost always wholly consequentialist, criteria. In this sense the deontological appeal to some hypothetical consent of individuals rests on a category mistake. Nozick's "acting in equilibrium" and Rawls's similar appeal to "what would be chosen" by individuals with "full deliberative rationality" (assuming these notions could be made sense of and applied – which I argue is not so) are typically irrelevant to evaluating the justness of social institutions and relationships. Although social relationships are partly produced and reproduced via the voluntary actions of persons, the relations

15 There are, no doubt, a great many further pertinent distinctions to be made in a
   thorough account of individual culpability.

among the various levels of relevant descriptions of such actions are seldom, and certainly not typically, transparent or direct. Leaving aside all the other difficulties of hypothetical contracts, speculation about what imaginary individuals would freely choose in imaginary conditions thus should not be expected to generate the relevant criteria for evaluating the justness of existing social institutions and relationships.

Trying to pin down what these criteria should be is extremely difficult, and very likely impossible at the scale of comprehensiveness to which writers in the modern liberal tradition aspire. We should expect this for two main reasons. First we should be suspicious of the claim that there are *any* neutral principles of social organization for a given society — let alone all historical and imaginary societies. Which social groups are hurt and which benefit from the operation of a particular principle are often determined by exogenous empirical conditions that vary greatly and often in unpredictable ways. The mere fact that all persons have a common interest in a particular good does not entail there is a neutral way of providing it. Moreover, the relevant empirical conditions presumed in arguments for different principles often (perhaps invariably) depend on counterfactual assumptions that are themselves ideologically loaded. For example, the move in Locke's argument from a positive community in which everyone has inclusive use-rights to the common to private individual rights of exclusive dominion requires there be no violation of the second proviso (that "as much and as good" be available to others). I have not defended Macpherson's view, for which there seems to be no textual evidence, that the nature of productivity is such that the proviso rapidly becomes "transcended" for Locke, but it is clear that Locke believed the productivity effects of enclosure and labor under conditions of private ownership would be such that the proviso would not be violated in practice. As our discussion of Nozick's account of justice in acquisition revealed, any argument for private property making use of Locke's arguments assumes some variant of this causal descriptive thesis, however implicitly.

Many would question this empirical assumption on the

grounds that capitalist economies based on private ownership of the means of production necessarily generate unemployment, thus there will always be some for whom the proviso is violated. If accepted, this argument might generate a Lockean case for a welfare state, or perhaps even for some sort of socialism, but many would not accept it. They might argue that unemployment results from the laziness of the poor, that it would be worse under any of the feasible alternatives, that in the long run there will be no unemployment, or that unemployment is not generated by the market system but by state intervention in it, to name a few common candidates. Leaving aside whether or not such questions will ever be settled decisively, the view taken of them is clearly pregnant ideologically, since it decisively shapes what the Lockean argument requires in practice. To adopt one or another establishment view of such questions may win a writer recognition from that establishment. It is likely, however, to weaken his credibility among others to whom he will appear to be peddling that establishment's values. This is, to a significant extent, what he will inevitably be doing—just because his counterfactual assumptions will be ideologically pregnant. This problem of inevitably loaded counterfactuals arises independently of the problem of inevitably loaded multiple descriptions. The latter no doubt compounds it in practice so they become mutually reinforcing in ideological debate.

A second, related, reason prompting suspicion toward the comprehensive theories to which writers in the liberal tradition aspire is that the kind of empirical knowledge necessary for the formulation of principles with so general a range is almost certainly beyond the capacity of a single person, if it is available at all. If political theorists are going to make use of empirical assumptions and theories about the workings of the societies to which their principles apply (which, it seems, they inevitably must), they are going to have to grapple with difficult and controversial causal questions and arguments about the possibilities available in a given situation. This is a monumental task for someone interested in formulating a general theory of distributive justice.

From this vantage point the debate between proponents of

the Kantian liberalism we have been examining and the "new communitarians" such as Michael Sandel, Alasdair MacIntyre, and Richard Rorty, is cast in a somewhat different light. These and other writers have increasingly argued in recent years that the major fault of the neo-Kantians is their failure to offer an adequate account of political community. This is an obvious (and acknowledged) source of the renewed interest in Aristotelianism we find in the writings of William Galston and MacIntyre, of Michael Walzer's attempt to give substantive content to the ideal of a liberal community, and of the growing interest in Hegelian political philosophy.[16] Several of these writers make much of the fact that substantive moral judgments about politics require acceptance of some notion of the good community as their basis. There is a blossoming debate between them and Kantian liberals over "community" versus "no community" in liberal theory.[17] This is no more, however, than a beguiling opposition of gross concepts. Of course substantive judgments about how communities ought to be organized and governed assumes accounts of how they are formed and reproduced, of what their goals and purposes might be, and of how they should limit community action, both internally, with respect to the individual actions of members, and externally, with respect to the needs and resources of other communities. We can no more make substantive judgments about politics without reference to the purposes of political life and the nature of political communities than can we make substantive judgments about food without reference to the purposes of eating. Because this is so, and writers in the deontological liberal tradition in all its variants have always made such assumptions, the argument should not be over whether community, but rather over what sort.

Many of the new communitarian writers appear to assume that community is synonymous with republican community,

16 Sandel (1982, 1984:81–96), Galston (1980), MacIntyre (1981), Walzer (1983, 1984:315–30), Rorty (1983:583–9, 1984a:1–19, 1984b:32–44), Charvet (1981), and Taylor (1979). For other examples of the revival of interest in the concept of political community, see Newell (1984:775–84), Beer (1984:361–86), Kateb (1984:331–60), Hirsch (1984), and Yack (1985:92–112), and, for a semi-popular account, Bellah, et al. (1985).
17 For one recent illustration, see Hirsch (1984).

and that this notion should be opposed, at a very high level of generality, to the neo-Kantian liberalism of Rawls, Nozick, and their progeny. Advocates of this view should keep in mind, however, that republicanism as an ideology has also proven itself serviceable to social and political repression, both historically and in the contemporary world, and that to embrace it as an abstract ideal is to say little useful from the point of view of articulating a viable alternative political ideology. Those interested in advancing this debate should shift it to a lower level of abstraction and seek to supply substantive content to the various communitarian proposals they advocate. They should consider how these are to be implemented in the capitalist economies of the late twentieth century, with their powerfully entrenched centralized bureaucratic states, and their seemingly inevitable participation in an ever more mutually interdependent international political and economic order. If these arrangements are seen as compatible with the various communitarian notions these authors defend, they must take seriously the burden of justifying them, and of dealing with the massive injustices they are thought by many to generate. If not, some account of how the new communitarian proposals might be implemented must be offered, in light of what we appear to know about the extraordinary stability of the centralized national states of the advanced industrial world.[18] Attractive as various romantic appeals to Aristotelian virtue, local communities, and republican conceptions of citizenship might be, if they are simply new variants of "ideal theory" they will turn out to be, on closer inspection, as vulnerable as the alternatives embraced by their opponents. If we want to avoid the inadequacies attending neo-Kantian answers, we have to refrain from asking neo-Kantian questions.

It is not my argument that critical thinking about general moral principles of social organization is avoidable or even ought to be avoidable. If it is going to be done intelligently it will require a range of sensitivity to empirical questions so difficult to achieve that it must inevitably limit the scope of our general moral claims. For instance, when Rawls asserts at

18 See Skocpol (1979:284ff).

the outset of *A Theory of Justice* that for his purposes society is viewed as a "closed system isolated from other societies," or in the Dewey lectures that a well ordered society is "a self-sufficient association of human beings which, like a nation-state, controls a connected territory" (1971:8; 1980:536), he is revealing what many would regard as so chronic a lack of awareness of how the world economy operates today, of how domestic policies concerning employment, growth, and wages are often, perhaps even typically for most countries, determined in large part by external events, of how even what Rawls conceives of as "primary" political liberties are often likewise overdetermined, it is difficult to see how a theory of justice based on his "isolation" and "self-sufficiency" assumptions can have much application to the problems of right and justice emerging in the actual world. There are many complex and ideologically loaded factual issues in international trade, for instance, concerning whether or not endemic problems of underconsumption in the metropolitan capitalist economies generate dependent relationships between themselves and third world countries, that in turn prevent in the latter balanced industrial growth, and in some cases all industrial growth: the so-called "development of underdevelopment" at the periphery as a condition for prosperity at the center.[19] Issues about the nature, causes, and consequences of this dependence are so controversial and so tremendously complicated, that someone professing to formulate a theory of distributive justice with some relevance to the contemporary world cannot ignore them by definitional fiat and expect to convince anyone who did not agree with him in advance.[20] To keep adding simplifying assumptions to a problem until it is theoretically "manageable" is all very well, but as these assumptions retreat from reality so, too, do the injunctions entailed by the theoretical model.

19 See, for instance, Baran and Sweezy (1965), Emmanuel (1972), Amin (1974), Cardoso and Faletto (1977), and Evans (1979) for pertinent discussions of these issues.

20 I am not suggesting that no liberal writers devote attention to questions of international justice. Beitz (1979), Shue (1981), and Barry (1982) exemplify something of a trend in this direction that cannot be evaluated here. For a review of recent liberal writing on this subject, see Dagger (1983).

It might be said that all arguments make assumptions and these writers could not be expected both to make their arguments and to establish all their assumptions, empirical and theoretical. So far as theories of right and justice are involved, the difficulty is that the assumptions are themselves inevitably loaded morally and politically, and largely determine the substantive results of the arguments based on them. To the extent that a writer constructs a model generating injunctions favorable to a particular establishment he will no doubt win recognition from that establishment and appear to others as an ideologue for it. This he will be, whether he intends it, as one suspects with Nozick, or not, as one suspects with Rawls, because he is presenting what is in fact an ideologically loaded and controversial model as a reasonable set of assumptions with a sound basis in the solid discoveries of psychologists and economists.

It might be thought that this attack on scientism is at variance with the realist view of social science I have outlined elsewhere,[21] but two points should be noted in this regard. First, the claim that the causal mechanisms constituting the social world are in principle discoverable must be distinguished from the claims of existing social scientists to have discovered the mechanisms they claim to have discovered. The realist claim is that the concept dependent nature of the social world does not make it in principle impossible to study scientifically, but the methodological problems arising in attempting to do so can be considerable, possibly even insurmountable. We assume there are causal mechanisms operating and try to discover their nature; of course we must expect the results to be at least variable and frequently unsuccessful. The methodological limitations inherent in studying causal mechanisms in the "open systems"[22] that constitute the social world

21 Shapiro (1982:563—78). For a comprehensive defense of this view, see Bhaskar (1978) and especially Bhaskar (1979).

22 This is Roy Bhaskar's term, intended to contrast the task normally faced by the social scientist with the experimental closure typical in most natural sciences (with the obvious exceptions of such sciences as astronomy, meteorology, and aspects of archeology, geology, and evolutionary biology). See Bhaskar (1978:64ff). For a summary of Bhaskar's views and those of other realist writers as they relate to the natural versus the human sciences, see Shapiro (1982:563—70).

are very great. I hold that there are good reasons for being skeptical of many of the proclaimed discoveries of the social sciences, particularly economics. The critical scientific attitude to the world consists in evaluating arguments and evidence, not in accepting the claims of proclaimed experts on faith alone. Complexities of technology and the inevitable constraints imposed on us by the intellectual division of labor severely limit the capacities of any given individual in this regard. This is no reason to turn blind faith in received opinion into a virtue.

Second, the realist makes an important distinction between the truth or falsity of a belief and its ideological function in the legitimation or delegitimation of relationships of power and authority. False beliefs can function ideologically as often as true beliefs, precisely because their ideological content is defined in terms of their function and not their truth content. Whatever the truth, assuming we can eventually discover it, about capitalist markets and productivity, different public assumptions about it will benefit different groups differently, and these assumptions will be used successfully to legitimate, or attack, various social practices relating to it.

This is not to say that questions about the truth of a proposition will be irrelevant to questions about its ideological function. I doubt that there are general rules concerning the relationship between them, but there usually is some relationship. Ideologies typically derive their persuasive appeal from the fact that they do make straightforward sense of some realm of experience, as suggested in Chapter 1. Once we suspect that claims about the productivity of capitalist markets serve a particular ideological end we become interested in their truth or falsity for two reasons. First, discovery of the ways in which a claim might be false, partly false, misleading, or misapplied may tell us more about its ideological force and why it is held to be true. We thus find ourselves grappling with the actual causal claim willy nilly. Second, to the extent that we might have an interest in criticizing a particular causal claim we think we have reasons for regarding as ideological, questions about alternatives to it inevitably arise. These force us to consider the substantive causal questions involved *as* causal questions. If establishment claims about the productivity of unregulated

capitalist markets obviously serve certain establishment interests and are simultaneously questionable empirically, questions
inevitably arise concerning the alternatives to them, whose interests they would serve, and whether they are viable. Thus
even though, in the realist view, there is no general or necessary relationship between the truth content and the ideological
function of propositions, it is unlikely we can understand the
latter without seriously studying the former.

III. CONCLUSION

I have argued that the liberal conception of individual rights
constitutes the skeleton of liberal political theory as it has
evolved in its dominant forms in the modern Anglo-American
tradition. I have treated this conception as an internally complex structure, and tried to sketch an account of the evolution
of its major component parts both historically sensitive and
useful for understanding its dominant contemporary forms.
Perhaps the greatest danger of this type of evolutionary explanation of contemporary ideas is that the whole process takes
on a teleological air many will find objectionable. There is a
vast difference, however, between the use of teleological explanations, in biology for instance, for heuristic reasons, and
the epistemologically loaded teleological view of history we
find in the writings of Hegel, and, in some interpretations,
Marx. In these latter there is a pregnant directed causal necessity inherent in events, a motor of history, that is driving in a
certain direction, if not predetermined at least inevitable. The
former type of teleological explanation makes no such assumption. Although later events are shown as evolving causally from earlier ones, and in that sense being determined by
them, there is no necessary sense in which they *had* so to
evolve. If some critical events had been different they might
have evolved differently. Biology offers good examples of
this: evolutionary biologists regularly employ teleological explanations as heuristic devices, yet this requires no questioning
of their assumption that biological evolution depends critically
on random events, or that organisms might have evolved differently than they have. The nature of the organism, its need

for survival, and the nature of its environment all place limits on the possibilities of adaptive change available to the relevant organism, but these are contingent limits that will vary with both organisms and circumstance.

The only sense in which the explanation offered here is teleological is in this weaker heuristic sense. This is not inherently implausible. It might be argued that all causal historical explanations are teleological in this sense. In claiming that the liberal view of rights evolved via processes of adaptive change importantly conditioned by, and functional to, the evolution of capitalist markets, I am not holding that this had to be the case, or that things might not have been significantly different, though this is difficult for us to imagine. Whether or not they could have is an empirical matter that could never be established with much certainty for obvious methodological reasons. We can speculate and argue, in terms of counterfactuals, about such questions. There are, further, conditional observations: the requirements of capitalist markets may be such that unless people in significant numbers hold certain moral and political beliefs, those markets will not be able to function. True conditionals of this form do not entail any necessary determinism, either in the sense that "since" capitalist markets "had" to function the relevant beliefs would become widespread (whether or not capitalist markets were bound to emerge and survive is a different, and also contingent, historical question), or in the sense that, if the conditional is true, the existence of capitalist markets "caused" the beliefs to be held. The actual causal process must have been vastly more complex, depending on mutually reciprocal mechanisms, elective affinities, and by-products of other historically parallel causal processes. A general theory of historical change which could tell us in advance how all causal mechanisms will operate is in my view unlikely to be forthcoming and certainly has not yet been discovered.

I have sought to show that the principal reasons for the tenacity of the liberal conception of individual rights, problems and all, are ideological: its Cartesian view of the subject of rights, its negative libertarian view of the substance of rights, its view of individual consent as the legitimate basis for

302

rights, and its essentially pluralist and utilitarian conception of the purposes of rights have, in their various formulations, combined to express a view of politics that is required by and legitimates capitalist market practices. As the needs of those markets have evolved so this ideology (in its most influential forms) has evolved with it, generating rationalizations for its imperatives and legitimating the particular institutional structures it has required.

The historical anthropology we have been engaged in has been an anthropology of establishment values. I have tried to show how the radical conservatism of Hobbes and Locke's liberal constitutionalism have been pressed into the service of the emerging liberal establishment and modified with the needs of that establishment. In pointing out the conservative tendencies (in this proestablishment sense) of this ideology from its inception and showing how, in its establishment forms, this doctrine has been stripped of potentially radical ideas such as thoroughgoing notions of participation, democratic community, and the labor theory of value, I have arguably downplayed the critical possibilities of some of the ideas discussed. Flatham (1976:184ff) has argued, for instance, that the widely shared assumptions about rights in liberal societies entail quite robust communitarian relationships. The practice of rights assumes shared rules and judgments, acceptance of common authority, and relationships of reciprocal dependence, so that individual rights presuppose "patterned interrelationships and interdependencies." From a different point of view Sandel (1982:133–83) has argued that if liberalism is to make good on its promise of a theory of justice acceptable to liberal sentiments, it must develop a stronger and more dominant notion of community than that offered either by Rawls's deontology or conventional utilitarian alternatives. From still a different point of view Walzer (1983) has undertaken an immanent critique of pluralism and tried to show that if adhered to consistently this doctrine entails conclusions many establishment liberals would, one suspects, regard as unacceptably radical.

This is not the place to pass judgment on these various arguments. Despite the reservations expressed earlier I certainly do not reject them out of hand. No set of substantive political principles, I have argued, is intrinsically radical or conservative: radical ideas in one context become conservative in another and sometimes vice versa. It may be that there is potential for very extensive internal criticism of liberalism; many of the arguments of the last four chapters might even be conceived of as such. My primary aim has been to show in as much detail as possible how conventional liberal values have come to function, and continue to function, conservatively in today's world, how they legitimate the two principal establishment ideologies of our time. I have also suggested that if these are to be questioned seriously, not only must we question the standard Cartesian conception of the subject, but also negative libertarianism and the view of individual and social action it presupposes, the artificial doctrine of individual consent on which liberal conceptions of legitimacy rest, and the pluralist and utilitarian view of social ends based on the identification of the good with the desired. We must recognize, as Galston, MacIntyre, and others have done, that morality is inevitably in part teleological, and that substantive conceptions of the good cannot be avoided in arguments of right and justice.[23] Unlike those writers, however, we must acknowledge that a theory of the good is inevitably in significant part empirical. This entails a more general injunction to come off the terrain of "ideal theory" and get involved in factual arguments about the causal structure of the social world which is where problems of social justice arise.

I have not argued that if all factual questions were resolved no moral questions would remain, but I do claim first that sensitivity to factual questions is a necessary condition for pertinent moral theorizing, and, second, that it is unavoidable in knowing what is possible. The one injunction from Kant that we really need to take seriously is that ought entails can. To engage seriously in moral argument within these constraints would, I think, produce a kind of moral philosophy substantially different from that examined in part III. It would be less ambitious in that it would try to answer fewer all-encompassing

---

23 For a more detailed discussion of this point, see Kane (1982:180–252).

moral questions. Indeed, it would be skeptical of the very possibility of general theories of right and justice. It would be more ambitious, however, in that it would require those theorizing about substantive questions of right and justice to involve themselves seriously in vast areas of the social sciences currently left to other experts in the intellectual division of labor.

Bibliography

Ackerman, B. A. (1980), *Social Justice in the Liberal State* (New Haven: Yale University Press).

Amin, S. (1974), *Accumulation on a World Scale: A Critique of the Theory of Underdevelopment* (New York and London: Monthly Review).

Anderson, P. (1974), *Lineages of the Absolutist State* (Norfolk: Verso).

Anscombe, G.E.M. (1958), "On Brute Facts," *Analysis*, vol. 18, no. 3, pp. 69–72.

(1969). "Modern Moral Philosophy," W. D. Hudson, ed., *The Is-Ought Question* (London: Macmillan Press), pp. 175–95.

Appleby, J. O. (1978), *Economic Thought and Ideology in Seventeenth Century England* (Princeton: Princeton University Press).

Arendt, H. (1958), *The Human Condition* (Chicago: University of Chicago Press).

Arrow, K. J. (1963), *Social Choice and Individual Values* (New Haven: Yale University Press).

(1973), "Some Ordinalist-Utilitarian Notes on Rawls' Theory of Justice," *The Journal of Philosophy*, vol. 70, no. 9, pp. 245–63.

Ashcraft, R. (1968), "Locke's State of Nature: Historical Fact or Moral Fiction?" *American Political Science Review*, vol. 62, no. 3, pp. 898–915.

(1978), "Ideology and Class in Hobbes's Political Theory," *Political Theory*, vol. 6, pp. 27–62.

(1980), "Revolutionary Politics and Locke's *Two Treatises of Government:* Radicalism and Lockean Political Theory," *Political Theory*, vol. 8, no. 4, pp. 429–86.

(1986), *Locke's Two Treatises of Government* (London: Allen & Unwin, in press).

Baran, P., and Sweezy, P. (1965), *Monopoly Capital* (London: Monthly Review).

Barber, B. (1975), "Justifying Justice: Problems of Psychology, Politics and Measurement in Rawls," N. Daniels, ed., *Reading Rawls: Critical Studies of A Theory of Justice* (Oxford: Blackwell), pp. 292–319.

Barbon, N. (1690), *A Discourse of Trade* (London).

    (1696), *A Discourse Concerning Coining the New Money Lighter* (London).

Barry, B. (1973), *The Liberal Theory of Justice* (Oxford: Oxford University Press [Clarendon Press]).

    (1982), "Humanity and Justice in Global Perspective," R.J. Pennock and J. W. Chapman, eds., *Nomos 24: Ethics, Economics and the Law* (New York: New York University Press).

Beer, S. (1984), "Liberty and Union: Walt Whitman's Idea of the Nation," *Political Theory*, vol. 12, no. 3, pp. 361–86.

Beitz, C. S. (1979), *Political Theory and International Relations* (Princeton: Princeton University Press).

Bellah, R. N., R. Madsen, W.M. Sullivan, A. Swidler, and S.M. Tipto. (1985), *Habits of the Heart: Individualism and Commitment in American Life* (Berkeley and Los Angeles: University of California Press).

Berlin, I. (1969), "Two Concepts of Liberty," I. Berlin, *Four Essays on Liberty* (Oxford: Oxford University Press), pp. 118–72.

Bhaskar, R. (1978), *A Realist Theory of Science* (Sussex: Harvester & Humanities Press).

    (1979), *The Possibility of Naturalism* (Sussex: Harvester & Humanities Press).

Blackstone, W. (1979), *Commentaries on the Laws of England*, 4 vols. (Chicago: University of Chicago Press).

Blaug, M. (1978), *Economic Theory in Retrospect*, 3d ed., (Cambridge: Cambridge University Press).

Bloom, A. (1975), "Justice: John Rawls vs. The Tradition of Political Philosophy," *American Political Science Review*, vol. 69, no. 2, pp. 648–62.

Bloor, D. (1983), *Wittgenstein: A Social Theory of Knowledge* (New York: Columbia University Press).

Bowden, P. (1967), "Agricultural Prices, Farm Profits and Rents," J. Thirsk, ed., *The Agrarian History of England and Wales*, vol. 4, (Cambridge: Cambridge University Press), pp. 593–695.

Bowley, M. (1963), "Some Seventeenth Century Contributions to the Theory of Value," *Economica*, vol. 30, new series, no. 118, pp. 122–39.

Brenner, R. (1973), "The Civil War Politics of London's Merchant Community," *Past and Present*, no. 58, pp. 53–107.

Browning, A. (1953), ed., *English Historical Documents 1660–1714*, vol. 8 (London: Eyre & Spottiswoode).

Buchanan, J., and G. Tullock. (1962), *The Calculus of Consent: Logical Foundations of Constitutional Democracy* (Michigan: Ann Arbor Paperbacks).

Cameron, D. (1978), "Economic Inequality in the United States," paper presented at the annual meeting of the Midwest Political Science Association (Chicago, April, 1978).

Cardoso, F. H., and E. Faletto. (1977), *Dependency and Development in Latin America* (Berkeley: University of California Press).

Cary, J. ([1765] 1696), *A Discourse on Trade and Other Matters Relative to It* (London).

Chappell, V. (1966), ed., *Hume: A Collection of Critical Essays* (London: Macmillan).

Charvet, J. (1981), *A Critique of Freedom and Equality* (Cambridge: Cambridge University Press).

Child, A. (1953), "Making and Knowing in Hobbes, Vico and Dewey," G. Adams, ed., *University of California Publications in Philosophy*, vol. 16 (Berkeley and Los Angeles: University of California Press), pp. 271–310.

Claude, R. P. (1976), *Comparative Human Rights* (Baltimore: Johns Hopkins University Press).

Coleman, D. C. (1956), "Labor in the English Economy in the Seventeenth Century," *Economic History Review*, 2d series, vol. 8, no. 3, pp. 280-95.

Daniels, N. (1975), ed., *Reading Rawls: Critical Studies of A Theory of Justice* (Oxford: Blackwell).

Dagger, R. (1983), "Rights, Boundaries and the Bonds of Community," paper presented at 1983 annual meeting of the American Political Science Association in Chicago, Ill. (September 1983).

Davenant, C. (1696), *A Memorial Concerning Credit*, reprinted in G.H.J. Evans, ed., *A Reprint of Economic Tracts* (Baltimore, 1942).

Davidson, D. (1968), "Actions, Reasons & Causes," A. R. White, ed., *The Philosophy of Action* (Oxford: Oxford University Press), pp. 79–94.

Delaney, C.F. (1977), "Rawls on Method," K. Nielson and R. Shiner, eds., *New Essays on Contract Theory, Canadian Journal of Philosophy*, sup. vol. 3, pp. 153–61.

Dickenson, H. T. (1976), "The Eighteenth Century Debate on the 'Glorious Revolution'," *History*, vol. 61, no. 201, pp. 28–45.

DiQuattro, A. (1983), "Rawls and Left Criticism," *Political Theory*, vol. 11, no. 1, pp. 53–78.

Dobb, M. (1973), *Theories of Value and Distribution since Adam Smith: Ideology and Economic Theory* (Cambridge: Cambridge University Press).

Downs, A. (1957), *An Economic Theory of Democracy* (New York: Harper & Row).

Drury, S. B. (1982), "Locke and Nozick on Property," *Political Studies*, vol. 30, no. 1, pp. 28–41.

Dunn, J. (1969), *The Political Thought of John Locke* (Cambridge: Cambridge University Press).

   (1984), "The concept of 'trust' in the politics of John Locke," R. Rorty, J. B. Schneewind, and Q. Skinner, eds., *Philosophy in History: Essays on the Historiography of Philosophy* (Cambridge: Cambridge University Press) pp. 279–301.

Dworkin, G. (1975), "Non-Neutral Principles," N. Daniels ed., *Reading Rawls: Critical Studies of A Theory of Justice* (Oxford: Blackwell), pp. 124–41.

Dworkin, R. (1977), *Taking Rights Seriously* (Cambridge, Mass.: Harvard University Press).

Emmanuel, A. (1972), *Unequal Exchange: A Study of the Imperialism of Trade* (New York and London: Monthly Review).

Evans, P. (1979), *Dependent Development: The Alliance of Multinational, State and Local Capital in Brazil* (Princeton: Princeton University Press).

Everitt, A. (1967), "Farm Labourers," J. Thirsk, ed., *The Agrarian History of England and Wales*, vol. 4 (Cambridge: Cambridge University Press), pp. 396–454.

Farer, T. J. (1981), ed., *The International Bill of Human Rights* (California: Entwhistle Books).

Finnis, J. (1980), *Natural Law and Natural Rights* (Oxford: Oxford University Press [Clarendon Press]).

Fishkin, J. (1975), "Justice and Rationality: Some Objections to the Central Arguments in Rawls' Theory," *American Political Science Review*, vol. 69, no. 2, pp. 615–29.

   (1979), *Tyranny and Legitimacy: A Critique of Political Theories* (Baltimore: Johns Hopkins University Press).

Flathman, R. (1976), *The Practice of Rights* (Cambridge: Cambridge University Press).

Franklin, J. H. (1978), *John Locke and the Theory of Sovereignty* (Cambridge: Cambridge University Press).

Furniss, N. (1978), "The Political Implications of the Public Choice–Property Rights School," *American Political Science Review*, vol. 72, no. 2, pp. 399–410.

Gallie, W. B. (1956), "Essentially Contested Concepts," *Proceedings of the Aristotelian Society,* vol. 56, pp. 167–98.

Galston, W. A. (1980), *Justice and The Human Good* (Chicago: University of Chicago Press).

(1983), "Defending Liberalism," *American Political Science Review,* vol. 76, no. 3, pp. 621–29.

Gardiner, S. R. (1889), *The Constitutional Documents of the Puritan Revolution,* 2d ed. (Oxford: Oxford University Press [Clarendon Press]).

Gewirth, A. (1982), *Human Rights: Essays on Justification and Applications* (Chicago: University of Chicago Press).

Giddens, A. (1976), *New Rules of Sociological Method* (New York: Basic Books).

Gierke, O. (1934), *Natural Law and the Theory of Society,* 2 vols. (Cambridge: Cambridge University Press).

Goodwin, A. (1979), *The Friends of Liberty: The English Democratic Movement in the Age of the French Revolution* (Cambridge, Mass.: Harvard University Press).

Grafstein, R. (1983), "Taking Dworkin to Hart: A Positivist Conception of Institutional Rules," *Political Theory,* vol. 11, no. 2, pp. 244–65.

Graham, K. (1977), *J. L. Austin: A Critique of Ordinary Language Philosophy* (Sussex: Harvester).

Grampp, W. D. (1965), *Economic Liberalism,* 2 vols. (New York: Random House).

Hare, R. M. (1975), "Rawls' Theory of Justice," N. Daniels, ed., *Reading Rawls: Critical Studies of A Theory of Justice* (Oxford: Blackwell), pp. 81–107.

Hart, H.L.A. (1961), *The Concept of Law* (Oxford: Oxford University Press).

(1975), "Rawls on Liberty and its Priority," N. Daniels, ed., *Reading Rawls: Critical Studies of A Theory of Justice* (Oxford: Blackwell), pp. 230–53.

(1979), "Between Rights and Utility," A. Ryan, ed., *The Idea of Freedom: Essays in Honour of Isaiah Berlin* (Oxford: Oxford University Press).

Hayek, F. A. (1960), *The Constitution of Liberty* (Chicago: University of Chicago Press).

(1976), *Law Legislation and Liberty,* vol. II, *The Mirage of Social Justice* (Chicago: University of Chicago Press).

Hexter, J. H. (1979), "The Myth of the Middle Class in Tudor England," J. H. Hexter, *Reappraisals in History: New Views on His-*

tory and Society in Early Modern Europe, 2d ed. (Chicago: University of Chicago Press), pp. 71–116.

Hill, C. (1961), *The Century of Revolution: 1603–1714* (New York and London: W. W. Norton).

(1968), "The Many-Headed Monster in Late Tudor and Early Stuart Political Thinking," in G.H. Carter, ed., *From the Renaissance to the Counter-Reformation: Essays in Honor of Garrett Mattingly* (London), pp. 296–324.

(1972), *The World Turned Upside Down* (Harmondsworth: Pelican).

Hirsch, H. N. (1984), "The Threnody of Liberalism: Constitutional Liberty and the Renewal of Community," paper presented at the annual meeting of the American Political Science Association, The Washington Hilton, September 1984.

Hobbes, T. (1966), *The English Works of Thomas Hobbes*, XI vols. (London: John Bohn).

(1968), *Leviathan*, C.B. Macpherson, ed. (London: Pelican Books).

(1972), *De Homine*, C.T. Wood, T.S.K. Scott-Craig, and B. Gert, ed. & trans., *Man and Citizen* (New York: Anchor).

Hodges, W. (1696), *The Groans of the Poor* (London).

Hohfeld, W. (1923), *Fundamental Legal Conceptions as Applied to Juridical Reasoning and Other Essays* (New Haven: Yale University Press).

Holdsworth, W. (1956–72), *A History of English Law*, 17 vols. (London: Methuen & Co.).

Holmes, R. L. (1981), "Nozick on Anarchism," J. Paul, ed., *Reading Nozick: Essays on Anarchy State and Utopia* (Totowa, N.J.: Rowman & Littlefield), pp. 57–67.

Isaac, J. (1986), "Was John Locke a Bourgeois Theorist? A Critical Appraisal of Macpherson and Tully," *Canadian Journal of Political and Social Theory*, vol. 10, no. 3 (in press).

Johnson, E.A.J. (1937), *Predecessors of Adam Smith* (New York: Prentice-Hall).

Johnston, D. C. (1981), The New Sovereign and the Modern Subject: An Interpretation of Hobbes's Political Theory (Unpublished Ph.D. thesis, Princeton University).

(1986), *The Rhetoric of Leviathan: Thomas Hobbes and the Politics of Cultural Transformation* (Princeton: Princeton University Press, in press).

Kane, J. (1982), Justice and the Good: The Logical Priority of Conceptions of the Good in Arguments of Right and Justice (Unpublished Ph.D. thesis, London School of Economics).

Kant, I. (1948), *Groundwork of the Metaphysic of Morals*, H. J. Paton, trans. as *The Moral Law* (London: Hutchinson University Library).

(1970), *Kant's Political Writings,* H. Reiss, ed., H. B. Nisbet, trans. (Cambridge: Cambridge University Press).

Kateb, G. (1984), "Democratic Individuality and the Claims of Politics," *Political Theory,* vol. 12, no. 3, pp. 331–60.

Kenny, A. (1979), *The God of the Philosophers* (New York: Oxford University Press).

Krook, D. (1956), "Thomas Hobbes's doctrine of meaning and truth," *Philosophy,* vol. 31, no. 116, pp. 3–22.

Landes, D. (1969), *The Unbounded Prometheus: Technological Change and Industrial Development in Western Europe from 1750 to the Present* (Cambridge: Cambridge University Press).

Letwin, W. (1972), "The Economic Foundations of Hobbes' Politics," M. Cranston and R. S. Peters, eds., *Hobbes and Rousseau: A Collection of Critical Essays* (New York: Doubleday), pp. 143–64.

Little, I.M.D. (1950), *A Critique of Welfare Economics* (Oxford: Oxford University Press).

Locke, J. (1824), *The Works of John Locke,* 12th ed., IX vols. (London: Baldwin).

(1958), *Essays on the Law of Nature,* W. Von Leiden, ed. (Oxford: Oxford University Press [Clarendon Press]).

(1959), *An Essay Concerning Human Understanding,* 2 vols. (New York: Dover).

(1963), *Two Treatises of Government,* P. Laslett, ed. (Cambridge: Cambridge University Press).

(1979), *Treatise of Civil Government and A Letter Concerning Toleration,* C.L. Sherman, ed. (New York: Irvington [1685]).

Long, D.G. (1977), *Bentham on Liberty: Jeremy Bentham's Idea of Liberty in Relation to his Utilitarianism* (Toronto: University of Toronto Press).

Lukes, S. (1977), "Relativism: Cognitive and Moral," S. Lukes, *Essays in Social Theory* (London: Macmillan), pp. 154–74.

Lyons, D. (1975), "Nature and Soundness of the Contract and Coherence Arguments," N. Daniels, ed., *Reading Rawls: Critical Studies of A Theory of Justice* (Oxford: Blackwell), pp. 141–67.

MacCallum, J. R., Jr. (1972), "Negative and Positive Freedom," P. Laslett, W. G. Runciman, and Q. Skinner, eds., *Philosophy, Politics and Society,* 4th series (Oxford: Blackwell), pp. 174–93.

MacIntyre, A. (1981), *After Virtue* (Notre Dame: University of Notre Dame Press).

Macpherson, C.B. (1962), *The Political Theory of Possessive Individualism: Hobbes to Locke* (Oxford: Oxford University Press).

(1965), "Hobbes' Bourgeois Man," K. Brown, ed., *Hobbes Studies* (Cambridge, Mass.: Harvard University Press), pp. 169–83.

(1973a), *Democratic Theory: Essays in Retrieval* (Oxford: Oxford University Press).

(1973b), "Rawls' Models of Man and Society," *Philosophy of the Social Sciences*, vol. 3, no. 4, pp. 341–7.

(1978), ed., *Property: Mainstream and Critical Positions* (Toronto: University of Toronto Press).

Maitland, F. W. (1920), *The Constitutional History of England* (Cambridge: Cambridge University Press).

Manley, T. (1669), *Usury at Six Percent Examined* (London).

Marx, K. (1969), *Theories of Surplus Value,* III vols. (Moscow: Progress Publishers).

(1973), *Grundrisse* (London: Pelican Books).

(1976), *Capital,* vol. I (Middlesex: Penguin Books).

Mayhew, D. R. (1974), *Congress: The Electoral Connection* (New Haven: Yale University Press).

Michelman, F. (1975), "Constitutional Welfare Rights and *A Theory of Justice*," N. Daniels, ed., *Reading Rawls: Critical Studies of A Theory of Justice* (Oxford: Blackwell), pp. 319–47.

Mill, J. S. (1950), *Mill on Bentham and Coleridge* (London: Chatto & Windus).

(1962), *Utilitarianism* (London: Collins).

(1974), *On Liberty* (London: Pelican Books).

(1975), *Three Essays: On Liberty, Representative Government, The Subjugation of Women* (New York: Oxford University Press).

Miller, R. (1975), "Rawls and Marxism," N. Daniels, ed., *Reading Rawls: Critical Studies of A Theory of Justice* (Oxford: Blackwell), pp. 206–30.

Minogue, K. R. (1972), "Hobbes and the Just Man," M. Cranston and R. S. Peters, eds., *Hobbes and Rousseau: A Collection of Critical Essays* (New York: Doubleday), pp. 66–84.

Misselden, E. (1632), *The Circle of Commerce or the Balance of Trade, in Defence of Free Trade* (London).

Moore, B., Jr. (1978), *Injustice: The Social Bases of Obedience and Revolt* (White Plains, N.Y.: M. E. Sharpe).

Mueller, D. C. (1979), *Public Choice* (Cambridge: Cambridge University Press).

Mun, T. (1623), *England's Treasure by Foreign Trade,* reprinted in J. R.

McCullock, ed., *Early English Tracts on Commerce* (Cambridge: Cambridge University Press, 1954), pp. 121–209.

Nasmith, D. (1875), *The Institutes of English Private Law: Book II – Things* (London: Butterworths).

Newell, W.R. (1984), "Heidegger on Freedom and the Community: Some Political Implications of his Early Thought," *American Political Science Review*, vol. 78, no. 3, pp. 775–84.

Nozick, R. (1972), "Coercion," P. Laslett, W.G. Runciman, and Q. Skinner, eds., *Philosophy, Politics and Society*, 4th series (Oxford: Blackwell), pp. 101–35.

(1974), *Anarchy State and Utopia* (Oxford: Blackwell).

(1981), *Philosophical Explanations* (Cambridge, Mass.: Harvard University Press).

Oakeshott, M. (1975), *On Human Conduct* (Oxford: Oxford University Press [Clarendon Press]).

OECD (1979), *Concentration and Competition Policy*, report of the committee of experts on restrictive business practices (Paris: OECD).

Ollman, B. (1971), *Alienation: Marx's Concept of Man in Capitalist Society* (Cambridge: Cambridge University Press).

Ordeshook, P. C., and K. A. Shepsle. (1982), eds., *Political Equilibrium* (Boston: Kluwer-Nijhof).

Outhwaite, R. B. (1969), *Inflation in Tudor and Early Stuart England* (London: Macmillan).

Panitch, L. (1977), "The Development of Corporatism in Liberal Democracies," *Comparative Political Studies* (April, 1977), pp. 61–90.

Parent, W.A. (1974), "Some Recent Work on the Concept of Liberty," *American Philosophical Quarterly*, vol. 11, no. 3, pp. 149–67.

Pareto, V. (1970), *Manual of Political Economy*, A.S. Schwier, trans., A.S. Schwier and A.M. Page, eds., (New York: Augustus Kelly).

Parker, R. B. (1979), "The Jurisprudential Uses of John Rawls," J. R. Pennock and J.W. Chapman, eds., *Constitutionalism* (New York: New York University Press).

Parkin, F. (1971), *Class, Inequality and Political Order*, (London: Praeger).

Paul, J. (1981), ed., *Reading Nozick: Essays on Anarchy State and Utopia* (Totowa, N.J.: Rowman & Littlefield).

Pennock, J. R. (1965), "Hobbes's Confusing 'Clarity'–The Case of 'Liberty'," K.C. Brown, ed., *Hobbes Studies* (Cambridge, Mass.: Harvard University Press), pp. 101–16.

Petty, W. (1899), *The Economic Writings of Sir William Petty together with the Observations upon the Bills of Mortality More Probably by John Grant*, C.H. Hull, ed., 2 vols. (Cambridge: Cambridge University Press).

Pigou, A. (1960), *Economics of Welfare* (London: Macmillan).

Pitkin, H. F. (1972), *Wittgenstein and Justice: On the Significance of Ludwig Wittgenstein for Social and Political Thought* (Berkeley and Los Angeles: University of California Press).

Plamenatz, J. (1965), "Mr. Warrender's Hobbes," K.C. Brown, ed., *Hobbes Studies* (Cambridge, Mass.: Harvard University Press), pp. 73–87.

Pocock, J.G.A. (1957), *The Ancient Constitution and the Feudal Law* (Cambridge: Cambridge University Press).

(1975), *The Machiavellian Moment* (Princeton: Princeton University Press).

(1981), "Virtues, Rights and Manners: A Model for Historians of Political Thought," *Political Theory*, vol. 9, no. 3, pp. 353–68.

(1984), "Verbalizing a Political Act: Toward a Politics of Speech," M.J. Shapiro, ed., *Language and Politics* (Oxford: Blackwell).

Polanyi, K. (1944), *The Great Transformation: The Political and Economic Origins of Our Time* (Boston: Beacon).

Pufendorf, S. von. (1710 [1672]), *De Jure Naturae et Gentium Libri Octo* (Lund, Sweden), B. Kennett, trans., as *Of the Law of Nature and Nations* (London).

Quine, W.V. (1953), "Two Dogmas of Empiricism," W.V. Quine, *From a Logical Point of View: Logico-Philosophical Essays* (New York: Harper Torchbooks), pp. 20–46.

Rae, D. (1975a), "The Limits of Consensual Decision," *American Political Science Review*, vol. 69, pp. 1270–94.

(1975b), "Maximin Justice and an Alternative Principle of General Advantage," *American Political Science Review*, vol. 69, no. 2, pp. 630–47.

(1979), "A Principle of Simple Justice," P. Laslett and J. Fishkin, eds., *Philosophy Politics and Society*, 5th series (Oxford: Blackwell), pp. 134-54.

Rae, D., D. Yates, J. Hochschild, J. Morone, and C.M. Fessler. (1981), *Equalities* (Cambridge, Mass.: Harvard University Press).

Ramsey, P. (1965), *Tudor Economic Problems* (London: Gollancz).

Rawls, J. (1951), "Outline of a Decision Procedure for Ethics," *Philosophical Review*, no. 60, pp. 177–97.

(1971), *A Theory of Justice* (Oxford: Oxford University Press).

(1975), "Fairness to Goodness," *Philosophical Review,* vol. 84, pp. 536–54.

(1979), "A Well-Ordered Society," P. Laslett and J. Fishkin, eds., *Philosophy Politics and Society,* 5th series (Oxford: Blackwell), pp. 6–20, originally published as "A Kantian Conception of Equality," *The Cambridge Review* (1975), pp. 94–9.

(1980), "Kantian Constructivism in Moral Theory," *The Journal of Philosophy,* vol. 77, no. 9, pp. 515–72.

(1982), "Social Unity and Primary Goods," A. Sen and B. Williams, eds., *Utilitarianism and Beyond* (Cambridge: Cambridge University Press), pp. 159–85.

Reik, M. M. (1977), *The Golden Lands of Thomas Hobbes* (Detroit: Wayne State University Press).

Riker, W. H. (1982), "Implications from the Disequilibrium of Majority Rule for the Study of Institutions," P.C. Ordeshook and K. Shepsle, eds., *Political Equilibrium* (Boston: Kluwer-Nijhof).

Riley, P. (1982), *Will and Political Legitimacy: A Critical Exposition of Social Contract Theory in Hobbes, Locke, Rousseau, Kant, and Hegel* (Cambridge, Mass.: Harvard University Press).

Roll, E. (1974), *A History of Economic Thought* (Homewood, Ill.: Irwin).

Rorty, R. (1979), *Philosophy and the Mirror of Nature* (Princeton: Princeton University Press).

(1980), "A Reply to Dreyfus and Taylor," *Review of Metaphysics,* no. 34, pp. 39–55.

(1983), "Postmodernist Bourgeois Liberalism," *The Journal of Philosophy,* vol. 80, no. 10, pp. 583–9.

(1984a), "Solidarity or Objectivity?" *Nanzan Review of American Studies,* vol. 4, pp. 1–19.

(1984b), "Habermas and Lyotard on Post-modernity," *Praxis International,* vol. 6, no. 1, pp. 32–44.

Rosenblum, N. L. (1978), *Bentham's Theory of the Modern State* (Cambridge, Mass.: Harvard University Press).

Rousseau, J-J. (1968), *The Social Contract* (Aylesbury: Penguin Books).

Routh, G. (1975), *The Origin of Economic Ideas* (London: Macmillan).

Ryle, G. (1949), *The Concept of Mind* (London: Hutchinson).

Sandel, M. J. (1982), *Liberalism and the Limits of Justice* (Cambridge: Cambridge University Press).

(1984), "The Procedural Republic and the Unencumbered Self," *Political Theory,* vol. 12, no. 1, pp. 81–96.

Sartre, J-P. (1969), *Being and Nothingness* (London: Methuen).

Schumpeter, J. A. (1978), *History of Economic Analysis* (Oxford: Oxford University Press).

Sen, A. K. (1970), *Collective Choice and Social Welfare* (London: Oliver & Boyd).

    (1975), "Rawls versus Bentham: An Axiomatic Examination of the Pure Distribution Problem," N. Daniels, ed., *Reading Rawls: Critical Studies of A Theory of Justice* (Oxford: Blackwell), pp. 283–92.

Shapiro, I. (1981), "Fiscal Crisis of the Polish State," *Theory and Society*, vol. 10, no. 4, pp. 469–502.

    (1982), "Realism in the Study of the History of Ideas," *History of Political Thought*, vol. 3, no. 3, pp. 535–78.

Shapiro, I., and J. Kane. (1983), "Stagflation and the New Right," *Telos*, no. 56, pp. 5–39.

Shue, H. (1981), *Basic Rights* (Princeton: Princeton University Press).

Sigmund, P. E. (1971), *Natural Law in Political Thought* (Cambridge, Mass.: Winthrop).

Skinner, Q. (1972), "The Context of Hobbes' Theory of Political Obligation," in M. Cranston and R. S. Peters, eds., *Hobbes and Rousseau: A Collection of Critical Essays* (New York: Doubleday), pp. 109–42.

    (1978), *The Foundations of Modern Political Thought*, 2 vols., vol. I: *The Renaissance;* vol. II: *The Age of Reformation* (Cambridge: Cambridge University Press).

    (1980), "The Origins of the Calvinist Theory of Revolution," B.C. Malament, ed., *After the Reformation: Essays in Honor of H. J. Hexter* (Philadelphia: University of Pennsylvania Press), pp. 309–30.

Skocpol, T. (1979), *States and Social Revolutions: A Comparative Analysis of France, Russia and China* (Cambridge: Cambridge University Press).

Smith, A. (1937), *An Inquiry into the Nature and Causes of The Wealth of Nations* (New York: The Modern Library).

Spiegel, H. W. (1971), *The Growth of Economic Thought* (Englewood Cliffs, N.J.: Prentice-Hall).

Stone, L. (1965), *The Crisis of the Aristocracy: 1558–1641* (Oxford: Oxford University Press).

Strauss, L. (1953), *Natural Right and History* (Chicago: University of Chicago Press).

    (1963), *The Political Philosophy of Hobbes: Its Basis and Its Genesis* (Chicago: University of Chicago Press).

Stroud, B. (1977), *Hume* (London: Routledge & Kegan Paul).

Supple, B. E. (1959), *Commercial Crisis and Change in England: 1600–42* (Cambridge: Cambridge University Press).

Tawney, R. H. (1961), *Religion and the Rise of Capitalism* (New York: New American Library).

Taylor, A. E. (1965), "The Ethical Doctrine of Hobbes," K.C. Brown, ed., *Hobbes Studies* (Cambridge, Mass.: Harvard University Press), pp. 35–55.

Taylor, C. (1979), *Hegel and Modern Society* (Cambridge: Cambridge University Press).

Thirsk, J. (1978), *Economic Policy and Projects: The Development of a Consumer Society in Early Modern England* (Oxford: Oxford University Press [Clarendon Press]).

Thomas, K. (1965), "The Social Origins of Hobbes' Political Thought," K. Brown, ed., *Hobbes Studies* (Cambridge, Mass.: Harvard University Press), pp. 185–236.

Tigar, M., and M. Levy. (1977), *Law and the Rise of Capitalism* (New York: Monthly Review).

Tocqueville, A. de. (1981), *Democracy in America* (New York: Doubleday).

Tribe, K. (1978), *Land, Labour and Economic Discourse* (London: Routledge & Kegan Paul).

Tuck, R. (1979), *Natural Rights Theories: Their Origin and Development* (Cambridge: Cambridge University Press).

Tully, J. (1980), *A Discourse on Property: John Locke and His Adversaries* (Cambridge: Cambridge University Press).

Walzer, M. (1965), *The Revolution of the Saints: A Study in the Origins of Radical Politics* (Cambridge, Mass.: Harvard University Press).

(1983), *Spheres of Justice: A Defense of Pluralism and Equality* (New York: Basic Books).

(1984), "Liberalism and the Art of Separation," *Political Theory*, vol. 12, no. 3, pp. 315–30.

Warrender, H. (1957), *The Political Philosophy of Hobbes: His Theory of Obligation* (Oxford: Oxford University Press [Clarendon Press]).

Wellbank, J. H., D. Snook, and D.T. Mason. (1982), *John Rawls and his Critics: An Annotated Bibliography* (New York: Garland).

Wernham, A. G. (1965), "Liberty and Obligation in Hobbes," K.C. Brown, ed., *Hobbes Studies* (Cambridge, Mass.: Harvard University Press), pp. 117–39.

Wiles, R. C. (1968), "The Theory of Wages in Later English Mercantilism," *Economic History Review*, 2d series, no. 21, pp. 113–26.

Williams, B. (1962), "The Idea of Equality," P. Laslett and W. G.

Runciman, eds., *Philosophy, Politics and Society,* 2d series (Oxford: Blackwell, 1962), pp. 110–31.

Winch, D. (1980), *Adam Smith's Politics: An Essay in Historiographic Revision* (Cambridge: Cambridge University Press).

Wittgenstein, L. (1958), *Philosophical Investigations,* G.E.M. Anscombe, trans. (Oxford: Blackwell).

Wolff, R. P. (1970), *In Defense of Anarchism* (New York: Harper & Row).

(1977), *Understanding Rawls: A Reconstruction and Critique of A Theory of Justice* (Princeton: Princeton University Press).

(1981), "Robert Nozick's Derivation of the Minimal State," in J. Paul, ed., *Reading Nozick: Essays on Anarchy State and Utopia* (Totowa, N.J.: Rowman and Littlefield).

Wood, N. (1981), "Thomas Hobbes and the Crisis of the English Aristocracy," *History of Political Thought,* vol. 1, no. 3, pp. 437–52.

(1983), *The Politics of Locke's Philosophy: A Social Study of "An Essay Concerning Human Understanding,"* (Berkeley: University of California Press).

Yack, B. (1985), "Community and Conflict in Aristotle's Political Philosophy," *The Review of Politics,* vol. 47, no. 1, pp. 92–112.

Yule, G. U. (1915), "Crop Production and Prices," *Journal of the Royal Statistical Society,* vol. 78, pp. 296–8.

Index